mindful
aging

Embracing Your Life After 50 to Find Fulfillment, Purpose, and Joy

Andrea Brandt, PhD, MFT

Published by
PESI Publishing & Media
PESI, Inc.
3839 White Ave.
Eau Claire, WI 54703

Cover: Amy Rubenzer
Editing: Hazel Bird, Jeanie Stanek
Layout: Bookmasters, Amy Rubenzer
ISBN: 9781683730781
All Rights Reserved.
Printed in the United States of America

***

The Library of Congress has cataloged this edition as follows:
Names: Brandt, Andrea, author.
Title: Mindful aging: embracing your life after 50 to find fulfillment,
   purpose, and joy / by Andrea Brandt, Ph.D.
Description: Eau Claire, WI: PESI Publishing & Media, [2017] | Includes
   bibliographical references.
Identifiers: LCCN 2017028494 (print) | LCCN 2017032538 (ebook) |
ISBN
   9781683730798 (ebook) | ISBN 9781683730804 (ebook) | ISBN
9781683730781 (pbk.)
Subjects: LCSH: Self-actualization (Psychology) in old age. | Older
   people--Conduct of life.
Classification: LCC BF724.85.S45 (ebook) | LCC BF724.85.S45 B73
2017 (print)
   | DDC 158.1084/6--dc23
LC record available at https://lccn.loc.gov/2017028494

Permissions are acknowledged in the Notes and Credits section on page
191, which constitutes an extension of the copyright page.

PESI
Publishing
& Media
www.pesipublishing.com

Praise for Mindful Aging

"If you're concerned about growing older, don't be. Andrea Brandt not only lays our concerns to rest about what awaits us as we age, she demonstrates how growing older can be the most fulfilling experience of our entire life."

— **John Tarnoff, MA,** Reinvention Career Coach; Author of *Boomer Reinvention: How to Create Your Dream Career Over 50*

"I used to worry that I would have to go back to school to learn how to age gracefully, but *Mindful Aging* has taught me all I need to know! It's a much-needed book and an empowering read that encourages reflection, self-discovery and personal change during a most precious time of life."

— **Theo Koffler**, Author, Educator, and Founder of Mindfulness Without Borders

"It's never too late to enjoy the rest of your life. With a learned approach to lifespan development, Dr. Andrea Brandt takes a wise and sensitive look at the process of mindful aging and concludes that while THE body must age, the mind can soar. *Mindful Aging* is inspirational and an insightful guide for all. A must read!"

— **Linda Metzner, PhD**, Life Coach

"Age and experience can be assets, rather than detriments, to living a happy, healthy, and empowered life. That's just one of the many uplifting messages Dr. Andrea Brandt writes about in this thought-provoking book, which is equipped with wisdom and a myriad of other inner resources that can only be developed with age. We are finally in our prime, uniquely ready to make our most significant mark on the world. *Mindful Aging* inspires and guides us to embrace the opportunities of our older years and to engage in what matters most."

— **James Gottfurcht, PhD**, Clinical Psychologist and President of Psychology of Money Consultants

"This timely and inspiring guide to aging with joy and renewal takes on special meaning as globalization and technological change in the 21st century beckons us to foster resilience and embrace life-long learning with pleasure, growth and fuller self-expression. Andrea Brandt's encouraging and informative work is long over-due."

— **Constance Kaplan**, Licensed Marriage and Family Therapist Faculty and Senior EMDR Trainer, Parnell Institute

"Beautifully written and providing a powerful mix of science, real-life examples, and heartfelt encouragement, this book offers the recipe for living our very best life after middle age."

> — **Sandy Michelson**, Marriage & Family Counselor, MA

"Thoroughly enjoyed reading this book. It poetically puts to paper concrete ideas and strategies for how to create a life worth living as a senior. I will refer to it again and again for myself and my clients."

> — **Douglas L. Gosney, MA, LMFT, SEP**, High Performance Coach and Past President of the Los Angeles Chapter of the California Association of Marriage and Family Therapists

"*Mindful Aging* offers a remarkable and optimistic strategy for the challenges and adventure of living as we grow older. It deserves a place on every bookshelf as a hopeful reminder of what is real and what is possible."

> — **Joel S. Satzman, MD**, Member of The Plato Society of Los Angeles

"This is not just another "feel-good" book. Brandt's clinical experience comes through as she explains clearly how to craft a life marked by health, purpose, creativity, and passion and offers exercises to bring it to life, literally."

> — **Katherine Carroll, NTP**

"*Mindful Aging* is an inspiring road map toward self-fulfillment in the "golden years" of life. Dr. Andrea Brandt has captured a vision and spirit of hopefulness for all of us and her exercises motivate us to engage in this wonderful process of aging. A must read book for all!"

> — **Dominic Cirincione, PhD**, President Organizational Fitness Associates

Flo Herman Golby, born in 1877, was my grandmother.
She was a mover and shaker long before the women's movement.
She exercised daily and flaunted her incredible style.
She was also an entrepreneur in the garment
industry and a private detective in the 1960s.
She married and divorced twice—the last time at 92 years old,
so she could have six more years of living a meaningful life.
She inspired me to write this book.

contents

Acknowledgments ix
About the Author. xi
Introduction: The Opportunity of a Lifetime. xiii

part | ONE

Preparing for the Adventure That Is the Rest of Your Life. 1

  1: Gaining the Mindset to Create Your Best Years Yet 3
  2: Letting Go of What Is No Longer Serving You 33
  3: Finding Your Joy and Living Your New Dream 65

part | TWO

The Fundamentals for a Healthy, Happy Post-Middle Age. 93

  4: Making the Connections that Make All the Difference 95
  5: Enhancing Your Body, Engaging Your Mind, & Expressing
     Your Creativity 123
  6: Developing Your Spiritual Side 147
  7: Transforming Your "Little Corner of the World" 171

Notes & Credits. 191
Bibliography. 203
Index 213

acknowledgments

I grew up in a very matriarchal family where the women thrived and produced well into their 90s. I noticed how others were in awe of how my family managed to look so good, work so hard, and feel so good … for example, my mother lost her eyesight at age 77 and went back to work nine months later for another five years!

In all my years growing up, I was curious about this phenomenon because I know these women had difficult lives; everything just wasn't coming up roses for them, and yet they managed to have a positive and productive attitude about aging.

As a result, I never saw old age as a state to avoid. Not that I haven't had periods of depression, but they were circumstantial, not because I was getting older.

This upbringing is the driving force that has led me to believe that life after 50 can be productive, meaningful, and joyful … if we know how to do it.

This book has emerged primarily from my background and positive beliefs about aging and my wonderful working relationship with my writing collaborator, Brookes Nohlgren. She put a great deal of herself into this book, and thoughtfully brought so many of her ideas and my ideas to life. Brookes is wise beyond her years and a dear, dear friend. Together we would like to thank Jacqueline Tasch for her writing and editing contributions that also added greatly to the book. We also thank those people whose real-life stories were used to illustrate ideas in the book; we appreciate their willingness to share so that others might be inspired by their examples.

I would like to extend my gratitude to PESI: To Teresa Fisher, who contacted me over two years ago about speaking on "mindful anger" to other therapists across the country, and to Karsyn Morse, who has shepherded this book on "mindful aging." They have both provided me with the opportunity to write and speak about areas of life that I am so passionate about.

I want to say "thank you" to Lisa Rivas for her enthusiasm and her smile, which she brings to whatever needs to be done.

Since we're all around the same age, I want to acknowledge my spiritual group because it's where I got some of my ideas for this book, and it's a safe place to talk about the challenges of aging … of which there are many!

To my Sensorimotor Psychotherapy supervision group, I am truly grateful for all your helpful support. And, to my friends and colleagues, I am indebted for your many nuggets of wisdom and creativity.

I am also deeply grateful to my patients, who have taught me so much over the years; they have provided me with an opportunity to continue developing my skills as a psychotherapist, and I so appreciate their trust and confidence in me.

To my husband, JP, for your endless love and support—I am lucky to have you in my life!

about the author

Andrea Brandt, PhD, MFT, has over 35 years of clinical experience as a renowned psychotherapist, speaker, and author. In addition to being a pioneer in the field of treating anger issues, she also works with a full range of emotional concerns that include anxiety, aggression, aging, the workplace, women's issues, and relationship dynamics. In her workshops, patient sessions, and presentations, Dr. Brandt reveals positive paths to emotional health that teach you how to reinvent and empower yourself. She emphasizes the mind-body-heart connection as a key to mental, physical, and emotional wellness.

A featured media expert, Dr. Brandt has appeared on numerous television programs, radio shows, and podcasts. She contributes to *Psychology Today* and has written blog posts for *The Huffington Post*, *Mind Body Green*, *Psych Central*, and more. She also trains therapists across the nation in a seminar titled *Mindful Anger: The Art of Transforming a Difficult Emotion into a Therapeutic Tool*. Dr. Brandt is the author of *8 Keys to Eliminating Passive-Aggressiveness* and *Mindful Anger: A Pathway to Emotional Freedom*.

For additional information visit www.abrandtherapy.com.

introduction:
the opportunity
of a lifetime

Welcome to the opportunity of a lifetime: to grow happier, more confident, more loving and better loved, and more engaged—at the same time as you grow older.

That's probably not what you've been hearing. The message society often sends is that old age is a waiting room for the next world, in which we are increasingly disabled and irrelevant before we disappear altogether. Or, alternatively, it's a playground for old people, where we engage in meaningless recreation all day. The media invite us to fantasize about retirement as a life of leisure, where we no longer have to work toward something, put out effort, or grow.

That's not how I see it. To my mind, that vision means we no longer get to experience the joys of being human: to discover, develop, and expand. There is no magical age at which we need to abandon our dreams and surrender our possibilities. Giving up a salaried occupation—if that's what we choose—doesn't mean giving up purposeful interaction with the world around us. Rather than take feelings of exhaustion and boredom to mean we need to retire, might these negative attitudes be more likely to indicate the need to reinvent ourselves—to explore new territory that brings us back to life and develops the skills we need to flourish there?

Through our youth and early adulthood, we taste a great many experiences and probably make more than one false start we live to regret. By age 50, we've accumulated the wisdom we need to place ourselves on more solid ground with a clearer sense of direction. As we grow older, we can contribute in a new way that is true to who we are *today*. That is the gift of the present moment. It is fresh and alive with possibility that is not bound to the past.

People are living longer than ever before. And those are healthy years—in fact, we can enjoy the best health of our lifetime, having discarded the bad habits that once held us back. Science extends our lifespan; it's up to us to make those additional years more rewarding to ourselves while we remain engaged with the world in a way that goes well beyond fun and games, although it does include play. As G. Stanley Hall observed, "We don't stop playing because we grow old; we grow old because we stop playing." "Playing," to me, means participating—being connected to, engaged with, and active in life. Having playmates, too. This is how we sustain our enthusiasm and joy—even as our bodies eventually slow down and our types and levels of activity change.

recognizing our value

Ours is a culture that deifies youth. This has not been the case in every time and every place. *Old man* is not a negative expression in Greece, where there is no stigma attached to growing older. Koreans have a special occasion to celebrate their 70th birthday, known as *kohCui* ("old and rare"). Many Indians live in multi-generation communities where the oldest people are the leaders. Other cultures also look to the wisdom of elders and hold the care of older people as a high value.[1]

In contrast, the Western view—dominant in Europe and the United States—is that growing older is about decline. In that stereotype, old people are ugly, forgetful, and cantankerous. Old age is a sequence of progressive illnesses and disabilities leading to death. We all have dementia or we will soon. A burden not just on our families but on society, we need to be shoved someplace where we can't be seen. Men with enough wealth can escape this stereotype, but hardly any women do.[2]

The truth—though—is that turning 50 marks the beginning of an extended middle age, and retirement—if that's what we choose—allows us to slip the harness of career and family demands and run free—free to pursue the interests and values that wisdom has brought us. From our 20s to our 40s, we tend to be preoccupied with the demands of others: birthing and raising a family, generating the funds and the work to care for them, developing job skills and pursuing a career. Ambition and discipline are key values, and too often we are obsessed with material things, not just what we need but what we think will provide us with the status we crave.

A friend of mine reached his mid-40s just about the time that newspapers were surrendering leadership of the information field to various digital media. Like many others, he was "down-sized." What seemed a catastrophe at the time turned out to be a blessing. At one level, it gave him the courage to pursue freelance projects—opening a world of constantly changing opportunities to explore his talents. More important, he began to think about what mattered to him—his creative life and his connections to family and friends.

At 70, he is "incompletely retired," still working on projects that appeal to him so that he can enjoy not only the work but also the travel he passed up in middle age because he was "too important" to leave his job for more than a week at a time. More significant, he has built a family of friends who value him for qualities that have nothing to do with status. He no longer defines himself by his job title.

As we turn away from the preoccupations of midlife, we have time to develop our answer to the question *What will I do with the time I still have left?* And, no matter how old we are, there is always time. Like my friend, many people in their 50s and 60s invest in career opportunities, but with a goal of achieving meaning rather than material success. Others turn to uncompensated pursuits that move toward the same goal. What some call the "longevity bonus"—years of relatively good health past 55 or 60—offers us a fresh start in many ways. If we are carrying regrets from things done—and undone—in midlife, we have an opportunity to heal relationships and to make our life whole.

While aging comes as a bit of a shock—who thought we would ever be as old as our grandparents seemed to us? It also brings a new understanding of how precious and fragile life is. With this wisdom, we can live every day in a value-oriented and meaning-filled way. We can bring that wisdom to the world. And, in its current state, the world certainly needs everything we can contribute as people who view wisdom and love as our guiding principles. Just as we must continue to steward our own lives, we need to steward the world. We have to continue to be the change we wish to see, or forfeit that role to others and hope for the best. If we wait for an invitation to step into this role, we will never receive it. Our potential for all the good we could do will be lost. The first step toward gaining respect may be commanding it. We do this by living a meaningful and engaged life.

flourishing in every decade

There's evidence that many people are doing exactly this: rediscovering the joy of life in its later decades. As witnesses, take the 340,000 people across the United States who answered a survey asking them to measure their overall sense of well-being on a scale of 1 to 10. The results showed that people in their late 40s and early 50s reported the least satisfaction, while those aged 70 or beyond were most likely to say they were happy—even compared to 20-somethings. The sense of satisfaction climbed with every decade after 50. In addition, levels of reported stress dropped sharply with age, and sadness stayed at about the same level from 18 through 85. In another American study, 70-year-olds rated themselves happier than 30-year-olds did. While older people are "normally seen as a burden on the economy and a problem to be solved," *The Economist* concludes, research "argues for a more positive view of the matter. The greyer the world gets, the brighter it becomes."[3]

Some of this effect has to do with the unavoidable fact that what's left of life is getting shorter. Observing what happened in my own life supports this idea. I was in my early 60s when two sudden, serious health conditions stripped me of my illusion of invincibility. They served as the wake-up call that made me realize I would have to live *and age* much more intentionally if I was going to have my best—happiest, healthiest, and most meaningful—life. The experience had multiple impacts. In my profession, it prompted me to finish one book I'd been belaboring for years and begin work on another.[4] I'd also always wanted to get out of my therapy office more and do public speaking and lecturing, and I decided to make that a reality. Today, I love the time I spend on the road, and it returns me to my office with a stronger connection to my patients.

Additionally, I've made some changes in my diet and exercise, but perhaps the most important changes were in my relationships. As an only child, I always thought I needed a lot of people around me. After my wake-up call, I realized that what I really needed was the intimacy and authenticity of a small circle of close friends. That's what made me safe and happy. I also came away with a greater appreciation for my husband, JP, and the unwavering and unconditional support he has always so generously given me.

Based on where I started in life—very isolated—I'm amazed at the support I've surrounded myself with. Now in my 70s, I have reached the happiest time in my life. Many people have a similar experience in their 50s and 60s: a cancer diagnosis, heart disease, diabetes, arthritis—something that triggers their recognition of mortality and inspires life change. Like me, many older people have found that health challenges and pain deepened their compassion for others and thus their ability to love and carry on meaningful relationships.

You don't need to go through a health crisis or the loss of a loved one to learn this lesson. Although we will all, sooner or later, face the difficulties of the body's waning years, we also have the gift of equally significant opportunities for benefit and greatness. If there's something you've "always wanted to do," why wait? Many of life's greatest lessons take at least half a lifetime to learn, and, as we gain in wisdom, we can move forward on projects that once seemed too ambitious. Drawing on a vastly deeper well of meaning and value and in a much more powerful way, we can exchange with others the kind of love and support we may have longed for, sometimes without success.

Of course, we must recognize our vulnerability and mortality, too—and even embrace them. The grand opportunity of mortality is to feel greater appreciation and urgency for the rest of life. Realizing that our days are finite, it's time, finally, to live like we mean it. To get life right. We experience an ardent desire to make the most of our life, to experience meaningfulness in all we do, to love like we never have before. The key question becomes: How do we do that?

That's what this book is all about. It involves a number of elements: knowing ourselves better and accepting our deeper truth, letting go of what no longer serves or uplifts us so we have the energy to pursue what does, getting clear about what we want—about what we'd love—and following through with actions to bring our dreams to life and effect change in the real world. We'll look at how to achieve these things in Part One. Then, in Part Two, we'll dive into specific areas of life that have proven to be the greatest source of happiness and well-being as we age: namely, relationships, physical exercise, continuous learning, creative expression, spirituality, and service to others. Each chapter includes selected research and personal stories that I hope will inspire you to reach your highest potential. Throughout, you'll see that mindfulness is the door to exciting and rewarding explorations that lead us to our truest dreams and most authentic selves. I'll be offering you general strategies for expanding into these key areas as well as exercises to develop new strengths you'll need there.

As the maxim says, today is the first day of the rest of your life. That's as true now as at any other point. Every day is a fresh opportunity for creating life anew. Whether you're coming to this book in your 50s—at the beginning of this opportunity-filled time of self-growth; in your 60s—turning the corner into full or partial retirement; or even in your 70s and beyond, you have the innate ability to change the years ahead. Think of it! You're not over the hill, you're at the top of the mountain. It's been tough work getting to this vantage point, but now you have a whole new world to explore. The good news is that it's never too late to grow stronger and happier and more confident. Or to have and pursue new dreams.

A temptation of the years beyond midlife is to overlook or ignore the opportunity to start anew and rather to just keep along the same old path we've been on, only with less vigor. To start winding down instead of gearing up. But we mustn't give in to that temptation if we wish to live our most full and meaningful life. Doing so would be to cut off so much of our potential. Did you know, for instance, that architect Frank Lloyd Wright was at his most prolific between ages 60 and 90? This can be true for all of us. That life is there for us, waiting, if only we will say yes!

If you are not engaged with life or others the way you'd like to be, if your perception of your future lacks vision or hope, if you feel restless, under-utilized, or bored—don't fret. It's never too late to move in a new, more positive direction. This book will show you how. Yes, it will take work—but it won't be arduous or depleting. Rather, I promise you, it will be uplifting and filled with joy. That's because what you'll be doing will be aligned with the true you, and bring you home to yourself.

All of the approaches advocated in this book lead to greater self-discovery and self-engagement, as well as greater engagement with the outside world. And they all engender emotional and physical resilience, which help us successfully face the unique challenges of older age. Indeed, this is a guide to embracing those challenges and taking advantage of the profound opportunities presented in aging and older age. It steers us to mindfully keep *becoming* who we really are—a journey we all can be on until our dying day. Won't you join me on the adventure?

part | ONE

preparing for the adventure that is the rest of your life

chapter | 1

gaining the mindset to create your best years yet

Some people seem to be authentically positive—optimistic, uplifting to be around, at peace with themselves—even though they may have, like all of us, lived through deeply challenging or hurtful experiences. We call them courageous. We marvel at their resilience. We love to be around them for the strength and personal power they exude. We'd like some of the secret sauce they've been seasoning their life with. They're not in denial about their troubles, but they're also not beaten by them. They seem to have truly accepted "what is" and yet they don't accept that this is the end of the road for them. They know that life is precious, keep their focus on what's working and good, and feel appreciation for all they have. And they know themselves. They know what they want, and they put their energy into having it, whether in a quiet, unassuming way or with an obvious passion that can easily be seen and heard. They live fully, fiercely, and in the moment, realizing it's all they really have. As a result, they feel vital and connected, and live happy, meaningful lives.

This is our goal. People aren't born this way (although some may be blessed with the genetics and upbringing that support resilience and positivity) and they aren't magically transformed by some genie they meet while they're out walking the dog, waiting for the bus, or taking out the trash. If you sat down and talked to them about their approach to life, you would almost certainly hear how hard they have worked at becoming who they are.

With or without the blessings of a relatively beneficent childhood, all of us have to work at the task of becoming people we admire and having a life we love. Some of us may have to work a little harder than others, but this is an achievable goal for everyone. Instead of letting our strengths become eroded by the stresses of life—or fortifying ourselves behind a wall in an attempt to keep the stresses out—we need to create a relationship with life that allows its flow to move through us rather than tear us down.

This is what I will call *realistic positivity*, a mindset that helps us to grow better as we grow older and to create a life we truly love.

realistic positivity: what does it mean?

You may have heard the term *realistic optimism*, first used by positive psychologist and thought leader Martin Seligman and now also used by others to mean "the ability to look realistically at what is, as well as what is possible, and choose a perspective that enhances one's ability to make the best of the moment and bring one's best to life."[5] Thus a realistic optimist is viewed as "someone who looks on the bright side of life but has a realistic grasp on the present and what to expect in life."[6] It tends to be a pushback against "Pollyanna optimism"—a "view of life that expects positive outcomes without regard for the options or the odds."[7]

While I agree with this thinking in large part, I don't want us to exaggerate our limitations or the obstacles we face or to underestimate our own capabilities. There is truly so much we are capable of—at any age—if we know how to go about it. Thankfully, science is validating this more and more every year, giving us exciting news about the seemingly unlimited potential of the human brain and body.

So, I'll be making a few distinctions between the existing term and my own, by going deeper and into the specifics of what I mean by each of the two parts of the equation: "realistic" and "positivity." For now, let me give you the quick version: Realistic positivity means seeing and accepting *what is now*—both in our inner and outer worlds—and then putting our focus on *what we would love*.

being "realistic"

How many times have you heard the phrase, *You have to be realistic!* "Realistic" is a slippery word, often a matter of perspectives and beliefs rather than facts. For example, when hearing about our weight-loss goals, even a good friend may ask us to be realistic, while at the same time we believe in our ability to get the result we desire. They are speaking for themselves, perhaps—what they believe to be true about *them*—but that doesn't mean what they believe is impossible for them will also be impossible for us.

The truth is that with the right know-how and application, *most* results—if they stem from our heart and are thus fueled by passion and joy—can be achieved. Not so sure? Just ask anyone who, driven by a true passion or love, has done what others believed to be impossible. Tao Porchon-Lynch is one example. At 98, she is the world's oldest yoga teacher. As of this writing, she teaches yoga classes most days of the week, travels nationally and internationally giving workshops and participating in retreats, and can still do many of the challenging yoga poses she mastered in her youth.[8]

You might argue that that's not so unrealistic, given that Tao has been conditioning her body to do yoga for *ninety* years, since the age of eight. While I'll grant you that, it doesn't explain away the achievements of other older athletes who have accomplished seemingly unrealistic things after starting well into their elder years—people like Fauja Singh, who ran his first marathon at 89 years of age and who today, at 106, is still at it. You'll be meeting Fauja and others like him who have defied what we thought was unrealistic, as we move through the book.

Our discussion of *realistic*, then, needs to start with the facts.

Being Realistic Means Knowing the Facts of How Things Work

Being realistic starts with recognizing and understanding factual reality—which can be a real challenge, as scientists and experts of all kinds are continuously making new discoveries and gaining new understandings about the intricacies of how the universe, and how we as part of it, work. Yet, this knowledge is key to our effectiveness in creating meaningful change. Just look at how important it is in treating a disease to accurately make the distinction between its symptoms and its cause. Obviously, we're not going to change the situation very effectively if we're confusing the two.

Before we knew about the existence of infectious microorganisms and their role in disease, for example, we thought fever was an illness and treated it with cooling cloths or even an ice bath. In fact, the fever was only part of the body's response to fight the microorganisms, and cold cloths did nothing to cure the infection that was the underlying cause.

We can make the same mistake in our own lives. For example, we may complain about fatigue and seek a cure for the disease. A cup of coffee may seem to help, but it's only treating a symptom. The real disease may be lack of exercise, a poor diet, or a life that has no motivation, inspiration, or joy. Amazingly, when we begin to address the real cause—say, starting a suitable exercise routine, giving the body much more nutrition and far less sugar, and spending time with people or doing an activity we love—our energy increases and our fatigue disappears.

Symptoms are easier to see than causes. That is why we are so often led astray. Choosing a mindset of realistic positivity means acknowledging the situation we find ourselves in, including its real cause, then focusing on creating what we'd like instead and discovering the pathway that leads to that end result. This can seem easier said than done, but I do believe that with openness and persistence we will get there—invariably learning valuable truths about ourselves and life along the way. That learning may be the very reason for the challenge in the first place.

I believe that there is always a pathway in the real world—though undoubtedly filled with twists and turns—between where we are and what we authentically desire to achieve. Accomplishing our goals may entail more than sheer effort; the road to our dreams often also requires curiosity, openness, and flexibility. A willingness to discover the way, which may lie outside of what we currently know.

Donna is an interesting example.[9] After pain in her abdomen and an inability to eliminate went on for a protracted period of time, she awoke in the middle of the night with an anxiety attack. Yet, that night's trip to the emergency room and the many subsequent medical consultations and tests could not pinpoint the cause, nor did the medication prescribed or the suggested treatments relieve the symptoms. The doctors told Donna she would just have to live with it. Many months of pain and discomfort ensued for this 69-year-old, who had been both health conscious and, up to then, healthy her whole life. At the suggestion of a friend, she decided to see a nutritionist.

Her research led her to an integrative medicine doctor in her area, who quickly ascertained the cause of the problem and promised her a cure—if she would follow the program he prescribed, to the letter. He also said that getting results would take some time. Though it sounded a bit extreme, she was desperate and, with no better options, agreed. After eight months of following a regimented program—consisting of exercise, meditation, acupuncture, and a highly restricted, anti-inflammatory, vegan diet—she was completely pain and problem free.

More than two years later, Donna continues this program as a way of life. Though she loves it and feels the best in her life, it wasn't comfortable or easy at first. Having had a career in U.S. healthcare management, alternative medicine was totally new to her. She knew nothing about it. And, though she'd always considered herself conscious of eating healthy, her diet had included meat, dairy, sugar, caffeine, the occasional drink of alcohol, and several other things she'd had to give up in order to get well.

Now, I'm not necessarily advocating being a vegan—I'm neither a vegan, a medical doctor, nor a nutrition expert—and I don't know if that route is the best one for everyone. I share the story to emphasize that there is a way, even when it's not widely known, even when it's off the well-worn path. Sometimes we just have to be willing to seek outside of what we already know.

While physical healing is beyond the scope of this book, knowing the facts about how our bodies and brains work is essential if we want to have some control over how we age. As John Ratey, M.D., says in his enlightening book *Spark: The Revolutionary New Science of Exercise and the Brain*, "Age happens. There's nothing you can do about the why, but you can definitely do something about the how and the when."[10]

To be able to achieve the things we want that turn our older years into a life we truly love, we need to understand the nature and capabilities of our body and brain and how we can work with them to bring about the change we desire. We will touch upon this throughout the book, but for now, let's talk about some of the best news to come about in decades: the discovery of neuroplasticity.

Our Plastic Brains

The field of neuroscience has put an end to the long-held notion that our brains stop developing after the first years of life, and that after that point no new neural connections can be made. Rather, our brains remain "plastic"—ever changing and able to make new connections—throughout life.[11] This means that we old (human) dogs can be taught new tricks. That we can continue to learn and grow until our dying day.

Research supports the notion that older age does not have to be a period of withdrawal, deterioration, and decline, but that—as with earlier stages of life—we can continue to improve and "become" who we authentically are and want to be. Knowing this is key to how we age. A "growth mindset," as coined by Stanford University psychologist Carol Dweck,[12] can have important effects on our achievements and social interaction. Indeed, there is tremendous power in knowing we can improve at what we put our focus on and effort into.

We've all heard that sitting is the new smoking. That if we rest we rust. Well, we're also learning that being too comfortable in general isn't good for us. We need mental and physical challenge—to work hard at something, which automatically entails grappling and struggling at times as we work to figure things out—in order to keep our brain functioning at its very best. Staying our sharpest requires some real effort. That's what a recent study at Massachusetts General Hospital discovered when comparing the brains of "superagers"—a term coined by the neurologist Marsel Mesulam to describe those "whose memory and attention isn't merely above average for their age, but is actually on par with healthy, active 25-year-olds"—to other people in the same age group.[13]

As you can see, what's considered realistic is a moving target; it is changing all the time. Science is continually showing us that we need to raise the bar in what we can expect from ourselves. To set truly appropriate expectations, we have to know what we are capable of. So often, it's more than we ever imagined, in part because we hardly allow ourselves to imagine at all—at least not the positive. We're good at envisioning the negative, though. As Mark Twain reputedly once said, "I've had a lot of worries in my life, most of which never happened." Sadly, many of us are much more likely to use our imagination to fuel our fears instead of our dreams. I hope this book will help to change that.

This brings us to the next part of reality to acknowledge as part of our new mindset: that of our perceptions.

Being Realistic Means Acknowledging Our Perceptions

In a scientific sense, reality is something that can be supported by facts. I know I have a chair because I can touch it and sit into it. It also is verifiable. A friend—or a stranger—can also touch it and sit into it. If you ask, "Is this a chair?" they will say yes. But realistic positivity stretches beyond this very basic material element to include what you think and feel when you sit there (is it a place where you go to relax or to settle yourself when you're agitated?) and perceptions of the chair that may be rooted in experience (does it remind you of a family member who owned it first, and were you sitting there when you received good or bad news?). All of this is a very real part of the chair to you, but your friend is unlikely to share these emotions and perceptions. Like a chain reaction, however, what we think and how we feel affects what we see and what we tell ourselves. In that way, this expanded reality drives the way we behave— the decisions we make and the actions we take in life—which means it greatly influences the results we get and thus our experience of life.

If, for example, we believe getting older looks and feels a certain way because of the elder role models of our youth or because of the picture society and the media paint of it, then that's what we'll expect for ourselves and we'll likely live up to it accordingly. It's what people refer to as a self-fulfilling prophecy. What we see and expect is what we get, because it's what we unconsciously end up creating.

Sadly, as in this case, our perceptions might be in direct contradiction to the facts of what is possible—and we limit ourselves unnecessarily. Rather than being based on objective reality—of knowing what's truly possible in the real scheme of things—our perceptions are based on experiences and the meaning (often inaccurate) that we made of those experiences at the time they took place. Let's look at how that happens.

Little Mapmakers

As children—in fact, starting as early as in the womb—we are little mapmakers. As things happen to us and around us, our developing brains do their best to interpret those events—to make meaning out of them—to keep us safe. "Safe" is a key word here; the whole mechanism is geared toward protecting us and ensuring our survival. That means protecting both our physical well-being and, because we are highly social creatures who survive better in a group, our ability to maintain harmony with others.

With each new message or experience, we add to the internal map we're charting of "how it is," in order to gain a sense of orientation in life and be able to safely navigate our world. We evaluate and then categorize each experience—whether a person, place, behavior, emotion, etc. (including our own thoughts and actions)—as "safe" or "unsafe," as "good" or "bad." This, then, informs us about what to seek and what to avoid in the future.

While the meaning we make often serves us in the short term—helping us to cope with, or in extreme cases actually survive, a confusing or painful experience—those interpretations often end up doing us a great disservice in the long run. They became a filter through which we come to view life, colored by our past, preventing us from being able to come at life with "fresh eyes," take each new experience at face value, and evaluate it for what it actually is. Because this map or filter is wired into our brain, we do all of this automatically—without conscious awareness.

Sadly, to gain a sense of control where perhaps we had none, we often assign responsibility for negative experiences to ourselves. All of our interpretations are imprinted on or "wired" into our developing brain, becoming "core beliefs" through which we see the world and ourselves as we go through life. The thoughts and beliefs created by childhood experiences can live on into our adult years, filtering our perceptions and driving our behaviors until they are discovered, challenged, and—if they are hurting us—released.

And, because it's all based on safety and survival, seeing through this filter makes us overly fearful and protective—overly sensitive to threats against our physical body and sense of identity/self that might make us unacceptable to "the group." We perceive threats where there aren't any, and we react accordingly, which often drives people, opportunities, and other goodness away.

For example, criticism and name-calling from an angry parent can create in a child a belief that they are stupid, worthless, incapable, or unlovable. As the child grows up and carries that belief as part of their self-definition, it will either greatly limit what they attempt in life or drive them to prove that belief wrong. In either case, they will be propelled to inaction or action in an attempt to be safe—to be okay—rather than to pursue a higher vision for their life. This is the opposite of free choice! Rather than creating our life based on what we would love for ourselves, we are on a treadmill, feverishly trying to change the past. But no matter what we achieve, it's never quite enough to resolve the angst. That's because, underneath, the belief is still there; we still believe it.

William Whitecloud, a creative development expert and the author of the best-selling book *The Magician's Way*, calls this reaction to our beliefs our "compensating tendencies."[14] We compensate for the belief that we don't belong, that we're not good enough, that we're unlovable, that the world isn't safe, and on and on—whatever our particular core beliefs may be. And, though we don't realize it, this keeps our mind and body—our brain and body physiology—in survival mode, in some degree of the famous "fight-flight-or-freeze" response, which is the opposite of the creative, innovative state we need to be in to create a life we truly love.

We can think of our emotions as the fuel that drives our decision-making and behavior—as "energy in motion." Though we can create amazing things fueled by fear, the result is never happiness. It's never the higher choice. In order to have true success—happiness and well-being—we need to create from the emotion of love.

Can you see just how important our perceptions are in a discussion of being realistic? If we aren't aware of what we think and feel in any given situation, we won't recognize how we may be preventing ourselves from pursuing and achieving what we would love. In this way, we have to make what's unconscious conscious, in order to give ourselves true choice.

We can take a big step in that direction by striving to see as much of the whole picture in a situation as we can. We'll look at that next.

Being Realistic Means Seeing the Whole Picture: The "Good" and the "Bad"

Rather than allowing our built-in negativity bias that's part of our survival mechanism to automatically cause us to see only the "bad" in a situation, or compensating for the same underlying fear by denying it and employing a Pollyanna approach that sees everything as "good," we need to strive to see the totality of "what is" and then choose how we want to respond. When we do this, we're able to expand beyond the limited view of our fear and see a brighter picture with more possibility.

Take Richard, for example, who met Lorraine in Oregon while he was visiting his daughter and grandkids 10 years ago. The two dated long distance for a couple of years, and then Richard proposed. While Lorraine loved Richard, she was very reluctant to move across the country and leave her home, family, and friends. As a compromise, Richard said that if Lorraine would live with him in Virginia until he retired in five years, he would move back to Oregon with her upon his retirement. She agreed.

Eight years later—three years past the time when he had promised to move to Oregon—Richard is still dragging his feet. He's got one excuse after another for postponing the move. Rather than delve into his feelings about moving, some of which are very likely fear, he avoids his feelings as much as possible. Instead, he compensates for them—drinking heavily every evening, spending hours and hours a day in front of the computer or television screen, and doing his best to avoid conversations about the move (and his avoidance of it). He procrastinates on the list of "to dos" that are his current reasons for not moving. Though he was recently diagnosed with an incurable progressive condition—making the matter more urgent—he still refuses to budge.

Rather than seeing the opportunity being offered him, which holds the potential for a better life—where he would be close to both of his daughters and grandkids and could create much more meaningful connections with them, where he'd be in both a house and a climate that would likely make his health challenge easier, and where he would keep an important promise that would make his spouse happier and remove strain from his marriage—he continues to view the situation as bad. He can only see giving up the house and community he is attached to. Rather than make decisions based on a vision he has for his life—which we'll discuss next in our section on positivity—he is operating out of a fear of loss.

Only when we have fully acknowledged the reality of a situation, including our thoughts and feelings about it, are we ready to effectively change it. Only then can we be free enough to see clearly and put our attention on what we *truly* desire. Only then are we ready for the second part of this powerful mindset: positivity.

what is positivity?

Positivity is sometimes defined as a way of viewing the world that focuses on that which gives us pleasant emotions, on what makes us feel good. It's about focusing on the "good," the positive in any situation. This definition takes us part of the way that I would like us to go. In the context of realistic positivity, I take the idea further, using the word to mean a focus specifically on what we would love—simply for its own sake, purely for the joy of having it. Because our emotions fuel our decisions and the action we take, with this meaning, positivity not only makes us feel good but also empowers us and influences what we do and create.

Though we certainly don't hear about this anywhere in mainstream life, the idea I'm proposing here isn't new. Werner Erhard, developer of the popular self-improvement trainings *est* and The Forum, said that we can live either based on our circumstances or from a vision we have for our lives.[15] William Whitecloud furthers that idea by proposing that this vision be based on what is true to the truest part of ourselves, our heart's desire—in other words, *what we would love.*[16]

If I could work with Richard, I would coach him to reflect on his situation so that we could uncover the negative feelings and beliefs that are causing his reluctance and robbing him of giving credence to the positive aspects of the move. I would help him tap into the higher part of him that knows his heart's desire, to help him craft a vision of what he'd really love for his life and then set out to accomplish that.

The entire mindset of realistic positivity hinges on this type of reflection—on our ability to become aware of reality as defined in the preceding pages and to choose positivity to create a life we love. Next, we'll discuss the tool we use to give us that awareness—it's called mindfulness.

the role of mindfulness in creating positive change

The key to understanding "what is" in any given situation—and that includes in both our inner and our outer worlds—is intentionally and nonjudgmentally focusing our awareness in the present moment. Leading mindfulness researcher and author Dr. Daniel Siegel defines the qualities of this state of mind with the acronym COAL: curious, open, accepting, loving.[17] All of these qualities are key to creating the safety that our psyche needs in order to see the reality of what is happening before us. Becoming the observer in this way actually allows us to step out of our "wired" perceptions and survival physiology, and, without our mind's chatter, to observe and be. Becoming more mindful isn't hard; it just takes the choice to do it and a small amount of effort to guide your attention in a way that may be unfamiliar. In the Exercises section of this chapter, I'll walk you through some basic mindfulness techniques.

Mindfulness can be—but doesn't need to be—about profound issues. One of my favorite exercises is to eat mindfully, focusing my attention on my sensory experiences as they are occurring. I like to use a flavorful food to practice with, such as an orange or grapefruit. Feel the texture of the fruit's skin with your hands and fingers, smell the scent as you cut or break the skin, feel the texture and firmness of the fruit in your mouth, and taste the unique flavor as you chew.

There are lots of books about how to be mindful. If you want to be trained more formally, attend a class or take an online course. Whether you seek formal training or not, the important thing is to spend time being mindful every day, by simply being present to whatever you do. You can make certain daily routines your practice ground for mindfulness—preparing and eating meals; sitting alone, inside or outside, and opening your senses to your surroundings; doing "conscious exercise" where you notice what you're experiencing in your body; and so on.

Many people think life just happens to us, but I fervently disagree. The more aware we become, the more clearly we will see how our own choices and actions affect what we experience. This is not about blame; it serves no purpose to beat ourselves up over past choices and the consequences they caused. Rather this is simply an invitation to take hold of the reins of your life and live more consciously so that you can create much more of what you want. To be who you truly are, you have to be awake!

In Chapter 2, we will apply mindfulness to observe our emotional world—a practice called emotional mindfulness. You'll find the word *mindful* or *mindfulness* in nearly every chapter of this book.

Mindfulness is essential for developing a mindset of realistic positivity—both for gaining the space we need to step out of our outdated and limited perceptions so we can see life more realistically and for shifting out of our survival physiology so we can focus on the positive, the direction we want to go.

Following are other strategies that will help you develop this mindset. They are both easy to implement and powerful for effecting meaningful and lasting change. As with all of the strategies offered in this book, practicing these and making them your habits will shift you in the moment into a positive frame of mind while also increasing your resilience and happiness long term.

strategies for developing realistic positivity

Put Your Perception in Perspective

In this chapter, we've talked about how our perceptions can affect us for good or bad. We may confuse them with reality, but they aren't facts and they aren't verifiable—everybody may have different perceptions. They represent our interpretations of events and the conclusions we've drawn, which are highly subjective and based on a number of different factors, the least of which may be factual reality. The good news is that we can change how we perceive ourselves and what's happening around us. To avoid getting stuck in false assumptions about "how it is" or "how things are" created by our own tunnel vision, it's important to broaden our viewpoint, especially in the face of a challenge.

One of the best ways to do this comes from University of Pennsylvania psychologist Martin Seligman, who teaches his clients to look at the worst, best, and most likely case scenarios in a situation. This strategy helps us steer clear of either catastrophic or Pollyanna thinking—so that we are neither overwhelmed by negative possibilities nor in denial of potential pitfalls—and makes us more able to envision and work toward a realistic, positive result. Say the weathercaster is forecasting heavy rain for tomorrow. Worst case, the rain could cause flooding and destruction. Best case, the forecast could be totally wrong and tomorrow full of sunshine. Most likely, the weathercaster is right, at least to some degree, but the rain won't cause any serious problems.

One thing I always like to remember when I'm going through something difficult is that "It could always be worse." On the surface, this may sound like a flippant brushing-off of the gravity of a situation, but it's actually deeper than that. If you've seen much of life—spent time in other countries, perhaps, and witnessed people who have far less than you do or known people who have been through terrible hardships—then you know how a broader perspective can instantly shift your perceptions about your own circumstances and engender resilience and newfound resolve. Following this statement, I remind myself equally that "It can always get better," and, in a more empowering formulation, "There is *something I can do* to make this better." We have a huge amount of agency in our lives and the lives of others we touch. Asking yourself, "How can I help here? What would make this better?" leads you to find the positive move that can make all the difference in the world.

When Melinda was diagnosed with breast cancer, she saw three different oncologists to confirm the diagnosis and asked each to prescribe the treatment he or she would recommend. Their views were remarkably similar. Melinda picked the doctor whom she felt the most kinship with, figuring that the connection would provide her with feelings of support during the treatment. She knew that the weeks ahead would be difficult, but she turned her attention to how she could organize her life to make it as comfortable as possible during that hard time. And she began to invest time in envisioning and planning what she could do after her body healed. Since travel was her love, Melinda enjoyed investigating several possible destinations throughout her months of chemo, surgery, and radiation. Settling on Barcelona, she developed her own itinerary—and, six months after she completed treatment, she was there, having one of her best trips ever.

Rather than succumbing to fear and feelings of hopelessness, she faced her fears and made positive plans. She disempowered her fears and empowered her dreams.

Set Your Sights Higher Than Mere Solutions

We all know that one of the distinguishing differences between optimists and pessimists is where they put their focus: optimists see possibilities where pessimists see problems. Since our focus greatly contributes to reality, it's easy to see where these different approaches will land us. The happier life belongs to those who acknowledge problems (i.e., are realistic) but then shift their attention to finding solutions (i.e., are positive). Becoming a "solution specialist" is popular and sound self-help advice that lifts us out of victimhood thinking and learned helplessness.

I'd like to take this notion a step further—or higher, if you will— where we put our focus not on the solution to our so-called problem but on the vision of what we *want*. The two are actually quite different. Take, for example, an illustration about health. If you are dealing with an illness, focusing on the solution would be looking for a cure. But, if your goal—your desired end result—is not just the elimination of that illness but rather vibrant health, removing the illness may not achieve that. Instead, you need to focus on what it is you are really after— excellent health—and go about discovering and doing what it takes to achieve that. As Buckminster Fuller famously once said, "You never change things by fighting the existing reality. To change something, build a new model that makes the existing model obsolete."

We are actually much more powerful creating something we love than trying to stave off problems. That's because the force behind our intention and action is love rather than fear. As an energy, love is always more empowering than fear. We are much stronger when working to create the positive than when working to avoid or fix the negative. The reason for this brings us back to focus: where we put our attention is what we end up creating. Instead of our focus being on the fear of dying, it's on the joy of living. I encourage you in any situation to cultivate a vision based on what you'd truly love and to concentrate on making *that* your goal. I'll be helping you to do that throughout this book. And because the mind envisions and creates in images, we do this most powerfully using our imagination—painting positive pictures of what we want to experience or create.

One small caveat: be sure your vision doesn't arise out of *shoulds* or what others want for you—who *they* want you to be. Haven't we spent—wasted—enough time in our youth pursuing that deadening and dead-end road? One of the great aspects of reaching post-middle age is that we begin to see that there is too little time to invest any of it in that rabbit hole; it's time to get this right once and for all—for ourselves. We deserve it. You deserve it. It's your birthright. Your life belongs to you and no one else. It's time, finally, to truly please your heart and truest self. So, whenever I'm talking about your heart's desire or doing what you love in this book, I'm referring to what is true for you and only you.

Use Empowering Self-Talk

A very important piece of maintaining a mindset of realistic positivity is our self-talk. This is where our dreams receive the rocket fuel they need to gain blastoff and reach their orbit or get shot down before they leave the ground. Most of us have an over-developed self-critic that does not seem to go away with age—unless we train it. If someone else heard our inner conversations, we would want to hide. Training the inner conversationalist can be a journey in itself.

We all have the ability to choose what we focus on as well as what we say to ourselves about it. This includes what we focus on and say about ourselves. Our self-talk influences every part of our life and might just be the most important thing we do all day—either building up our confidence and self-esteem for going after what we want in life or reducing us to a pile of rubble where we waste precious time and energy reciting all the reasons we can't. Similarly, decreasing the amount of negative thinking we do about others and the world also propels us to act and take risks, as it increases oxytocin, a neurotransmitter that greatly affects our confidence.[18]

A key to living your best life at any age is to adopt self-talk that reminds you that you are in the driver's seat, that you are actually very powerful and have a huge capacity to grow, and that you have the ability to choose and the inner resources to effectively handle challenges. You can create your life the way you want it to be. For example, just look at how differently you feel when you replace "have to" with "get to" or "choose to," or when you replace "problem" with "project": "I choose to get up and go to work today," and "I have a health project." If you can embrace the idea that every challenge truly is an opportunity to learn about yourself and life and to become wiser, more authentic, more courageous, more loving, more compassionate, and otherwise more of the person you would like to be, you will look for the lesson or gift in your suffering and find new, meaningful ways to expand.

Positive self-talk helps us build on our successes. Acknowledging your efforts, progress, and achievements will create a momentum that then takes on a life of its own. You'll also want to be specific rather than offer yourself general praise, for the greatest effect. "You're great—I love you," is less effective in developing confidence to keep stretching and tackling the next challenge than, say, "Look at how thoroughly you cleaned and organized the garage." This will help you stay connected to the pleasure of a job well done and spur your enthusiasm for climbing the next hill. Our self-talk is also crucial to developing a growth mindset. Again, focusing on your efforts rather than your talents will remind you of your immense capacity to grow and learn. People who succeed aren't always naturally gifted, but they are always willing to *do*—they take action, fear or no fear.

Become a Beauty Aficionado

Part of using our focus to create more of what we want in life means looking for what makes us happy, brings us joy, or pleases us on some level of our being. I put these types of experiences into a general category called "beauty." We want to become an aficionado of beauty as we go moment to moment through our day.

Every moment—in all circumstances and situations, in all people, not only in material things—will have aspects that we like and don't like. Becoming an aficionado of "beauty" means seeing and accepting "what is"—the good parts and the bad—while actively looking for and consciously recognizing that which we appreciate. Another name for this would be becoming an "apprecionado"—recognizing that "where there is life, there is beauty." Choosing to see and then focus on the good and say thanks brings us untold rewards.

Make Gratitude Your Foremost Attitude

Once you find the beauty, feel grateful for it. We hear and read about gratitude all the time. It's covered in nearly every personal development book on the market. That's because it's one of the most powerful tools there is for being happy and healthy. By my estimation, it may even— quite literally—be divine! My theory is that gratitude connects us to the highest energy we have available to us—the energy we know as love. With gratitude, we push a button that instantly releases feelings of elation and peacefulness throughout our being, and suddenly all is right with the world.

Having an attitude of gratitude doesn't mean you override your internal judge, critic, or complainer. Part of realistic positivity is to notice these aspects of yourself and give them a voice. But then you are free to tell them that they don't get to run the show. You get to consciously choose what to focus on and where to put your energy. By making it your habit to focus on what you like, appreciate, find beauty in, and even love in any situation or circumstance, your happiness, peace, and fulfillment levels will instantly rise. Your health, too, will improve. Research has shown that people who keep a gratitude journal, where they record things they feel grateful for, "enjoyed better physical health, were more optimistic, exercised more regularly, and described themselves as happier than a control group who didn't keep journals."[19]

Find Inspiration in Role Models

Finding others we admire as people and adopting them as role models is a realistic positivity strategy that has tremendous potential to lift us up. Whether we appreciate their achievements, qualities they possess, or ways in which they have endured, overcome, and grown from challenges, other people can be a huge source of inspiration for us and the catalyst for developing resilience. Some of the seniors I most admire, many of whom are in their 80s and 90s, are fully active, happy, and making substantial contributions to society. They are magnificent role models. Seeing what's possible via others' examples, we gain new reference points for setting our own intentions, expectations, and goals.

This should never, however, lead us to make comparisons or beat ourselves up for not "living up" to what someone else has done. As Theodore Roosevelt reputedly said, "comparison is the thief of joy." Rather, it's about giving ourselves a positive vision for our own goals and expanding our thinking about what is possible for us. It's about making the impossible possible by first changing our *beliefs*. Even the consideration of what is possible starts to create change.

As we look to others for inspiration, we, of course, know that no one is perfect. That's okay. We can take the positive and inspirational we see in others and leave what is less than healthy and functional behind. By developing in ourselves the qualities we love and admire in others, we build ourselves and our life into a mosaic of what we value most. While you may have done a lot of this in your lifetime already, ask yourself whether there are still places to explore, develop, and grow. Learn about people you look up to, and make them your heroes. After identifying and incorporating a lesson that benefits you, move on to the next.

Become Fearless by Facing and Disempowering Your Fears

Part of putting our perception in perspective and not mindlessly allowing it to rule how we live is recognizing when we are in safety/survival mode and reacting on autopilot to our fears. Emotions are part of our human survival wiring. The purpose of emotions—which, as mentioned, you can think of as "energy in motion"—is to prompt us to act. They are designed to move us to do something about our situation. The problem arises for us when we experience our emotions but don't figure out what they mean and address them with constructive action. Rather, because of our aversion to the discomfort they cause, we try to suppress them and, in doing so, become even more ruled by them, often to the point of being paralyzed.

Melinda gave herself some time to experience the grief and anguish of her diagnosis, while at the same time she was looking ahead to treatment. When she felt ready, however, she moved forward emotionally, knowing that she would need to call on her strength to heal.

Fear is a powerful emotion. We have more aversion to it than to almost any other feeling. Yet avoiding it keeps us severely limited in what we experience and create for ourselves in life. When we're caught in the perceptions of our fears, we rarely can see the reality of a situation. But, in order to act productively in a way that will help us create a life we love, we must be willing to look honestly at a situation, accept our thoughts and feelings about it, and only from that wider viewpoint make decisions about how to act.

If the fear of death, for example, keeps us so preoccupied that we're living in constant anxiety, without joy, then we cut our potential vastly short. As psychologist Carl Jung said: "As a physician I am convinced that it is hygienic—if I may use the word—to discover in death a goal towards which one can strive; and that shrinking away from it is something unhealthy and abnormal which robs the second half of life of its purpose."[20] While thoughts of death are inevitable, we can either allow them to keep us in bondage, unable to live freely, or remain fully and fearlessly in the present, which is the place where we experience joy.

When we stay stuck in fear, in effect paralyzed, at best we waste our potential for a fulfilling life, and at worst we damage relationships and our health. Today science clearly recognizes the link between mind and body, understanding that emotional stress can result in physical symptoms,[21] with chronic stress linked to six of the major causes of death.[22] As with everything else, we are greatly served by approaching our fears with a mindset of realistic positivity. Realistic positivity gives us the tools to dismantle our fears and move into the present, where we can refocus our energy on what we love. Let's take a look at this and other significant fears that are likely to affect us more intensely as we age.

uncertainty, the unknown, change

Remember Richard? I believe change is one source of his fear. Now in retirement, he has already lost one of the pillars of his middle-aged life. This happens to many people as they grow from 50 through 60 to 70 and beyond. Our job provides us with a setting that gives us a sense of competence and control. We are assured of a regular income, which also supports our sense of safety.

Living in a new place, as many older people do after retirement, can bring more uncertainty and with it a diminished sense of control. On our home turf, familiar people and places are touchstones that tell us we are safe. We may not like our neighbors, and we may wish the restaurants had better food, but still, we know them. At the most basic level, we are so familiar with our surroundings that we don't have to turn on the lights if we need the bathroom or a snack in the middle of the night. We may also worry that change will necessarily mean that things get worse.

Seeing the Gift of Change

Innovation—new creation—comes from stepping into the unknown. Retirement may bring us fresh opportunities to explore our talents and confirm our competence in new arenas—whether they're paying jobs, entrepreneurial efforts, or volunteer work. New places and new people can be stimulating and refresh our joy in life. As we grow older, new settings can provide additional supports in terms of services—a condo takes care of mowing the lawn and handling major repairs, and assisted living often provides house cleaning or meal services—that free us to spend more time doing what we love.

Viewing Change with Realistic Positivity

We are creators in every moment, with a large degree of agency over our lives or, at the very least, over what we think. This means more than choosing the outer circumstances of our lives. If you can hold your vision of what you'd love while sitting in the discomfort of not knowing and not being in control, an answer will emerge that will lead you down your desired path. This takes courage and the willingness to surrender control, as well as the willingness to fail—knowing that failure is only feedback and a necessary step along the road to creating what we really want.

loss

Another feature of life as we get older is loss—of physical characteristics, of our abilities, or of loved ones—and that can lead to grief, loneliness, and despair. Anyone who has gone through a divorce, the death of a loved one, or the loss of a limb or major bodily function knows this. You may wake up in the morning with an overwhelming sadness that starts before your conscious mind has even kicked in to remind you what has taken place, that it wasn't just a bad dream. At a less intense level, we may lose our hair—women, too, may suffer some thinning—and some of our strength. We inevitably lose some of the beauty of youth, even though we remain attractive. Losing a driver's license and the mobility that goes with it can be a terrifying prospect.

Seeing the Gift of Loss

Through loss, we learn to value life in this moment and to live and love fully, knowing that we may not get another chance. We learn that every moment counts. This knowledge is priceless; it makes all the difference in the choices we make and thus our experience of life. We also learn not to be as attached to material things that don't really matter in the big scheme of things, and not to define ourselves by whether we have them or not. In some ways, loss is an impetus to meet new people and explore new ways to achieve the affirmation and love that we need.

Viewing Loss with Realistic Positivity

This is where the expanded vision of realistic positivity can contribute greatly to our enthusiasm for life and our vitality to move forward. The impermanent nature of life and everything in it is a fact. We have to acknowledge that we don't "own" anything, that nothing actually "belongs" to us. We are merely borrowing it, and we can't control how long we'll have it. Knowing the truth that "the only constant is change," and that change often entails loss, makes us more resilient in the face of loss and enables us to be more proactive about replacing losses when they occur.

Sometimes life fills in the void without our intervention. The key is being open to and emotionally holding the space for the possibility for something to take its place. A friend of mine is a good example. One day as she was having lunch with a friend, she experienced the sudden and complete loss of hearing in her left ear. In the space of an hour or so, that side of her head became dead to sound. Neither medical nor alternative treatments brought it back. While she grieved her loss—and this grief is an important part of realistic positivity, as an acceptance and acknowledgment of "what is"—she came to appreciate the neuroplasticity of her brain for "rerouting" sounds to her right ear, yet hearing them on her left side. Looking back, she realized that she had treated one of her favorite activities—listening to music through headphones—as though it would always be with her. Now she finds herself being grateful for the things that still work, acknowledging that they, too, may not always be there for her.

Other times we have to fill in for the loss ourselves, and it's best to view the void as a space for something new and wonderful to enter our life. The loss of a job or career, whether by choice, layoff, or enforced retirement, carries within it the opportunity for new ventures, such as purpose-filled entrepreneurship or volunteerism. The loss of a loved one creates an opportunity to deepen existing connections or forge new ones.

illness and pain

By the time you reach 50 or 60, you will be exceptionally fortunate if you have not already experienced illness and pain. Some people seem to think that old age is preoccupied with both, yet research tells us that many people live in good health even in advanced years.

The Gifts of Pain

Besides making us grateful when we are pain-free, which is a huge gift in itself that allows us to live life with greater urgency and appreciation, pain can be a pathway into our deeper self. As we'll continue to explore throughout this book, science has now confirmed the mind-body connection. This means that what happens in our body is not separate from our mind, and that by learning to listen to our body, we can discover that our illness or pain has something to teach us about how we've been living our life. This, again, isn't about blame. Not at all. It's about self-discovery and self-knowledge, about listening and taking care of ourselves to see whether our illness or pain is revealing a deeper need. It's also why just taking a pill may not resolve an issue. It is worth exploring why it is that we have that pain and lovingly addressing what we find.

Viewing Pain with Realistic Positivity

When we are facing illness or pain, a good strategy is to stop worrying and get the facts. Too many people speculate endlessly about what might be wrong with them, when the only thing wrong is a negative use of their imagination and the stress it puts them through. While medical doctors are a good place to start for this part of the process, they likely won't be the place to stop. As counterintuitive as it might sound, I highly recommend going into your illness or pain, and seeing what it has to teach you about your life. Like my own example in the introduction of this book, illness was for me a tremendously valuable wake-up call— one that, because I embraced its message, greatly improved my life. While I'm sorry that I had to get ill in order to become more aware, I'm truly happy that it happened because it led to that end result.

Many people express becoming more thoughtful, loving, and compassionate after going through loss, illness, or other suffering. It's very often the fire of these types of experiences that burns away what is false and not serving us, and in rising from the ashes, we become our truest, best selves.

> "The most beautiful people we have known are those who have known defeat, known suffering, known loss and have found their way out of the depths. These persons have an appreciation, a sensitivity, and an understanding of life that fills them with compassion, gentleness, and a deep loving concern. Beautiful people do not just happen."
>
> —Roy Nichols and Jane Nichols[23]

death

We may act as though we'll live forever, but the truth is that we will die. Sooner or later, but inevitably. It's part of being human, and the older we get, the closer we are to that final fact. Friends and family who are critically ill or dying remind us of this. As we age, it is nearly impossible to ignore our thoughts and question marks about illness and dying, or our future. How we treat these thoughts is another matter.

Seeing the Gift of Death

There is a benefit to recognizing our mortality. It helps us to take stock of what we've done and to give fresh consideration to opportunities the future may hold. We may decide it's time to do now the things we've been leaving for some future date. We may reevaluate our achievements to determine what we need to do to enhance the meaning of our lives. Many people have the gift of a life-threatening diagnosis, followed by recovery. This wake-up call can help us to live more consciously every day.

Viewing Death with Realistic Positivity

Something magical happens when we finally, fully admit to ourselves that it's not likely that we'll be the one to defy the current laws of nature and not die. It pushes us right into a corner and asks us to make a choice: "What will you do with that knowledge? How will you choose to live your life?" The fear of death varies among people depending on how they view death, what they expect to happen, and how much they have enjoyed their life. We fear losing all that we love, including the people we will leave behind. My advice about handling fear is to simply acknowledge it. Write about it. Share your fear with someone who can listen effectively without fueling the fear. This could be a trained therapist, counselor, pastor, or the like. Explore what the fear of death has to teach you that will make you happier today and from here on out. Let that fear inform you as to how you might better live life.

I hope this look at fear has helped you get a sense of what realistic positivity is all about, and how embracing it can reduce stress, remove limitations, and pave the way for newfound joy to flood your life.

exercises

Timeline Review: Aging

In this exercise, take a few moments to evaluate your experiences to date with aging and to see what perceptions you have about the process of aging, about what older age looks like, and specifically about yourself as you age.

1. Take a blank piece of paper or new digital file and write "Aging and Older Age" at the top. Think back to when you first started having thoughts about yourself being "older"—when aging began to surface as a new reality in your life. How old were you? Was there a triggering event or circumstance that seemed to usher in what you considered a new phase of life? For some it's turning 50, when "over the hill" jokes and cards start to turn up or a younger person calls us "sir" or "ma'am." For some it's physical change, like wrinkles on our face or on the other end! For some, it's turning 60, regardless of how we look or feel. Write about the initial experience or timeframe when aging became part of your current reality.

2. Now take a few minutes to think about how aging has continued to bring waves of changes to your life. On a new page, draw a line vertically down the center. At the top of the left column, write "Dislike"; at the top of the right column, write "Like or Love." Under each heading, make a list of things about aging that you dislike or feel good about, respectively.

3. Take three to five entries from your "Like or Love" list and write a few sentences explaining why you like them.

4. When you've finished, notice how you feel having focused on these positive aspects of aging. Make notes about any observations you have.

Practice Basic Mindfulness

1. Find a quiet place where you won't be disturbed, and seat yourself in a comfortable position.

2. When you're ready to begin, take several slow, deep breaths, gently observing the expansion and contraction of your belly and chest as you take air in and out.

3. Once you feel relaxed, close your eyes and allow your mind to wander. At first, you may want to just see what floats to the surface. As you become more adept, you may want to focus your thoughts on a particular emotion or event.

4. Imagine those distracting thoughts are bubbles—let them float away or burst.

5. Don't judge the images that present themselves. Just examine them and pay particular attention to how they make you feel— both physically and emotionally.

You may want to include journaling in your mindfulness practice. Before you start, note the date, time of day, and any particular area you are hoping to explore. If you are writing about a particular event— perhaps a conversation with your partner—describe the scene. Who was there and what happened? When you end your session, make a few notes about your experience and participation in the event: What thoughts came to mind? What emotions and sensations were stirred?

Shift from Self-Doubt into Confidence, from Fear into Love

Shifting out of our perceptions of fear and self-doubt doesn't have to be a long and arduous trip. Following are some steps that can feel like magic, making it happen within minutes.

1. Write down your thoughts, feelings, and self-talk that occur when you're feeling insecure, stuck, or afraid.

2. Once you've written all of them down, turn the page over or skip down a few lines, leaving some white space. Write the heading: "What I Love."

3. Begin listing what you love—about anything. It can be about life in general, something that's happening in your life right now, people, animals, activities, works of art—anything. Keep listing and writing until the feeling in you shifts. It won't take long. Soon you'll be viewing your circumstance, and your ability to handle it, in a much more empowered way.

4. This exercise is one of the best for creating the life you want. If you can employ this whenever you are feeling weak or low, you will almost instantly shift the way you feel and move yourself into

a much higher energy for taking positive action that will produce results you want.

The Gratitude-Appreciation One-Two Punch

Develop your gratitude and appreciation muscles by expressing gratitude for even the simplest act or thing of beauty around you.

1. Become aware of what is around you and express appreciation or gratitude, both in your self-talk and outwardly to others where desired, as you *genuinely* see beauty, recognize goodness, and feel joy throughout your day. (Be truthful with yourself here—no faking it. Only express appreciation for what genuinely pleases you.) This expression can be as simple as a smile.

2. At the end of each day, reflect on how this practice makes you feel—about yourself, others, and life in general. How is this different from how you felt before you began to do the exercise?

3. If you like (and I highly recommend it!), continue this practice for 21 days, to cultivate the neural pathways that will establish it as a habit and a new way of life.

Go from Challenge to Possibility: Part 1

1. Look at a challenging situation from your life and write a short phrase that encapsulates it.

2. Next, evaluate the worst, best, and most likely scenarios for how it will turn out.

3. Finally, journal about how pondering each outcome makes you feel. How did your fears shift as you broadened your perspective about the possible outcomes?

4. What new insights, if any, came from the exercise?

Go from Challenge to Possibility: Part 2

1. Continuing from the previous exercise, turn your paper over or give yourself a new blank page.

2. Taking the situation you used in that exercise, step into a place of simply *not knowing* what the outcome will be. This place of not

knowing might look in your imagination like a blank page, an empty space or void, darkness, or something else that represents to you the unknown. Tell yourself that you don't know—and *don't need to.*

3. Be still and rest in that place for a moment or two.

4. Then, when you're ready, let your imagination wander to what you'd *really love* in this aspect or area of your life. What is your highest dream? Untether this vision of what you want and let it be free from the situation and experience you've been having. Instead, ask yourself: "What is it that I would love here?"

5. Write down the insight you get.

6. Spend a few minutes thinking about what would happen if you made *this* your goal in the situation—if, instead of working to solve the problem at hand, you put your focus on and energy into this. Write down any thoughts you have about it.

***

The tools you have learned in this chapter will help you to make immediate shifts in how you feel about yourself, others, and the world. They will lay new neural pathways in your brain and release neurochemicals that will both instantly and progressively increase your happiness, health, and overall well-being in the moment and, if practiced regularly, in the long term. The approaches and practices that together comprise a mindset of realistic positivity also pave the way for a deeper healing to occur—a healing that is essential in our being able to be fully in the present moment and free to make new choices to create a life we truly love. That healing is the focus of Chapter 2.

chapter | 2

letting go of what is no longer serving you

I want you to take a little imaginative journey with me. Let's pretend you're going about your usual business—maybe sitting and reading a book, working at your desk, placing the dishes in the dishwasher—when the phone rings. You turn to go to the phone, and you find you can't move in that direction. Or maybe you turn, but you can't walk any further. You might even get to the table where the phone is waiting, but you can't reach out to pick it up. Your arm will only move so far. You want to answer the call, but you simply can't move the way you need to make it happen.

This may be exactly what's occurring in your emotional life. Invisible strings are tying you to the past and keeping you from being fully functional in the present—limiting all that you do. I call these invisible strings "tether points." What you need to do is look inside to discover where these strings are attached and cut yourself loose from them so that you can move forward freely, with true choice.

In Chapter 1, we learned that we *can* change—that at any age, in any life stage, we absolutely have the capacity to learn, grow, adopt new habits, and make new choices to create a life we truly love. *Realistic positivity* is the mindset that is key to letting us do this most efficiently and effectively, and we explored what it means and how we can develop it for ourselves. Now we're ready to take the next step in creating that life, which is a bit like taking the car in for a tune-up. Using what we learned about being realistic, it's time to find out "what is" for us in our inner world and change what is restricting our movements and limiting

33

our choices. It's time to make conscious what is unconscious, so that we can release whatever is no longer serving us and make new, more empowering selections.

We won't go randomly excavating in your past to dredge up old sorrows or pain. Instead, we'll be looking at what isn't working well in your life *now* so we can learn what that reveals to us about the unique perceptions you've been holding. Where do you experience pain? Where do you feel unpleasant emotions such as anger, sadness, or anxiety? How about guilt or shame? Or do you feel numb and out of touch with your emotions—as though you're disconnected from your heart and living only in your head? Hunting down the tether points will take us into your past, yes—and that's okay. Until we become aware of where they connect and how they hold us back, we will be run by those old unconscious forces. It's time to take our power back.

This chapter is about self-exploration and self-understanding— getting to know ourselves at deeper and subtler levels—and releasing anything that is no longer serving us. I'll be helping you to process and let go of the beliefs, memories, judgments, and regrets that are keeping you bound to the past and unable to fully engage in life in the present with freedom of choice. It takes energy to maintain those connections, and the tremendous energy and resilience that this will unleash will catapult you into a whole new level of living.

Self-exploration is a lifelong adventure. Some of us may start exploring sooner than others, but there's wilderness territory in everyone—no matter our age. This wilderness may contain long-standing mysteries that upon discovery can set us free from self-doubt, limitation, and unnecessary pain. The work we'll be doing is a major leg of the journey in becoming a truer—and happier—version of ourselves. Let's get started.

understanding our tether points

In our earliest days, we humans learned that social connections—living and working together—overcame our relatively weak physical strength compared to environmental threats such as lions and tigers and bears. Being so wired to function in a social group for our very survival created in us a need for belonging and acceptance by others. As a result of this need, any time we aren't validated in precisely the way we think we should be by someone else, we feel threatened and experience a wound to our sense of self.

Our tether points originate with experiences that were hurtful and damaging to our sense of self—I'm going to use the word *trauma* for these events. In my use of the term, a trauma doesn't have to be severe, though it can be. In this context, trauma means "injury" and the degree of wounding is always subjective—the same event or experience will affect people differently, based on many factors, including genetics; previous experiences, mindset, and beliefs; the social support received in the wake of the trauma; the duration of the trauma; and the type of trauma it is.

We experience myriad small and large "injuries" to our sense of self over our lifetime—from the time we are developing in the womb until our dying day. These become critical points on the "map" we make of the world and affect how we navigate life. The meaning we make of these events will either weaken us or build our resilience—either create a tether point that limits our present and future or give us new depth and insight into ourselves that helps us create a life we love.

To make this more tangible, let's look at an example. Christina was only nine years old when her mother died. They had been very close, and she suffered deeply from the loss. In Christina's family, expressing grief was seen as a sign of weakness, and her father scolded her whenever he saw her crying. Like other people who are mourning a lost loved one, she also sometimes felt anger at the mother who abandoned her, which then made her feel guilty for having such feelings. In suppressing her mix of emotions, she acted out in school, where she was again scolded into silence. Christina's response was to turn away from emotions—to try to shut them off. More than anything, she wanted to protect herself from feeling so much hurt ever again. She made an unconscious vow that she would never love anyone as deeply as she had loved her mother.

Christina grew into a very attractive woman, and many men were drawn to her. She chose, however, not to open herself up to another person for fear of suffering the pain of another loss. Instead, she had a series of brief affairs. Sometimes she chose to partner with men who were married or otherwise unavailable for a serious relationship. If she mistakenly became involved with someone who cared for her more deeply, she found an excuse to end the relationship.

As an elderly woman, she was quite alone and unhappy because of it. She came to therapy seeking some answer to her isolation from other people, of which she had little understanding. She didn't know that the source of the problem was 65 years in her past. She had never realized the choice she made as a little girl, let alone questioned whether it continued to make sense for her in the long term. Instead, she had unconsciously lived her entire life based on this early event.

In therapy, I worked with Christina to finally mourn the loss of her mother and experience her feelings of grief and anger, which had been residing within her, beneath the surface of her life, the whole time. Eight months after our work together ended, she called to tell me about her new relationship. For several months she'd been dating a man who was both unmarried and emotionally available. They were having a good time together. She said she didn't know what would happen in the future, but that she was happy and more comfortable being close to someone than she could ever remember being.

Christina was in her 70s when she processed the trauma of her childhood loss and turned the corner to creating a life she would love. Her story shows us that it's never too late to gain awareness of the thoughts, beliefs, and emotions that are lurking in our unconscious, determining the path of our life, much like an airplane that's on autopilot, flying according to a programmed flight plan, even though it's set for a destination we don't want (surviving rather than thriving) and on a course sure to be filled with turbulence (seeing things and people as a threat when they aren't).

As you can see from this example, the key to healing, as I've alluded, is experiencing the emotions that we weren't able or allowed to feel at the time of the event that produced them.

the energy of emotions

Traumas generate emotions, and unless these emotions are processed at the time they occur, they become stuck in our system—both mind and body. They stay with us as energy in our unconscious, affecting our life until we discover them and process them out. Whether at the time they occur or decades later when they are discovered, the healthy flow and processing of negative emotions such as anger, sadness, grief, and fear is essential. When something bad happens, we need to recognize the violation to our sense of self, feel the natural emotions that follow, realize the violation doesn't say anything about us personally (and thus not make negative meaning of it), and take appropriate action informed by the emotions we felt.

So, why doesn't this processing happen naturally? Because these emotions are painful—and because things like crying or confronting others with something they've done are often not socially acceptable— we choose to suppress them rather than feel them and work them out. Eventually, we get so good at this, we may not even notice what we are doing. When we deny and run from our feelings, however, the underlying issues never get resolved. As we saw with Christina, suppressed emotions don't just go away. If they are not properly processed, they become toxic and cause us serious harm. They will keep showing up in our lives, in some form of dysfunction or unhappiness, until we resolve them. Throughout life, "feeling our feelings" is one of the healthiest and most productive things we can ever do.

The process can be somewhat counterintuitive and uncomfortable, but it isn't actually hard. To get you started on this path, in this chapter I'll walk you through some of the basics of getting in touch with your inner world and bringing what's been largely unconscious into your awareness. I promise it will be a very rewarding journey—one that will give you tremendous freedom and energy to put into creating what you would love instead. It's never too late to "right the wrong" by getting the emotions unstuck from our mind-body system and letting them go.

the need to "feel what we feel"

As I've said, when we are children, we often don't learn how to feel our feelings. This can happen for a number of reasons. Meaning well and hating to see us hurting, our parents may rush in after an upsetting episode, such as an argument with a friend or the loss of a favorite toy. How many of us have heard the words, "Don't feel bad—it's okay," when it isn't okay? Parents and others may have had good intentions, hugging us as they said the words, but the truth is that we may need to feel bad for a time and maybe even think about why we feel the way we do. Or, like Christina's father, our parents may have been stern, imposing a social standard that finds expressed feelings—such as anger or sadness and crying—unpleasant or unacceptable, so that the "comfort" felt more like an order or reprimand. In either case, we don't learn how to productively feel our feelings. We don't learn that they are temporary and fleeting—that they have a predictable beginning, middle, and end—and thus don't need to be feared or avoided or interpreted as being the end of the world.

In addition, our parents may not have been good models for us, either hiding their emotions or letting them out in explosive—and frightening to a child—episodes. Angry and abusive parents inflict untold damage on the children they raise. We may learn to mimic them, or we may decide to suppress emotions entirely because they were so troubling to us. As we get older, some of us try to talk ourselves out of what we feel—"I'm overreacting" or "I'm just making myself feel bad" are common self-talk messages. Others deal with feelings by immediately leaping to other thoughts where they feel safer.

As children, we can't distinguish between our feelings and our "self"; we think our feelings *are* us. If our feelings aren't acceptable in a particular situation, we may decide that we ourselves aren't acceptable—adding shame to an already bad equation. All of this feels so bad that we become averse to feeling our feelings at all. In turn, we may create a *false self* who meets what we see as the requisites of social acceptance and safety. We contort ourselves and conform to others' expectations in order to stay safe—we smile when we are unhappy, we swallow our anger, we avoid disagreeing and expressing our true thoughts. To please our parents and other powerful people in our lives, to gain their approval and love, we play a role—of the good girl or boy, the helper, the people pleaser, the martyr, the perfectionist, the entertainer, the funny one, and so on. But, while it may serve our interests in the short term, as we continue to present this false self to the world, it becomes ingrained, and we lose our sense of our true self. Indeed, the false self may become quite real, even to ourselves.

No matter how many years have gone by since they were originally generated, the feelings we suppressed or denied remain in our psyche until we process them. Feeling our true feelings reverses this dynamic by bringing us back in touch with our truth—our true self.

My experience as a girl followed this pattern. When I was a child, my mother worked six days a week, so I really looked forward to her day off and to plans we made for it—to go shopping, to dine out, or sometimes to go to the zoo. Often she would cancel those plans, citing exhaustion, and when I seemed disappointed or angry, my mother was quick to respond: "After everything I've done for you, how could you be so angry with me?" The message was clear: your emotions are not okay with me and should be suppressed.

After many of these painful interactions, I began to change my behavior. To get my mother's attention, I developed my sense of humor. On the outside, I was constantly in a good mood, laughing with people, making jokes, even if I didn't think either the jokes or I were very funny. I was really good, and really fun, and who could tell that I was seething underneath? That became my false self.

It was many years before I realized my pattern and did something to change it. In therapy, I came to see that I might be laughing, but I wasn't feeling funny or happy at all. To change the way I was behaving seemed dangerous, however. I thought: "What if I'm not funny? No one will like me or love me. If I'm not the life of the party—or making somebody else feel like they are because everything they say is so hilarious—I will be alone, rejected." It was really scary to give it up. But I knew it was the path to my freedom and happiness. After all, I didn't like myself very much when I saw how dishonest I'd been—not only with others but with myself, too. Little by little, I began to discover a more authentic self and share her with the world.

Obviously, the degree to which we are in touch with our feelings is the degree to which we can be authentic and connect deeply with others. Our ability and skills in productively handling our emotions are also the foundation of other invaluable qualities such as perseverance, fortitude, and resilience, which make an enormous difference in what we dare to go for in life and therefore our experience of it. This area of our lives has huge ramifications for everything we create, so it's vital that we learn how to productively process our emotions, no matter our age.

In a moment, I'll give you a step-by-step tutorial that should make it simple, though not necessarily easy, to do. But first, we need a quick recap on the tool that will make the process possible, our discussion of which began in Chapter 1—that of *mindfulness*.

the healing power of mindfulness

You'll recall that in order to step out of our limiting perceptions—our thoughts, feelings, and beliefs—in any circumstance, and stop them from unconsciously driving what we do, we need to observe them nonjudgmentally. We need to bring them into conscious awareness. In doing so, we actually shift to using a different part of our brain: a less reactive part, a part whose job—rather than fighting, fleeing, or freezing to ensure our survival—includes exploring, discovering, and innovating to create a life we love. You'll also recall that the qualities we'll need in our observation spell the acronym COAL: curiosity, openness, acceptance, and love.[24] The psychological safety this approach engenders enables our psyche to let down its guards and reveal what it has locked inside.

When focused on our inner world of sensations, emotions, and thoughts, we call this kind of observation *emotional mindfulness*. This self-awareness is fundamental to understanding and being happy with ourselves, forming close bonds with others, and recognizing our motivations so we can take action and create our life based on what is true for us rather than out of the insecurities of the false self.

"Feeling what we feel" will also open us to a pool of creativity that lies where we are immersed in reality rather than our perceptions or beliefs. That's where emotions take us. They are helpful companions on the journey of life. We need to make friends with them, to interact with them in a loving rather than a fearful way. The following steps will help.

feeling our feelings, step by step

Dr. Susan David, a psychologist and the author of *Emotional Agility: Get Unstuck, Embrace Change, and Thrive in Work and Life*,[25] designed a four-step process to help children learn how to go through—rather than around—an emotion. What a great idea! It's exciting to imagine how this will prevent wounding that otherwise might have occupied people's entire lives. And, while this is a good system for handling an emotion as it is happening, it can also be the basis for a good recipe for processing old stuck emotions that are the result of childhood or other wounds. That's our task in this chapter. Although my approach to feeling our feelings contains a few additional steps, I think you'll find it very straightforward and easy to follow. Every step is essential, so give each one your all. I guarantee you'll be pleased with the results.

Step 1: Ground It

To feel and process emotions, you must be in your body and in the now. To begin, sit comfortably with your eyes closed in a place where you won't be disturbed. Take several deep breaths in and out, and bring your awareness inside your body. Squeeze the muscles in your pelvic floor, belly, heart, and throat. Feel a heaviness in your elbows, as if weights are pulling them down. Cross your arms and, using your fingers, knead the opposite forearm. Next, imagine a stream of energy going from your tailbone all the way down into the center of the earth. Visualize roots extending downward from the bottom of your feet, planting you deeply into the ground. Once you feel that you are "in your body," move on to the next step.

Step 2: Recall It

Call to mind an issue, conflict, or situation that you've been upset about recently. To start, don't choose the most traumatic event in your history; find something that provoked a mild to strong emotional reaction, or that you think should have provoked such a reaction even though you felt "numb." Review what happened or what it was about in as much detail as possible, envisioning yourself back in that time and place and experiencing it with all your senses. When feelings begin to arise, go to the next step.

Step 3: Sense It

Continue to breathe deeply in and out and, after a quiet moment of relaxation, mentally scan your body for any sensations. I call this activity "percolating" with a feeling; we want to get the emotion bubbling and stirring inside us, the same way coffee percolates in an old-fashioned coffee maker. As it does, observe any bodily sensations—physical feelings—that accompany it, such as tingling, vibrating, tightness, cold, itchiness, burning, queasiness, and the like. Also notice any thoughts, memories, images, and other inner experiences that come up with the sensations. These are bits of information we need in order to understand our past experience—to know "what is" for us—and ultimately process it, thereby letting it go. Explore the sensations with your awareness, and describe them to yourself silently in as much detail as you can.

Step 4: Name It

Now, associate an emotion with the sensations. For example, is the tingling in your chest anxiety? Is the quickly rising energy from your belly to your heart and throat rage? Is the pressure in your throat and behind your eyes sadness or grief?

In my book *Mindful Anger*, I divided emotions into the two broad categories of "comfortable" and "uncomfortable" and listed many different variations of each. (These lists can also be found on my website at abrandtherapy.com/mindful-aging-book.) For example, are you angry or bitter or irritated? Recognizing the sometimes subtle distinctions between emotions will give you a greater sense of your experience and a richer knowledge of yourself. And, very importantly, because the role of emotions is to drive behavior, knowing more precisely what you feel will also inform you about how you'd like to act.

Becoming sensitive to the nuances in our emotions is also key in identifying the emotional fuel that's motivating us to act in any given moment or circumstance: Are we being driven to do something reactively, out of fear, or proactively, out of the pure passion of what we would love to experience or create? Both can feel like "tension"—one in the form of anxiety and the other excitement. This is a question we need to continuously ask ourselves if we are to create a life we love.

Step 5: Love It

As part of our mindful approach, which creates emotional safety, we need to fully accept everything that we feel—without judgment of any kind. In his landmark book *Learning to Love Yourself,* Gay Hendricks coaches us to actually love ourselves for feeling what we feel in any moment, no matter how unpleasant the emotions or how much we dislike feeling them.[26] I completely agree with this approach, as it allows for a deep level of acceptance that prompts us to heal.

Therefore, whether it's true to your thinking mind in this moment or not, say, "I love myself for feeling _____ (angry, sad, anxious, etc.)." Do this whenever you have an emotion of any kind, and especially the harder ones.

Step 6: Feel/Experience It

Just sit with the emotion and any of its sensations, letting the feelings percolate and flow. Don't try to affect them; rather, just observe them. Gay Hendricks advises giving feelings the space to simply be.[27] Notice whether the feelings waver in intensity. Do they move? Welcome any discomfort, knowing that it will be fleeting and will help you to heal. Allow your body to respond the way it seems to want or need to. If you need to cry, do so. If you need to say or yell something, or do something physical—for example, shaking out your arms to get your energy moving or punching into the air to simulate punching a person—do it.

Remember that the role of emotions is to prompt decision making and action. They signal to us that there is something we need to do. That follow-up action getting thwarted is another spot where things typically get stuck. To free the energy of the emotion from our body and psyche, we need to express the emotion, including taking the action that it dictates.

Failing to show our emotions at the time they occur (or soon thereafter, while the event or issue is still fresh) is a key point at which the processing of our experiences gets thwarted. Therefore, expressing our emotions—in a productive way—is key to getting the stuck emotions moving inside us and to fully processing them out.

Step 7: Receive Its Message/Wisdom

Does the sensation or emotion you're experiencing connect with one or more experiences in your past? Does it give you any insight into the root of the trauma, or a belief that is negative and thus limiting? This is like discovering gold. To get all the information the energy of your emotion holds, you may need to return to these experiences in one or more additional sessions, until you feel complete.

You might be thinking, "I'm not getting anything." Go with whatever shows up as obvious. Don't be afraid to make it up! Use your imagination if need be. Ask yourself: "If this sensation or emotion were going to say something to me, what would it be?" Simply set the intention that whatever you need to see or hear right now comes forward. If you still have trouble, do free-form writing, where you journal about what the feeling means for a full 10 minutes without stopping your pen or your fingers on the keyboard. Again, be willing to make it up and just see what comes out.

Step 8: Share It

Find someone you feel safe sharing your reflections with, or just write about them on your own. Describe what happened, how you reacted at the time, and what you've come to see about it now. This will help to keep the energy of the situation moving out of you, with a momentum toward being released. Talking about our experiences and the emotions they create with someone who can listen objectively and bear witness to what we've gone through is an important step in the healing of emotional wounds. I'm referring to a therapist, counselor, clergyperson, or other professional trained in this skillset. I also highly recommend writing about your experiences and emotions as a way of "sharing" them. This certainly doesn't have to be for public consumption (like in a book or blog) or even for anyone else to read, though it can be if that feels safe to you. Journaling privately for yourself and writing letters (but not sending them) to those to whom you originally needed to express your emotion can be very effective methods for knowing "what is"—bringing the unconscious into the conscious—and moving the emotion out of your system.

Step 9: Let It Go

Visualize the energy leaving you, or perform a ritual of physical release to symbolize letting this emotion go. I'll provide ideas for doing this a bit later in this chapter.

***

Allowing feelings—anger or loneliness or fear or grief—to wash over us, and sitting with them for a while in this accepting and nonjudgmental manner, is a profound method of handling our troubles. Though we sometimes imagine the worst when thinking about feeling our feelings—that they will last forever and maybe even cause us to go right off the deep end to a place from which it might be hard to return—this isn't the case. Eventually—usually within 15 minutes or so—the feelings will subside, and a peacefulness will descend in their place. How to deal with the person or decision who triggered the feelings in the first place may seem easy and obvious after this process. If not, some thinking is acceptable, now that you've honored the feeling itself.

Discovering our true feelings and giving them a voice in this way can shed light on other things we need to release that are not serving us in creating a life we love. These include *agreements*—made either consciously or unconsciously by the false self in trying to keep ourselves safe—that are no longer or never were true to us, *faulty thinking* and *limiting beliefs*, *attachments* and *memories* that keep us stuck in the past instead of living vibrantly in the present, *resentments*, and *regrets*. Let's look at each of these.

untrue agreements

The false self we create to "get along" in the world sometimes makes agreements—with ourselves or others—that don't serve us or them. Perhaps: "If you'll love me, I won't outshine you," or "If you don't call me on my addictions, I won't call you on yours," or "I'll live according to your rules if you promise to never leave me." These agreements come right out of our survival thinking. At some point, they may have helped us stay safe in a situation, but they actually can prevent us from thriving today. They limit us and keep us small; they disconnect us from our true selves. And they create baggage we don't want or need. If an agreement isn't true for us, we'll inevitably end up with regrets or resentments that rob us of vital life energy we could be using to create the life we love.

When we conform to these agreements made by our false self, our heart is not engaged. Instead of promoting love, these agreements value safety above all else. Therefore, the agreements aren't going to serve us in achieving what we want to create. Instead, we need to enable ourselves to feel the emotional weight or pain that will help us to uncover those agreements, examine them, and release what our true self doesn't accept. I'll help you do that in the Exercises section at the end of the chapter.

For now, take a look at your life today to see where you are most unhappy. Have you entered into an agreement—with people, or an employer, or even with yourself—to do something that simply isn't true for you? If so, you need to fully acknowledge it, feel your feelings about it, and let it go. Then you'll be free to make a new choice that is right and true for you. In doing this, we sometimes worry that we'll let others down, but when we are doing anything without our heart being in it, we're not really serving anyone very well. We'd do far better to spend the time, effort, and energy doing something that *is* true for us. In doing so, we'll make a far greater difference in the world.

limiting beliefs and faulty thinking

We've talked about the mapmaking we do as children and actually continue to do as we go through life. Often the meaning we decide to make of an experience is one that gives us more control over the situation. We blame ourselves, or decide something happened because of a fault or deficiency of our own. This is where we go off the rails—thinking that what happens to us is about us: what we did wrong, what we deserved because we are bad somehow, and so on. These assumptions become limiting beliefs and faulty patterns of thinking that we carry forward, and they begin getting in the way of our creating what we would love in life.

For example, as a child, if our father doesn't spend time with us, or say supportive things, or show affection and let us know he loves us, we might develop a belief that he treats us this way because, somehow, we just aren't good enough. To compensate, we may take on the false self of the "achiever" in hopes of getting his love and validation. This can lead to a pattern of perfectionism, where we always zero in only on what is wrong or bad with what we do rather than on what is good or right. No matter what we've done, we can't feel happy; all we can do is find fault. At best this robs us of joy and satisfaction; at worst it creates anger, helplessness, and the fear of failure. This can get so bad—where we begin to dread the feelings that are generated when we attempt to do anything—that we procrastinate endlessly or altogether fail to act. Perfectionism is a type of faulty thinking that holds many people back from living a life they love.

There are lots of types of faulty thinking that can develop out of our childhood experiences and the beliefs that form around them. Review the following chart, and see if any of these sound like you.

Types of Faulty Thinking[28]

Self-flawed thinking	Nothing I do is good enough. Something is wrong with me; I am inadequate, unworthy, and unlovable.
Perfectionist thinking	Things have to be perfect for me to be happy, and nothing I ever do is good enough.
All-or-nothing thinking	If I cannot be all things to all people, then I'm nothing. I can either spend time with my family or financially support them—not both. I'm either the best or the worst; there is no in between.
Telescopic thinking	I always feel like a failure because I focus on and magnify my shortcomings and ignore my successes.
Blurred-boundary thinking	It's hard for me to know when to stop, where to draw the line, and when to say no to others.
People-pleasing thinking	If I can get others to like me, I'll feel better about myself.
Pessimistic thinking	My life is chaotic and stressful and full of misery and despair; that's just the way life is.
Catastrophic thinking	My life feels out of control and something terrible might happen, so I can't relax. I must be prepared by always expecting the worst.

Helpless thinking	I am helpless to change my lifestyle. There is nothing I can do to change my schedule and slow down.
Victim thinking	Other people and other situations are to blame for my overdoing, my stress, and my burnout.
Resentful thinking	I am full of bitterness and resentment, and I will never forgive others for what they did to me. I am a victim of a demanding job, a needy family, or a society that says, "You can do it all."
Resistance thinking	Life is an uphill battle, and I must fight to enforce my way, resist what I don't want, and cling to things to keep them as they are.
Wishful thinking	I wish I could have the things I cannot have because the things I have are of no value. If only my situation would change, I could slow down and take better care of myself.
Serious thinking	Playing and having fun are a waste of time because there's too much work that needs to be done.
Externalized thinking	Happiness can be found in the external world. If the outer circumstances of my life would change, it would fix how I feel inside.

Attachments, resentments, and regrets are other items we need to release to free our emotional energy and bring ourselves fully into the present, where we can use that energy to create a life we love. We'll look at those next.

attachments and memories

Whereas Buddhism, along with some other Eastern religions, warns against the power of attachments to distract us from the spiritual world, Western culture glorifies these connections to people and things, and even our own bodies and feelings. Some of these attachments—for example, to friends and family—are normal. In our materialistic world, other attachments—the need to collect objects to prove our status or to beautify our body in an obsessive way—have an obvious downside. Here we'll look at how good attachments can become sources of pain when we fail to recognize that we live in a changing world and are unable to let go.

Objects

One reason we may become attached to objects is if they link us to a time or a person. I'd bet that some of you have, tucked away in a closet, a dress or pair of jeans that you wore in that youthful time when everyone has a natural beauty. Even if you could wear the garment again—and, for many of us, that's a large *if*—it wouldn't restore you to that period of your life. We may also keep objects that belonged to a loved one who is no longer part of our life. The problem is that trying to hold on to something also makes our energy stuck. We are meant to live in the now; when we try to keep ourselves in a different time and place, life becomes stagnant.

The best choice is to let go of these objects: to make ourselves available for what the present has to offer and live fully today. We can show our gratitude to the people and times we want to remember and send them on their way to a new life so that we can make the most of *our* new life.

One of my friends is Cynthia, aged 79, a semi-retired university professor who had a rare and valuable collection of books related to her field in the fine arts. Since her retirement, she hadn't touched them, and they were taking up space in her home. They were old friends; she had delighted in discovering and purchasing them one by one. They had aided her through an exciting and fulfilling career for several decades. It was hard to part with them; they felt like a part of her—of who she had been. Yet they were her past. She wasn't using them to learn or to teach others anymore. They were doing nothing to support her in who she is today. Realizing it was time to let them go, she decided to find them an excellent new home—a place where they would be used by many and valued, even honored, for how special they are.

Cynthia lived in Europe and quickly realized that the institutions there would not have the need for the books, as they were not doing the kind of research the books supported. But, after giving a workshop at a university in the United States, she saw that it was a perfect fit. She asked the head of the fine arts department if he would be interested in the books, and he jumped at the offer. The department features them as a special collection in its library.

Of course, not all of our possessions will be so special or rare, despite their sentimental value to us. But we can feel better by finding them a good new home where they will be of value to someone else and be put to use supporting someone else's "present." Charities such as the Salvation Army and Goodwill are always ready to receive just about anything and can give your treasured objects a new life.

As we grow older, many of us will downsize our residence, at least once. This is especially true if we had a house full of children that is now mostly empty space. Trying to choose which objects and furniture will go to the new space is a difficult task—but it moves us into a future where more of our time and energy is freed from housekeeping to enjoy the many opportunities open to us.

Another difficult choice is objects we've kept—a shawl, a sweater, or a favorite cup—to connect us to loved ones who are no longer with us. There is a happy medium here where one or two items can support that link without taking up all the space in our new life.

Loss of People

Deaths of family, friends, and partners can be so devastating that our whole orientation in life feels lost. We simply can't accept what has occurred. Think of a parent who has lost a child, who wants to keep the child's room exactly as it was the day the child died. It's heartbreakingly understandable to try to capture the life that was and freeze it in time or to deny that the room will not serve its original purpose. But this kind of holding pattern, where we remain in the past, traps us and, over time, can even make us sick.

Our material things can call to mind a person or an experience that we have loved who is no longer here and only part of our past. We feel they keep us connected to what we once had. But if they keep us reliving the past rather than being in the present, they are not only dust catchers but also energy zappers—taking up our space and energy rather than providing us with the inspiration and adding to the vitality we need to live fully today.

I know letting go of the past—and the people in it we have loved so dearly—is easier said than done. But it's a requirement for living our best life now. That doesn't mean we can't remember and thank and send love to those who have meant so much to us who are no longer here. We can and should do that as much as we feel the need to. That's how we can connect in a positive way, rather than ruminate on what is lost, which only induces pain. A helpful approach is to recognize how those we have loved are still with us because of who we became by being with them; they truly are part of us and live on through us. An important way to honor them is to live our best life, strengthened and more resilient because of the love they gave us.

As a simple exercise to help you see how much you are living in the past, notice your thoughts and discussions—how much is about the past versus the present or future? It might help to keep a journal handy for a day and just make a quick note whenever you think or talk about the past. Mark the time and the topic you were thinking of or talking to someone else about. Then, look over your notes and evaluate the amount of time you spend in the past. Do you see how this is keeping you from being in the present and living your life fully today?

We can't take away grief—the emotion that comes from missing someone or something essential to us after a loss—and we shouldn't try to. Love lost is painful. It just is. And it takes time to heal. However, we can make sure we don't add to our grief by ruminating rather than simply honoring and feeling the feelings when they come. This we can control.

The past can have a particularly strong pull where we have highly negative emotions such as resentments and regrets.

resentments:
responding to perceived harm

Someone harmed us—they crossed a boundary that kept us safe or failed to help us meet a need. They took something that we had deemed as ours: a loved one, a career, a home, material possessions, money, an ability of our body or mind. The anger we feel over an injustice is normal and healthy if we use its energy to do something positive for ourselves or others. But it is unhealthy if we just continue to recycle it and ruminate rather than become stronger and more resilient as a result of what we have gone through.

My husband, JP, experienced extreme—but understandable—resentment when a mistake during surgery on his spinal cord left him with no control over his limbs. As he explains it, he would try to move his hand and end up punching himself in the eye. Lying in the hospital,

JP would think about ways to commit suicide and—even more—how to get back at the doctor. He settled on breaking the doctor's hands. While he imagined becoming strong enough to carry out his plans, his anger became transformed into a determination to recover. "It got me moving," he says. Although the forecasts of his doctors were not encouraging—predicting he would never walk again—JP's determination in physical therapy paid off, and he eventually made a near-full recovery.

Just as important, he was able to forgive the doctor who had done his surgery—not only forgive but make friends with the man, who had shown significant remorse. "For the first time, I learned about forgiveness," JP says. "It was the biggest lesson from the experience." Ironically, watching someone I love fight so hard to come back from a great loss, it has been harder for me to forgive the doctor than it was for JP.

Resentment is a particularly corrosive emotion if it's left to fester very long. My husband experienced the gift of forgiveness, which is the best antidote we have for this poison. Others never find that gift.

A friend recently told me about her next-door neighbor, Pete, in his late 60s, who is a good example of resentment that has never been let go. People don't see the resentment, however; instead, they see an angry man.

Pete is hostile and verbally abusive to most people, launching tirades in the middle of the street if someone makes a minor infraction of the parking rules in his neighborhood. He has yelled at neighbors' grandkids for playing in a tree that sits between his and his neighbor's property. My friend says that in 10 years of living there, she has never seen a soul visit him.

One day, my friend had a guest who happened to arrive as Pete was washing his car in the driveway. She admired it—an expensive Italian sports car—and said her late husband had had one just like it. Apparently, those were the magic words to get Pete to open up and share. Pete told my friend's visitor that he, too, had lost a mate—that his fiancée had been killed over 40 years earlier in a plane crash. He said the Italian sports car in his driveway was nice but that he would have rather spent the money it cost on the children he and his bride-to-be might have had.

There's no question that what happened in Pete's life was heartbreaking. And equally heartbreaking is his response to it. Here's a man who has spent four decades walking around with a huge resentment toward life and seemingly most of the people in it. Pete's behavior is his way of expressing the anger triggered by his belief that life has done him wrong. It's also his unconscious way of keeping himself safe from ever getting close to anyone again—because people can't stand to be around him.

regrets:
missing out or hurting others

Over the course of a lifetime, we will no doubt make choices that take us away from opportunities that may have led us to extraordinary experiences. Perhaps a possible partner whom we turned down—or, conversely, a partner we chose despite knowing from the start it was not a great love. We may also cause pain to others through our choices, our anger, or, perhaps worst of all, our neglect. Sometimes a regret becomes the core of a cluster of emotions—sorrow, grief, remorse—that can seem overwhelming.

To focus excessively on these past events holds us back from living as our best self and creating our best life today. Rather than wishing we could go back in time, what we should ask ourselves is whether we can take steps in the present to heal what was done in the past. This is particularly important if our regret involved a person who is still living. If that's the case, you might think about approaching this person, expressing your regret, asking for their forgiveness, and seeking a way that you can atone for your past offense.

For example, Edna and Marianne were good friends in college, but, as they moved into their 20s, they seemed to be always quarreling. Edna had married right after graduation and was in the midst of her child-bearing years, while Marianne was building a career and looking for a partner. Eventually hard words were said: Marianne disparaged Edna's husband, and Edna said Marianne was so prickly she would never find a mate. A few months went by without any contact, then a few years. Soon three decades separated them, but Marianne, in particular, regretted the loss of her good friend.

In her 40s, she had sought out a therapist and had learned that much of what Edna had said was true. She did have a sharp manner and a judgmental attitude toward others that was leaving her in isolation. Thanks to this help, she was able to change her life, and eventually, she found a part-time partner—they chose not to live together, but they saw each other regularly and were best friends and lovers. Marianne found herself wanting to tell Edna.

So she did. She found Edna on Facebook and left a note on her wall suggesting a phone conversation. Then she crossed her fingers. As it happened, Edna also had some regrets about that time, and the two of them shared apologies and laid the foundation for a renewed friendship.

Sometimes, letting go of regrets and resentments can happen suddenly, like a balloon popping, when we've ruminated to the point that even we are so bored or sick and tired of it that we just snap: "No more! Enough time spent on this. I have a life to live beyond this. It's done. It's past. I can't change what happened, and I'm not willing to spend any more of my precious energy or time on it." I've seen this happen with old wounds, patterns, and even addictions. Sometimes, enough is simply enough.

But in most cases, it's a process. Marianne's approach offers a helpful model. What could you do to repair a situation that has left you feeling such regret? What could you learn from this experience that would allow you to live more happily and more healthily, love more freely and deeply, and give more of yourself to make a difference in others' lives today? We may need to mindfully revisit what occurred, taking greater responsibility (if applicable) for our own role in how things played out, and, most importantly, accept that the past is over and choose what we want to do and experience now. The sooner we realize that we can't change the past, the more quickly we are motivated to do something of value for ourselves and others now, in the present moment.

The last step is often forgiveness, which we'll take up in the next section.

strategies for letting go of what is no longer serving you

Make Your Healing a Project

Healing is a process of self-exploration, one that can provide infinite benefits no matter what life stage you are passing through. It's never too late. Don't approach it with fear. No matter what you find as you learn more about yourself, you will tend to love yourself more rather than less. This emotion of love fuels us to behave in ways that then increase our feelings of joy and self-love, creating a positive reinforcing cycle of thoughts, feelings, and behavior that expands and uplifts us, helping us to create a life we love. By knowing and loving ourselves, life gets better in every way, fast!

As we were doing research for my book *8 Keys to Eliminating Passive-Aggressiveness*, my collaborator, Brookes, was alarmed to discover that the long list of common characteristics of passive-aggression almost identically matched the long list of complaints her mate had about her! These were things like agreeing to do something but feeling anger and agitation when doing it, talking in a circular fashion and changing the subject as if others could read her mind, never directly answering a question, and saying "I don't know" when pressed to answer something she felt uncomfortable about while at other times acting like an expert even when she didn't have enough information. Until the overarching pattern of passive-aggressiveness was revealed, these behaviors had always seemed to Brookes like unrelated quirks rather than signs and symptoms of a larger issue with anger. Self-critical, she often felt like she was "wrong" but was not sure how to change to be "right."

Upon this self-discovery, she set the goal of having a much better relationship with anger, which is a normal, healthy emotion. Using the strategies in *8 Keys to Eliminating Passive-Aggressiveness*—mindfulness being a key one—along with the strategies in *Mindful Anger*, my previous book, she did just that. Within months, her partner commented on how much better the relationship felt to him and how much less stress there was day to day. Today, Brookes still has to stay vigilant about her natural tendency to avoid conflict and anger, which was part of her imprinting in early life. However, it's not nearly as difficult as it used to be for her to address or express her anger in a productive way when it is triggered or to take care of her needs in the first place, which eliminates much of the anger she used to experience. With the new model for dealing with and communicating anger in place, she simply doesn't need to be passive-aggressive anymore.

As you begin your project, you may want to read some of the quality self-help books designed to help you work through specific "issues" you see in your life: for example, if you know you have an anger problem—because you either feel angry a lot, suppress your anger, or feel afraid of anger in general—you could read my book *Mindful Anger*, which will help you understand your anger and teach you how to heal it at the root. If you know you act passive-aggressively, try my book on that topic and break that incredibly destructive pattern once and for all. For just about every "problem" under the sun, someone has spent their life's work studying it to understand it better and help people with the issue find their way back to a healthy life. Be persistent and you'll get the answers you seek. You may also want to work with an experienced guide: find a compassionate therapist or coach you feel confident in and comfortable with who has this expertise.

Set the Intention to Release
What Is No Longer Serving You

As you set out on your "project," I recommend as your first step making a sincere intention for your healing. This includes the intention to become aware of what you do not yet see about yourself and your pattern, as well as the inspiration for, or vision of, a new, healthy model to replace it with. If you are spiritually inclined, your intention might take the form of a prayer for guidance and clear vision.

Once you set the intention, allow yourself to expect the means of your healing to start coming about. Remember, focus contributes greatly to reality. When we're on the lookout, we find what we expect to find. So, look for life to begin opening doors and sending opportunities your way that you might not have noticed before. It might come in one big insight or, more likely, as breadcrumb after breadcrumb leading you down a new path. Follow the breadcrumbs!

Forgive, to Help Yourself Heal

There are three possibilities with anger: to ask someone else to forgive you, to forgive someone who has hurt you, and to forgive yourself. Forgiveness doesn't mean you're wiping the slate clean. "Forgive and forget" are not natural partners. You need to recognize the truth of what happened, then find a way to move forward. And you don't always have to express your forgiveness to the person you feel caused the wound. Before you can forgive, you need to experience and express your upset emotions—anger, sadness, grief. Sometimes writing a letter—that you never mail—expressing how you feel can help you let go of the negative emotions. But forgiveness is important. It may help you to know that the forgiveness is really for your benefit, so that you can let go of the regrets or resentment that are eating up your valuable life energy.

Forgiving yourself is sometimes a more difficult matter. You need to recognize what you did and the damage it caused others or yourself. And you need to realize that you made a mistake—or years of them— and that ultimately, if you knew then what you know now, you would have made a different choice. But life doesn't work like that. We don't get that luxury. The best we can do is accept what has happened and make the very best of the situation now, no matter how much time has gone by. Using mindfulness, explore why you did what you did, and express your gratitude for moving toward change. Atonement, to either the person you harmed or someone who can be their symbolic representative, is a powerful way of moving into self-forgiveness.

Forgiveness is easier if you take a more realistic attitude about the vulnerability and fallibility of the human race. The fact is that the earth is an imperfect place, and being human is an imperfect condition. We all know that to err is human … but we don't like that very much! Unfortunately, however, nothing could be more true. In order to forgive ourselves and others, we have to soften our stance on being human; we need to understand that people are fallible—and that's simply a reality we have to accept.

As a psychotherapist who's worked with thousands of people over 35 years, I can tell you without a doubt that when people know better, they do better. The caveat to that, of course, is that "knowing better" means more than simply being told. We have to truly *get* it, and that could require being told a thousand times through different experiences until the thing we're being told becomes something we *know*. We see this with addiction all the time: simply understanding that you're an alcoholic doesn't stop you from drinking. A person most often has to "hit rock bottom" before they truly see and comprehend the devastation they are making of their own and, very likely, others' lives.

The more we know about and understand the culminating forces behind someone's choices and actions, the more clearly we see that they are another variation of the "perfect storm" that is being human. There is always a reason for everything, whether we can see it or not. Having compassion but with clear, firm boundaries as to what we will expect and accept or not allow is the best way to give anyone a chance to make amends and rehabilitate. Beyond that, the choice to do that or not do it and the work it takes to become well are up to them.

We're all on a hero's journey, but our starting points, our destinations, and the struggles we encounter along the way are unique to each of us.

Find Meaning in Your Suffering

Letting go of regrets and resentments—in essence, doing forgiveness—requires learning from our suffering. We transcend suffering by making meaning out of it and getting what it has to teach us—by making ourselves better for having gone through what we have endured. As author Haruki Murakami tells us, "When you come out of the storm you won't be the same person who walked in. That's what this storm's all about."[29] Let yours and others' pain and suffering not be in vain—by learning and growing from it.

Use Rituals to Help You Release and Let Go

Remembering that we are body as well as mind and spirit, it can be helpful to create a meaningful physical ritual to let go of the harmful belief or pattern of behavior, the emotion or memory, the resentment or regret that you are leaving behind. If you live near a body of water, one ritual might involve selecting a stone or symbolic object to represent what you are shedding, and then tossing it as far as you can into the water.

Lighting a candle is another nice way of releasing, either to symbolically burn away whatever we're declaring to be finished now or to honor someone or something and say goodbye. You can also write a phrase on a piece of paper that represents the assumption, agreement, or attachment and toss it in the fireplace and watch it burn, saying the intention to release it. A friend I know burned things that represented what she desired to release: a cigarette for her smoking habit, a newspaper headline for the career she was ending, and a thistle for the inner self-critic she hoped to leave behind with the other two.

exercises

Timeline Review: The False Self

In this exercise, we're going to look back over your life to identify the significant factors and events that caused you to abandon what was true for you and take on a "false self." By seeing where we have been and continue to be false to ourselves, we can make the choice now to live truer to who we really are. We're looking for events, experiences, and messages—whether explicitly told to us in words or implied by someone's actions—that taught us that it wasn't safe or "good enough" to be the way we naturally were.

1. On a blank sheet of paper or digital file, divide the page by decade.

2. Taking as much time as you need, go through each decade, thinking about where you were and what was going on for you during that time period. Following are some examples of ideas to reflect on. Make notes about any thoughts or memories you have about the answers to these questions in the space for the decade in which they occurred.

   • Who were you living with?

   • What were your relationships like?

   • What were your biggest struggles or stresses at the time?

   • Did you experience traumatizing events?

- What strong emotions do you recall feeling on an ongoing basis during this time?
- What negative limiting beliefs do you remember having about yourself that started then?
- Which, if any, of these thoughts and emotions can you see are still alive and active in your life today?

Examine Your Thinking

Many forms of faulty thinking can come out of our limiting assumptions and agreements, and these often stay with us for a lifetime, despite the harm they cause. Since the first step in making change is awareness, use the list of "Types of Faulty Thinking" offered in this chapter to help you recognize which patterns of thinking are still limiting you today, and do the following steps.

1. On a clean piece of paper or digital file, note which of the faulty thinking patterns you can see in yourself.
2. Reading through the descriptions of those items again, choose just one to use for the rest of this exercise.
3. Knowing that this thinking pattern originally came out of a desire to protect yourself (keep you safe) or help you get a need met, can you identify what that protection or need was? Take your time with this, sitting with it as you reminisce.
4. Now, reflect on whether you still experience the same lack of safety or unmet need in your life today, or is it really an experience just of the past? If it still exists, can you think of a more productive, less limiting way to create safety or get your need met today?
5. What would you like to do?

Timeline Review: Resentments and Regrets

Resentments and regrets rob us of life energy, weaken our immune system, and can tax us to the point of damaging our health. It's crucial for our own well-being that we release as many of these as we can today.

Ask yourself the following questions:

1. Who are you upset with? Even if it's yourself, note the source of the upset.

2. How long have you been upset? Plot on your decade timeline when this particular problem with this person (or yourself) occurred or began.

3. What are you upset about? Identify the need of yours that this person didn't fulfill or the boundary they breached. What did they take from you that you thought was yours? If it's yourself you're upset with, what did you do or not do that you feel regretful about?

4. How has being upset over this incident or relationship seemed to serve you? How has it limited you or your happiness?

5. Knowing that releasing this resentment or regret will free up emotional energy that you can use to create more of a life you love, are you willing now to let it go? If yes, use this incident in the release exercise below.

What Do You Want to Release, Once and for All?

As long as we're still able to think, we have the opportunity to evaluate our life and to identify and shed that which is no longer serving us. Isn't it time to lighten your load? What, really, have you got to lose? In fact, by not shedding what isn't serving us now, we lose the most—in potential health and happiness, loving and meaningful connections, and the fulfillment of our purpose at this stage of our life. So, despite any reservations you may have about letting go of what is no longer helpful or true for you, I assure you, you won't miss it.

1. Take a clean sheet of paper or digital file and orient it horizontally. Draw vertical lines to create seven columns across the page. Label these "Beliefs/Assumptions," "Agreements," "Attachments/ Memories," "Resentments," "Regrets," "Reactions/Patterns," and "Objects." A blank table is provided for you.

2. Spend a few moments reflecting on each of the headings and, as you do, below each, write some ideas about how you might benefit from releasing them and lightening your emotional load.

3. Give yourself plenty of time to do this in a relaxed, reflective way. If you need to, put the list aside for a while and come back to it as ideas arise for you throughout the day.

4. At the end of the day, review your list. Thank each of these items for the role they have played in your life and tell them they are no longer needed.

5. Take a moment to imagine how you would feel if freed from the emotional weight and pain they represent, and commit to releasing them once and for all.

6. Do a ritual of release for each of them individually and send them on their way.

The work you've done in this chapter, though possibly challenging, will reap rewards equal to the effort. With fewer tethers keeping you bound to the past, you'll now have much more energy and enthusiasm for living fully in the present. Next, we'll explore what will make the present the most meaningful and fulfilling as you discover what gives you joy and craft a vision for a life you'll love.

Beliefs/Assumptions	Agreements	Attachments/Memories	Resentments	Regrets	Reactions/Patterns	Objects

chapter 3

finding your joy and living your new dream

For many people, turning 50 is just the beginning of great things: Pablo Picasso was 55 when he painted *Guernica*, and much of his best work was still ahead of him. Enlightenment philosopher John Locke was a few years older when he began to publish the culmination of a lifetime of study and thought, including his "Essay Concerning Human Understanding."[30] Other historical and cultural figures made new starts when they were even older. Although Cornelius Vanderbilt had already made a fortune in steamships, he was 70 when he bought his first railroad. And J. R. R. Tolkien was 62 when he published *The Lord of the Rings*.[31]

Less famous people also take on new challenges in later life. Barbara Hillary, a retired nurse and two-time cancer survivor, decided at 75 that she'd like to see the North Pole and raised $25,000 to make the trip, becoming the first African American woman to visit there.[32] Taking up mountaineering in his 70s, Bill Painter became the oldest person to reach the summit of Mount Rainier at age 81. He made the climb an annual event—the last time he was 84.[33]

Given these accomplishments and adventures past midlife—*well past*, in some cases—it's surprising that the media-fed fantasy of "old age" features beach walks and golf and a life of leisure. If you're buying into these daydreams, be warned. Research suggests they're not all they're cracked up to be. A British study showed that boredom set in as soon as 10 months after retirement. While many people make financial plans for their post-career life, they don't address a key question: What will you do all day once you have no job to go to?[34]

"The questions people ask at earlier stages of life become more profound at these later stages," says Stewart Friedman, founding director of the Wharton Work/Life Integration Project. "Am I living the life I want to live? What is most important to me? *Who* is most important to me? You see the end, and so you think about what you want to do with the time that you have remaining. There is the question of: now what?"[35]

The failure of fantasy to deliver what it promises is not particular to our older years. From beginning to end, Western culture promotes dreams of wealth and power and beauty attached to possessions and what we call "free" time, instead of focusing on what truly makes us happy. At older ages, we've grown too wise to buy that line. The truth is that people feel happiest when they're engaged with the world, enmeshed in a social group, and excited by the prospect of compelling activities. Besides thinking about how you will pay for life after your career, you need to be thinking about how you will spend your time. And, more importantly, how will you find the social connections and mental challenges that are so crucial to thriving at any age?

creating a vision

Let's take another imaginative trip. This time, we're attending our own memorial service. Who would be there? What would they say about you? What interactions with you would they remember? What affectionate and funny stories might they tell? How would they describe your accomplishments? Was there a single thread that best defined your life and your passion?

If your answers to these questions leave you feeling disappointed, you have time to create a brighter scenario. As Les Brown says, "You are never too old to set another goal or to dream a new dream."[36] A mindful life is one in which we remain aware that the day of our eulogy will eventually come and let that awareness guide our choices. It's never too late to craft a new vision, and we're never too old to pursue it.

If the stereotypes about aging aren't what we want our older years to be, we need to create a new vision for the life we will lead starting right now. We need to redefine older age for ourselves, looking anew at what "the good life" means to us at this stage. Only we can decide how we, uniquely, define and measure "success."

We need a vision that will actually bring us the satisfaction and love we want, rather than someone else's notion of what we *should* want or love. Focusing on the *qualities* we want to experience—authenticity, vitality, loving connection, fulfillment, adding meaning to other people's lives—will help us achieve our desired result. Having this kind of intention without knowing exactly how we might accomplish it makes way for the most free and innovative part of us to contribute in the creative process, leading to a much more rewarding journey than our rational mind might devise.

setting aside limiting beliefs

What we believe we *can* do has a huge impact on the goals we set, the course we follow, and thus what we achieve. It's important to expose ourselves to new, positive reference points that disrupt our limited thinking about age, expand our expectations, and help us craft new visions of what is possible. Here are just a few examples.

Allan Stewart was a retired dentist who went back to school in his 80s. He set a Guinness World Record when he completed a law degree in Australia at the age of 91—and another record when he got a master's degree in clinical science at 97.[37] Nola Ochs of Kansas interrupted her college career—for about 70 years—but she got her bachelor's degree at age 95, graduating alongside her 21-year-old granddaughter. She got her master's degree at 98 and was a graduate teaching assistant on her 100th birthday.[38]

A diagnosis of Parkinson's disease at age 55 threatened Linda Berghoff's lifelong love of dance—but not for long. Encouraged by her longtime friend, Laura Karlin, she signed up for a dance class anyway. Together they developed a dance class for people with Parkinson's, modeling it on a pioneer program at New York's Mark Morris Dance Center. At 65, Berghoff is leading a class in the Los Angeles suburb of

Venice, one of five programs she and Karlin have established in Southern California.[39] Some small-scale research studies suggest that—in addition to the joy it inspires—dance may help physical symptoms, too.

If there is something you dream of doing but you think you're too old or you lack the talent or skills, dare to discover otherwise. Challenge your assumption, knowing that people of all ages—people *just like you*—have done and are doing simply amazing things. The stories I've recounted here provide just a taste of the energy and spirit of those who have the strength and determination to stay healthy, happy, and relevant regardless of expectations or diagnosis. These people are following new dreams—dreams they never knew they had until they became propelled by a need and a mission to stay vital. You, too, can be one of them. The older we get, the more crucial it becomes to savor every moment. More than ever, we need to live like we mean it. If not now, then when? What are you waiting for?

So far this book has been building toward an answer to that question. In Chapter 1, I shared with you the strategy of realistic positivity. Part of that is becoming more aware of the beauty that lies within every moment—whether in a person, an exchange, or a sensory experience. Looking for beauty is a fundamental way of tapping into the happiness and well-being that are always available inside us, as part of our nature. In Chapter 2, we learned how to release false ideas and perceptions we have about ourselves and what happens as we grow older. We set a goal of reconnecting with our authentic self and living with that heart and those eyes.

Both of these projects prepare us for this new task: finding our joy and making it a part of our life every day. In her delightful books about organizing your home, *The Life-Changing Magic of Tidying Up* and *Spark Joy*, best-selling author Marie Kondo emphasizes that we should keep in our lives only those things that elicit our joy. The end result of her method is "a living environment filled with the things we love."[40] I would underscore this message: By shedding what's no longer serving us and consciously adopting what uplifts and expands us, we begin to build a life we truly love.

That's what this chapter is about: helping you begin to discover what you'd like—no, *love*—to do with the incredible gift of time you've been granted, so that you experience your most fulfilling and rewarding life in older age. Then, you can craft a vision for a life you would love and adopt an approach and strategies for bringing that vision to life.

In this chapter, we'll turn to the authentic self we've been uncovering over the previous two chapters and ask some questions that can set us off on a new journey—under the guiding star of realistic positivity.

finding the life you love

Joy is a natural part of us; we're wired to feel it. Sadly, too many of us lose our sense of joy as we grow older. We no longer experience delight on a daily basis. We may even forget what it feels like. Dictionary.com defines joy as "the emotion of great delight or happiness caused by something exceptionally good or satisfying; keen pleasure; elation."[41] Other synonyms and related emotions include bliss, jubilation, exultation, glee, and appreciation. We experience these emotions as physical sensations: buoyancy in our whole body, a tingling in our chest, an irrepressible smile on our face. Like passion and inspiration, joy creates a positive excitement that uplifts and expands us.

Marie Kondo also includes fascination and attraction in her definition of joy, as well as the feeling of being at ease and an internal sense of rightness. When coaching her clients on how to decide what to keep and what to throw out, Kondo has them hold each article—a piece of clothing, a book, a photograph, or another household item—and see how it makes them feel. If they're dithering, she has them look at all the things they've laid out and quickly pick out the three that give them the most joy. When compared against other items, those that create joy are easy to recognize.

I'd like to approach the self-exploration we're doing here in much the same way. As you go through the day or mindfully recall other times in your life, what creates joy should jump out at you. Joy's message is, "Choose this! This is true for you!" When you're considering who and what to keep in your life as you grow older, a key criterion must be what sparks your joy.

"And every day, the world will drag you by the hand,
yelling, 'This is important! And this is important! And this is
important! You need to worry about this! And this! And this!'
And each day, it's up to you to yank your hand back, put it on
your heart and say, 'No. This is what's important.'"

—Iain Thomas, *"The Grand Distraction"*[42]

Feeling the spark of joy is an indication that we are in touch with our true self. That's why joy is an excellent barometer for making decisions and setting goals. As you'll recall, emotions are energy. Their job is to attract our attention to what is going on for us in the present moment, prompt us to make decisions, and give us the fuel to act. Before we can make joy a goal and get our radar set for it, we have to know what we're looking for. If experiences of joy have been few and far between for you, I hope this chapter will help change that.

opening yourself to joy

To begin, we need to get rid of the layers of resentments, regrets, false agreements and assumptions, limiting beliefs, and patterns of negative thinking and fear that may be masking what would bring us joy. This was the task we took on in Chapter 2. The good news is that no matter what and how much we pile on top, joy is still there within us, ready to be tapped and experienced. It's part of our essence, who we really are. When we connect with this inner resource, we feel much more at home with ourselves, and any loneliness we may have been experiencing disappears.

To find what we truly love, we also have to get beyond the barriers of the rational mind and experience from our heart. This requires being in a state of wonder or innocence. Some spiritual traditions refer to this as "beginner's mind"—a mind not tainted or occupied by past experiences and therefore free from categorizing a new experience before we can explore it more fully for what it is. The only way to give our *heart* a chance to respond is to get the *mind* out of the way.

Like a dog on a walk, venturing wherever his senses and curiosity take him, we need to intentionally be awake to the details all around us and find the wonderful in the ordinary. If you want to see joy, go to a park or schoolyard where little children are fully engaged and delighted in the present moment. Notice that it doesn't take anything particularly special to evoke this feeling for them. It doesn't have to be Disneyland. It can be an ordinary playground or even their own backyard.

The same is true for us. Almost anything in our day-to-day routine can recall to us the continuous state of wonder we experienced as children. The fact is, we too often don't take the time to experience what's around us: to look up from our keyboard to see the sunset outside our window or listen to the rain, to put a book aside and play with the cat or the dog, to savor the components of our dinner instead of just shoveling them down so we can get on to something "more important."

The elements of joyful experience are all around us. We just need to open our eyes and our hearts so we can see them. We need to be open to mystery, including the seeming magic of synchronicity and serendipity, where events inexplicably line up, and life itself appears to be confirming our choices or nudging us in a certain direction for our own highest good. Thus, letting go of rationality, opening up to our imagination, and listening for and following our intuition are powerful tools for discovering and living a life we love.

Here are some strategies that will help you to begin discovering what brings you joy.

strategies for finding your joy

Use Mindfulness and Observe Your Life

The practice of mindfulness is a key resource for finding the life we love. While at first we may need to set aside a special time and place to focus on the present moment, with time we will find that we can slip into and out of a mindful state quite easily, even as we go about our daily routine. All it takes is being open both to the sensory input we are getting from the world around us and to the emotions and sensations that input generates.

Be fully where you are in this moment. Is it light or dark, cold or hot? If you're not comfortable, why not? If you're smiling, what stimulated that good feeling? In Chapter 1, I shared a technique for eating mindfully, using the example of an orange or grapefruit. Practice that with different foods you enjoy, and I guarantee you'll become aware of new levels of unexpected delight! Part of a friend's daily routine is to go to a local market. It gives her joy to look at the faces, particularly the children, and to invite interactions with others. She usually comes home with most of what she needs—but a big part of the errand is to engage mindfully with the social world. Another friend began taking a walk in his neighborhood. In no time, he began to know the houses where dogs or cats were hanging out and to note the progress of gardens as the yearly cycle of growth and decay moved forward. He took pleasure in the workings of his body as he moved along.

Whatever your scenery or experience, indoors or out, take time to enjoy it. It's all part of being human, and you can savor it as such. If we embrace and move through each day with gratitude, we can live a happy and fulfilling life, no matter what is happening. We need to begin with a real acceptance and appreciation of the whole human journey, before we can note the things that give us particular joy.

Meditate

To bring us a step further toward our authentic selves and our truth, we can turn to meditation, a specialized form of mindfulness. Although Westerners were originally introduced to it through religious and spiritual practices, it no longer appears only in that realm.

Meditation can take many forms. The simplest perhaps is sitting in silence and observing your breathing, without trying to control it. When thoughts arise, as they will, you observe them without getting attached to them, and then gently draw your attention back to your breath. The Chopra Center prescribes using a mantra—a repeated word or phrase—to give your mind something to hold its attention, so it less frequently turns to your thoughts.[43] Chanting symbolic words on one pitch is common to many religious practices. Because our minds are so active, many people find it easier to chant than to focus on breathing or silence. If you're more of a visual learner, you might find success in looking at a candle flame as your focal point for the meditation.

So, how long to meditate? While the experts seem to agree that 20 to 30 minutes twice a day is ideal, even a few minutes a day is beneficial. Any of us can do that!

By the way, walking can also be highly meditative if done as a mindfulness practice, where you are present in your body, senses, and environment rather than ruminating in thought. Some of the great creative figures in history have used walking as a means to relax the lower, reactive brain and access the more innovative, solution-oriented brain, and also as an experience in adventure and discovery in and of itself.

Meditation frees the creative thinking, visioning, clarity, and problem-solving capabilities essential to creating a life we will truly love. It gives us the mental and emotional room to hear from ourselves and to inventory the personal resources that lie beyond our reactive thoughts and emotions—resources such as intuition and wisdom. Like mindfulness, meditation doesn't deny or suppress our thoughts and emotions; rather, by enabling us to observe them, it helps us gain the perspective that we are *more than* those thoughts and emotions, which can make all the difference in how we respond to them. It has a profound effect on the life we create.

Revisit Your History

The inspirations for joy are remarkably consistent over a lifetime. You might want to give mindful consideration to where you found joy in your childhood and youth. How can you revive that joy now? Here are two interconnected examples of how joy traveled through time.

John Orne Johnson ("JOJ") Frost had always loved storytelling. After the death of his beloved wife, Frost needed outlets. He wrote columns for the local newspaper recounting the area's history, and then he discovered that pictures were another way to share his love of history. He was an untrained folk artist when he began painting at age 70, in 1922.

Using house paint and wallboard, Frost captured his boyhood memories as a fisherman from Marblehead on the Grand Banks of Newfoundland, as well as the heroic, historic deeds of Marbleheaders from the colonial days through the Civil War. In the six years prior to his death in 1928, Frost created more than 100 paintings and numerous wood carvings to show future generations what life had been like in earlier days in the Massachusetts seaport. Although townsfolk laughed at the childlike pictures of the untrained artist, the art world discovered him after his death, and he is now considered in the same league as Grandma Moses, another creative senior.

Among his admirers was a school librarian from Ohio named Priscilla Moulton, who moved to New England in 1959 and visited the Marblehead Historical Society. She was intrigued and moved by Frost's paintings, which were like little stories depicting the busy and sometimes dangerous lives of colonial fishermen and townspeople. She began to imagine a book for young people illustrated with the paintings; she even created a first draft that captivated a classroom of third graders. But Priscilla was busy with her family and career. The story went into a box with her working papers.

Fifty years later, when she was moving out of her house in 2009, she reopened the box. Her dream of using the paintings and the stories they told to touch young readers excited her again. In a project with her 60-year-old daughter, Bethe, Priscilla co-authored the historical fiction book *Molly Waldo! A Young Man's First Voyage to the Grand Banks of Newfoundland, Adapted from the Stories of Marblehead Fishermen of the 1800s.*[44] The freshly printed books, featuring Frost's paintings, arrived on Priscilla's 90th birthday and were soon being used by a fifth-grade teacher in Marblehead's public schools.

We'll hear more of Priscilla's story later in this chapter—it's amazing how big a dream can grow from the tiniest spark of joy. Unlike some physical attributes that decline with age, creativity is not age-dependent. In fact, the older you are, the deeper is your well of raw material crying out for self-expression. Also, the sense of mortality that comes with longevity can be a catalyst; some elderly people have an urgent need to create something that will outlive them.

Stay Vigilant to Please Yourself

Following your heart's desire, your "bliss," as mythologist Joseph Campbell called it,[45] means being committed to doing what brings you joy. If you are someone with a strong pattern of people-pleasing or being overly concerned about what other people think, take this opportunity to leave that pattern behind. The greatest reward for you will be living your own life. And that's the way it should be—it is *your* life! The fact of the matter is we are most powerfully helpful to others when we are coming from our true self. To do that, we must know what's true for us and live and act from that place. Shedding our concerns about others' opinions is often one of the blessings of older age.

The truth is that no one cares about what you're doing with your life nearly as much as you do. What other people will say, what they might think, isn't nearly as important as how you feel about your life, day by day.

Look for the Laughs

Have you laughed recently and found yourself realizing that it had been a long while since you laughed that hard? Did it make you feel like you need more humor and joy in your life? As adults, we simply don't laugh enough. We aren't intentional about including humor and laughter as an important part of our life. And yet, it makes such a difference when we do. Studies show the great benefits to laughter and laughter therapy, including decreasing stress hormones and boosting our immune system. By triggering the release of endorphins, the body's natural feel-good chemicals, laughter promotes an overall sense of well-being. It's even been shown to temporarily relieve pain.[46]

I invite you to go on a treasure hunt for what tickles your funny bone. Watch comedies more often, read the funny papers, buy joke books, watch little children play. Look for the laughs and find them, whatever they are for you. Make them a part of your life every day.

Choose Based on What You Love

We talked about this at length in Chapter 1, but it bears repeating here as we embark on finding our joy, creating our vision, and bringing both to life. We are always making choices, every minute of the day—not just by what we do, but also by what we *don't* do. What are your choices committing you to? What are they choosing in favor of? To create the life we love, we must stay vigilant to ensure that our choices come from what we love or will love rather than from our fears, insecurities, and self-doubts. Ask yourself, "What is motivating me here?" Set your new standard as making choices that go toward what you love and be disciplined in adhering to it. It will make all the difference.

If you lapse, that's okay. In fact, it's going to happen. Remember, it's in our biology to live in a state of fear, guarding against threats. But we also have a higher nature that we can call on and use instead of the lower, instinctual one—if we're aware of it and make a conscious choice. This is how we use the mind in pursuit of our heart's desire. We must do this as consistently as possible in order to create our very best life.

Our gifts and true nature are enduring. Even if buried or abandoned or seemingly forgotten, when we touch upon them they light us up with their energy, and we feel that spark of passion or joy. Our truth resonates within our body and emotions. We must allow our brain to register this communication rather than block it. The exercises that follow can help.

exercises

Timeline Review: Joy

1. Do a timeline review to recall, by decade, what in your life has evoked the most joy. Look back at the exercises in Chapter 2 for a reminder of how to do this. While I will be asking you to do this in later chapters as well in specific areas of life, for now, do a general review. This might include activities, people, travels, peak experiences, and so on.

2. Make notes about each joy that comes to mind. Take your time and list as many as you can.

3. In your notes, be specific about the source of the joy—what in particular you enjoyed about what you experienced: Was it the freedom you felt when traveling solo across Europe after college or driving cross country on a motorcycle with the wind in your face? Or the immense love you felt holding your newborn for the first time? Or the sense of timeless flow you felt when painting for hours on end?

4. Look over your list, being mindful of any sensations and emotions that arise. How do you feel? Do any items on the list evoke more feelings than the rest?

5. Consider whether there are any items on the list that might be dreams you'd like to pick back up at this point in your life.

Stepping into Wonder and Finding Your Joy Today

To open ourselves to and find what gives us joy, we may need help quieting our rational mind so that our heart is free to engage with the world. This exercise will help.

1. Begin by calming your body through mindful breathing—counting "one, two, three" as you inhale deeply and then again as you exhale. Repeating this for a few moments will shift your physiology out of survival mode, where it will be much more receptive to exploration. Get grounded in your body as you learned to do in Chapter 2, rooting yourself through your feet into the floor, feeling a heaviness that draws your elbows downward, and kneading the skin on your forearms using the opposite hand.

2. Now, scan your body, and then explore and name whatever feelings are present; fully acknowledge and embrace "what is" in your current reality. Don't try to deny or disown anything; instead, allow it all and then love yourself for feeling it, whatever it is.

3. Imagine giving yourself a shower in golden light that washes away all that you know and also any *need to know*. In other words, step into curiosity, wonder, and innocence.

4. When you're ready, open your eyes and look at the world anew. Gently go through your day and look for what brings you joy—for what gives you energy and uplifts you. If you can, get outside; be around nature. Do something different from your norm. Expose yourself to new people and scenery.

5. When you find that you are experiencing joy, feel gratitude for it. This will increase your positive feelings exponentially.

6. *Repeat*—again and again. Make this a daily habit, a new way of being.

Evaluating Your Joy

This exercise will allow you to see where you have joy in your life and where it is absent. It's designed to bring mindful awareness to the choices you've made that have created your present life. The purpose is to give you the power to make new choices that increase the joy you experience as you consciously craft your new life.

1. List the activities that represent how you spend your time. Include elements from all parts of your life. List them down the side of a page and write the numbers 1 to 10 across the top.

2. Now rate your level of joy for each activity (with 1 being the lowest and 10 the highest level of joy). An example (my own chart) is below.

Joy Rating	1	2	3	4	5	6	7	8	9	10
Working with therapy clients and groups										X
Doing professional supervision									X	
Writing books and articles									X	
Giving workshops and webinars										X
Attending professional seminars										X
Reading for work										X
Doing administrative tasks					X					
Attending spiritual group gatherings										X
Doing physical therapy						X				
Working out at home						X				
Walking in the neighborhood								X		
Pole dancing									X	
Traveling for vacation										X
Watching TV with my husband, JP										X
Going to plays and movies										X
Eating at new restaurants										X
Cooking						X				
Spending time with family and friends										X
Making new friends									X	
Having dental work done			X							

3. Now fill in your own chart. (See page 80.) List all the things you regularly spend time doing.

4. Review your chart, and identify which activities have a joy level of 6 or less, with the goal of phasing these activities out as you spend more time doing what brings you a higher level of joy. (You'll see from my chart that I have worked at eliminating activities

that have a joy level of less than 7 for me. Awareness of your current levels of joy, and the recognition that you have the power to change how you spend your time, can help you create a life where you experience high levels of joy too.)

5. As you explore new activities, you can create a similar chart to rate them. If something doesn't deliver the joy you thought it might, first ask yourself if course-corrections might make the activity more joyful (doing it in a different setting or with different people, for example) before you cross it off the list and move on to the next inspiration.

6. The goal is to end up with a chart where nearly everything you spend time on scores a 7 or higher. This may require revisiting Chapter 1, where we discuss seeing the beauty and finding joy in whatever you're doing, through mindfulness.

Troubleshooting

If you're having trouble finding your joy, you may still be stuck in your false self or in your perceptions about what it means to be your age. The false self is built from notions we have about who we *should* be. Although it's mostly created in childhood, it can last a long time until it's almost a learning disability, barring us from seeing ourselves and the world with realistic positivity.

1. In Chapter 2, we talked about agreements that no longer serve us: choices we have made to limit ourselves in order to maintain a relationship with someone else. Settling yourself into a mindful consciousness, think about the agreements in your life and how they might have outlived their usefulness.

2. One relevant unconscious agreement might be that we would age the way our parents and grandparents did: that we might live our older years in leisure activities, shunning work, for example. Or that "women our age" should only dress a certain way or enjoy certain activities. Consider the societal or familial stereotypes that might be limiting what you can discover for yourself.

3. We don't want to design our life according to what we *should* be. Instead, we need to start with "what is" and discover what we love.

Joy Rating	1	2	3	4	5	6	7	8	9	10

If you are having trouble developing an image for this new phase of your life, simply intend for it to be revealed to you. A colleague I know did this exercise in therapy. The only image that came to mind was stacks of paper on a table by a window. It meant nothing to her at the time, but 10 years later, she was writing a book that made her a sought-after speaker and expert in her specialty. And her desk was next to a picture window overlooking a park.

Put your focus on discovering what is a reflection of the true you and be COAL—curious, open, accepting, and loving—as you go through your daily life. Observe your inner reactions to what you experience. Most obviously, what is true for you will evoke a response of aliveness, passion, and/or joy.

living your dream

Once you know what brings you joy, you have to convert it into a meaningful plan that you can implement in your daily life—a plan that will infuse every day with joy. Begin doing it "on purpose." Create a mantra for yourself that names it and allows you to own your love for it and to pursue it—whatever it is. Here are just a few examples to illustrate what I mean:

- "I love painting"
- "I love to dance"
- "I love playing bridge"
- "I love petting my dog"
- "I love walking in nature"
- "I love spending time with family and friends"
- "I love helping young people by sharing my wisdom"
- "I love being a voice for women's empowerment"
- "I love performing random acts of kindness"
- "I love being an instrument and messenger of love"

Go ahead and name what lights your fire. The more you own it, the more focus you will put on it, which will help you create it more solidly in the world. And this is key, because a dream isn't real until you're living it. While that doesn't mean its reality depends on completing the job or arriving at the finish line, it does mean that you're actively *doing* something to move in that direction. Action is what ultimately brings dreams to life. Without action, we're just dreaming. And dreaming the dream, though it may feel safer, is not nearly as satisfying as living the dream. To have a life you love, you must actively live your dreams.

a life that supports your dream

A dream can only come about within a life that supports it. In his wonderful book *The Great Work of Your Life*, Stephen Cope talks about "creating the right conditions" that would support us in doing our "great work," that would allow our unique contribution to "come forward" into the world.[47] I would extend this notion to developing the life that is true for us—a life we'd love. I like to think of it as building a *structure* to our life—the architecture our life is built on—that is in sync with what we value and desire. Only then can we experience true well-being and happiness.

Connecting to ourselves—to our own truth—is the linchpin. That's because what isn't true for us isn't going to be viable in our life in the long run. Ultimately, if it's false, it cannot be sustained. For us to thrive, the foundation of our dreams must be viable and sustainable, and that will only be the case when they are true to who we really are.

So, what makes up our life's structure? Since our life is the sum total of all of its parts, the structure is the infinite number of building blocks that make up our life and those blocks' relationships to each other. The structure is everything our life is built on—from the thoughts we think to the choices we make to the conversations we hold to the actions we take. It really includes everything about us: our mindset, imprinting from childhood, genetics, behavior patterns, what's running us unconsciously as well as what we have made conscious. It's also our routines and habits, our relationships or lack thereof, and the quality of those relationships in nurturing and supporting us. And it's the level of support we receive and the degree to which we give and receive love. Finally, it's how much we're stuck in the past versus living fully in the present.

A good place to start is to look at our habits, as they form an important part of the structure of our lives. I'm sure you've heard the saying, "First we make our habits, and then our habits make us." Some habits support us in living a life we love, and some don't. It's cause and effect. For example, criticizing someone will make them feel attacked and will likely cause them to have negative feelings toward us. Conversely, giving feedback in a supportive, positive way constructively communicates complaints that need to be addressed. The former tactic creates a structure for disharmony in the relationship; the latter builds safety, harmony, and closeness. A lifestyle of sitting all day creates illness and disability, whereas getting regular exercise creates health and well-being in body and brain. Focusing on the negative makes us stressed and unhappy; addressing reality and then focusing on what we do want makes us feel safe, uplifted, and energized to do something productive about the situation.

Most habits aren't conscious. They were established some time ago, and we continue them without giving them any thought. Therefore, to change them, we need to bring our habits into conscious awareness and evaluate them, choosing to let go of those that don't serve our values and desires and replacing them with ones that do.

One way to become more mindful about our habits is something psychologists call *pattern interrupts*. We all have a morning routine that we do without thinking. Bathroom, feed the cats, put the coffee on, brush your teeth. Whatever it is, throw a wrench into the middle. For example, I sometimes stand on one foot while I'm brushing my teeth. Not only does this strengthen muscles that promote balance but it also puts me in a state of mindfulness about the rest of my routine. This may sound silly, but you'll find that it makes you aware of the present moment whereas before you were on autopilot moving through your life.

Of course, it's easier to adopt new habits than to break old ones, so the key here again is to put our focus on what we want to create and where we want to go, rather than on what we don't want and wish to leave behind. To break an old habit, you might think of replacing it with a new one. You may be a person who has the habit of saying nothing when someone hurts your feelings. Next time it happens, do the opposite of your usual behavior, even if it's only to say, "Ouch." Or if you have deep concerns about the consequences, practice first with yourself. Later, we all think of what we could have said—so, when you think of it, replay the situation in your head, with your desired response. In time, you may feel ready to speak up in the moment something occurs.

If you're the doer rather than the "done to," you have more control. The antidote to a relationship torn down by criticism and contempt, for example, is appreciation. The simple act of genuinely looking for and appreciating something about what someone else does will instantly begin to heal the damage and turn the relationship around. To offset the damage that can result from sitting too much, experts recommend getting up frequently, even if that means simply standing. The recommended ratio is: for every 20 minutes of sitting, stand for 10 minutes and move for 2.[48]

As this last example shows, our habits of self-care are especially important to our well-being because they support us in everything else we do. Did you know, for example, that getting enough sleep enhances your creativity, ingenuity, confidence, leadership, and decision-making? Just getting a little extra sleep can actually increase the volume of your brain, and getting too little can make you feel lonelier and more helpless.[49] The bottom line is that we are happier and more effective when we've had enough sleep. Throughout Part II of the book, we'll look at several key activities, habits, and regimens of self-care and beyond that help us to live our happiest and function at our best. These include diet and exercise, continuous learning, creative exploration and expression, spiritual connection, meaningful engagement with people and community, and giving of ourselves through service. When we have a structure that is composed of these building blocks, we cannot help but love our life.

Habits are supported by routines and procedures—structures within our building blocks. Examples include keeping healthy, delicious options in the house so we can stick to our desired food program; putting our exercise clothes on first thing in the morning so that we build momentum that pushes us toward the gym; joining a gym or exercise group that is near enough to be convenient; and setting aside some time each week or each month to explore new social connections in our community. Structures like these greatly reduce the need for sheer willpower to keep ourselves on track. Yes, it requires the use of our will and follow-through to make any positive choice, but we can work *with* rather than *against* ourselves to make this easier.

dealing with fear and resistance

With any dream, it's a guaranteed biological fact that internal resistance will raise its ugly head at some point or even many points along the path. The hold of our fear-based survival system is that strong. No sooner have we formulated our true vision than our rational mind will begin questioning its validity, our authority and ability to pursue it, and the availability of opportunities to go forward—before we even begin. Understanding this and expecting it is part of a realistic positivity mindset.

When the fears and rationalizations start, hear them, thank them for trying to keep you safe, then set them aside and place your attention back on what you would love. Remind yourself that the real purpose of life is to truly live. You will need to be ruthless with this, trust me. And you won't get it right 100 percent of the time. That's okay. William Whitecloud calls this "the Battle of Evermore." Choosing our heart's true desire over our fears and insecurities may be a challenge until our dying day. Reinforced moment by moment, day after day, it's the most important choice we ever make.

Another opposing force we will have to conquer is an interesting phenomenon called *counterwill*. It's the innate resistance to being controlled. No one likes to be forced, cajoled, manipulated, or otherwise coerced into behaving a certain way. Although the resistance may not be expressed openly, it still remains, generating anger that may also be suppressed. While this occurs mostly in the context of relationships with others, it can also turn up in dealing with ourselves. Rather than try to force ourselves to do something the way we think we should, we would do better to be more flexible and creative while still keeping our eyes on our goal.

If you fully acknowledge "what is," you gain the power to change it. If you deny it or keep it hidden from your view, you will be helpless to make change. As part of this, remember to allow yourself to feel all of your feelings, and love yourself for feeling them. This takes the power out of the fear and self-doubt and allows you to move forward, pursuing what you'd love instead.

strategies for beginning to live your dreams

Start Right Now

"There is no time like the present" becomes truer with every year we live, and every moment is a potential starting point for creating change. Start now and start small. Whatever it is you are going for, first "lean in" to it by putting focus and attention on it, then break it down into bite-sized steps. If a dream or goal doesn't seem "realistic," it's likely because we're trying to take in too big of a picture all at once. As an old proverb instructs, we eat an elephant one bite at a time. Even giant, "unrealistic" goals can be accomplished if done step by step, a little at a time.

Looking at your goal right now, what is the most obvious tiny first step? Is it researching, writing an outline of ideas, reaching out to someone to ask their view, buying supplies or a piece of equipment, or signing up for a class? No matter what your dream is, you can do something *right now* that will take you the next step on your path toward it. Besides giving you time and space for intuiting what is needed next as you focus on the end goal, small strategic steps compel your dream out of the clouds and ground it here on earth. That is where you'll experience the joy, satisfaction, and exhilaration of pursuing and doing that which your heart says is true to you.

Create a Workable Plan

We met Priscilla Moulton earlier in this chapter, as she completed the first step of her dream to bring JOJ Frost's vision of history to youngsters. Actually, she may have thought she was done, but then she had a surprise. Visiting a classroom and seeing the children engaged in Frost's world and his art, Priscilla got the idea for a new project—reuniting Frost's paintings, which have become scattered in the holdings of museums and collectors throughout the United States. Her vision is to use the Internet to display them together, virtually, so that viewers can see the chronological panorama of American history that Frost created almost a century ago. At 93, Priscilla is still pursuing her dream, which interestingly will also fulfill the dream of Frost himself, to inform future generations through "stories on the wall."

"Project JOJ Frost" has delivered meaningful rewards. It has allowed an elderly woman with limited vision, hearing, and mobility to become immersed in a network of curators, archivists, and art collectors. Using her acute mind to collect and share information and images of an important American artist has brought satisfaction and fulfillment beyond measure. Although 1,000 miles apart, Priscilla and her collaborator-daughter, Bethe, debate daily about how to bring JOJ Frost's pictures to the world; they celebrate their partnership and the growing circle of Frost advocates who have contributed to their work. Let's look at the steps they took toward implementing their dream.

1. Looking for a complete list of Frost's works, Priscilla and Bethe began with the local Marblehead Museum, whose director, Pam Peterson, had written *JOJ Frost: A Gallery Guide*. While it had illustrations and descriptions of the museum's holdings, Priscilla wanted to track down the paintings *outside* of that institution.

2. An Internet search revealed that an art student named Martha Katz-Hyman had done her master's thesis on Frost in 1971. It included an outstanding bibliography and list of the Frost paintings known at that time. When Bethe called the author as a courtesy to inform her of their work, she learned that both had attended Marblehead schools and had shared the same best friend. Two years later they would attend the same high school reunion and meet for the first time—just one example of the personal satisfactions that came out of Project JOJ Frost.

3. Through the Internet, Priscilla and Bethe built a list of museums that own Frost paintings, and Priscilla began an email correspondence with these institutions. Over the next two years,

she visited each location and met curators and archivists. Because she no longer drives, these trips were shared with her daughter or her granddaughter (bringing one more generation into the project).

4. The Moultons also visited the important archives that had files about the artist, including the Smithsonian Institution's Archives of American Art. On two visits there, Bethe used her iPad to capture over 1,500 images of letters, newspaper articles, unpublished notes, and old photographs.

5. The Moultons recruited two retired friends who love history and research to help Priscilla gather material from New England archives by scanning and transcribing documents, as well as seeking out genealogical information from the web. Now the Moultons have their own valuable archives.

6. With the research phase of the project largely finished, the Moultons have built a network of Frost advocates. Soon, a newly renovated gallery at the Marblehead Museum will educate young and old alike, encompassing the story of Frost's works near and far. As others are inspired, new dreams and new legacies will take shape.

Their project is not "done" and never will be, but they are having great fun and finding a good deal of fulfillment as they connect the people who care about these paintings. They are confident that those connections will eventually lead to the reunification of the artist's works in various ways, through books, exhibitions, and the Internet.

Be Flexible

As you work toward your dream, allow yourself some flexibility. For example, to complete this book on time for the publisher, my collaborator, Brookes, and I set a schedule to write by, with monthly and weekly milestones to meet. The milestones were not really negotiable if we were to meet our goal. Exactly how we accomplished them, though, was flexible. This included the time of day we wrote and where we worked. If you've ever done anything creative, especially a large project like a book, then you know that, for many writers, it can be easy to procrastinate; plenty of things are easier than writing, and, when you need to write, those things all come to mind and try to tempt you away from your work. In the professional world, however, deadlines are deadlines. So even when the project is ultimately of our choosing, it can feel like we're being forced to do something, like we lack control. Having choices gives us a greater sense of control.

So, I find it beneficial when I need to get something done that isn't really an option (because it's something I truly want to do) to give myself choices surrounding what I'm doing, so that my counterwill is appeased. In the example of writing this book, this meant choosing where to write, what time to work day by day, which sections to work on and in what order, and even what to eat. It also included what kind of exercise to do each day (I like walking, dancing, and working out at the gym; Brookes likes swimming, dancing, and yoga), taking frequent stretch and rest breaks, and having food both that was healthy and that we each liked to eat.

Our bodies are of course an integral part of everything we do, and that means accomplishing our goals and dreams. Though it may sound a bit strange, I think you'll find that it works well to include your body in the decision-making and ask what it would like each day (and throughout the day) as you work toward your goals. The body isn't a slave; it's a partner. We need its cooperation. To get that, we need to make sure it is healthy and happy. This, again, will reduce the need for sheer willpower alone to keep us on track.

Be Proactive and Resourceful

Being proactive and resourceful is good advice for your life as a whole as you approach your older years. Part of being a good steward of your life and your dreams is anticipating your needs. Educate yourself about the common challenges typically faced when people move into different age stages, and be proactive in creating a structure that will allow you to thrive rather than merely survive. For example, depression is a problem for many people as they age. While depression has many causes, proactively creating a life we love will have positive effects.

All of the chapters in this book will help you to do that. In addition, the proliferation of information today—and our access to it—provides opportunities to learn about whatever you like. Do you have a passion for the Beatles and want to learn more about why they are considered the greatest musical group of all time? Do you want to know what you can do to have a fulfilling sex life at age 65, 75, 85, or 95?

Or perhaps you want to know what your options are for ensuring your financial well-being, even though you've retired? Susie and David had put money away for retirement and were financially conservative all their lives. Still, they wondered whether what they were spending each month would cut too deeply into the resources they needed for the duration of their lives. When Susie, 70, saw an ad for a retirement planning workshop, she signed up along with her daughter, who was in her 40s and had not yet started saving for retirement. The workshop opened her eyes to the reality that, without an actual budget, she and her husband were operating on hope. She discovered new approaches that would enhance their investments. She and her husband signed up with the financial planners and began making the changes that would allow their money to go further.

Being resourceful may entail being creative and persistent. If at first an answer, solution, or pathway forward doesn't appear, keep intending to find it and continue to look. Don't be afraid to try different things or to fail. We all know that the path to success is littered with failure. Persevere until you find what you are looking for.

AARP is a wonderful all-round resource for so many issues related to aging. I highly recommend both the organization and the book *Disrupt Aging*, by AARP CEO Jo Ann Jenkins.[50] The organization seems truly passionate about improving life in the United States for the population aged 50 and over, having long been an advocate for America's seniors. In addition to offering discounts and benefits related to travel, dining, shopping, and the like, AARP actively lobbies the government on issues related to seniors and offers resources for finding volunteer opportunities and doing projects that give back to the community. The minimal membership fee even includes a subscription to the organization's magazine, which covers both meaningful and entertaining topics relating to aging.

Build a Circle of Support

Priscilla Moulton was able to find initial support for her project in her daughter, Bethe, and over time they built a much larger network of people who shared their dream. As your notion of the life you love takes shape, look around to see if any local organizations are moving in the same direction. AARP, again, is a great resource; you can post your opportunity on its website to find interested volunteers. You might also share your dream with friends and family. You never know how the ripples of your idea may spread.

Let Go of Notions of Success and Failure

Worrying about how you're doing and what others will say about your efforts detracts from your focus on what you love. Instead, just go for your vision—your desired end result—with all your might, as if, as the maxim goes, you could not fail, or as if the worst has happened and you have already failed and now have nothing to lose. The truth is, we can experience life only in each finite moment, and, by living fully according to our heart, we cannot fail, no matter the outcome. We are successful in the most meaningful sense of the term because we are living our dream.

You will face a number of challenges as you move forward to create the life you love. Here are some exercises that will help develop your "fitness" for this endeavor.

---

exercises

Hearing the Voices of Your Fear and Your Love

1. On a new piece of paper or digital file, make three columns. Write the headings "Activity," "Motivation," and "Fear/Love," from left to right.

2. Now, choose two of your more active days from the past week or so, and list what you did with your time in the "Activity" column.

3. Going one by one, spend a moment considering each list item and what motivated you to spend your time that way. In the "Motivation" column, write the reason you did the activity.

4. Being mindful and honest with yourself, evaluate whether the energy that fueled the choice and behavior was some variation of the emotion of fear or whether it was driven by a vision of creating what you love. Write your conclusion in the final column.

Coming Up with Your Next Three Action Steps

1. Write down one dream or goal that has come up for you during the course of reading and working through this chapter. Writing it down now doesn't mean you are committing to it, so don't worry. For now, we'll just be using it to practice breaking a goal down into "realistic" action steps.

2. Evaluate whether your dream or goal can be done in a single action. Probably not. In fact, probably far from it. If not, take several minutes to begin listing the most obvious smaller action steps that would be needed to accomplish the larger goal.

3. If these steps are still too large in and of themselves, continue to break each down until you have three bite-sized action steps that you could take right now.

4. If this goal or dream is something you would like to commit to trying so that you can see how joyful and meaningful it will be, take these first three steps and feel the excitement and fulfillment of pursuing your new dream!

5. Keep repeating this exercise until you achieve your goal, always looking for the small next steps that seem the most obvious to take.

***

No matter what your desires are, the strategies in this chapter will help you get in touch with them and achieve them. Take this knowledge and approach into the remaining chapters of the book, which highlight key areas that have been proven highly worthwhile in older age for the health, happiness, meaning, and fulfillment they create.

part|TWO

the fundamentals for a healthy, happy post-middle age

chapter | 4

making the connections
that make all the difference

Most of us enter our 50s and 60s embedded in a social network: the parents, siblings, and other kin who were part of our youth, supplemented by the friendship circles we built and extended through school and career, and—especially close—our partners and our children, even grandchildren. The amount of love and support we draw from them may vary but the links are essential.

Bob married Sarah when he was 23 and she was 21. Approaching the 50-year mark in their marriage, both have wide social circles that include at their outer edges work colleagues, neighbors, and "hobby" friends—golf buddies for Bob, book club for Sarah. At the core, however, is a much smaller group. Besides Sarah, Bob's includes their daughter Alice and his brother Sam. Sarah's core is a bit larger: Bob, all three of their children, and her best friend from childhood, Louise.

Louise chose not to marry. Three close friends (Sarah, of course, is one) and her brother, Mike, are at the core of her circle. Until her mother's recent death, Louise was also very close to her. She regularly "prunes" the outer rim of her network. For Louise, each connection requires a lot of energy to support, so she keeps the number at the maximum she feels she can invest in completely.

You may recognize yourself in one of these relationship patterns—or you may have your own. While everyone may have a separate approach to relationships—how many, how deep, how long-lasting, who relies on whom—our happiness and health will depend on that network and especially the inner core.

Some relationships may need work to take their place in the loving circle that will nourish and enrich your life as you grow older. Both genetics and early life experiences greatly influence our abilities in the social realm, but, as we've seen with other areas of life, we have the capacity to learn and grow in how to positively connect with others. While Bob and Sarah remain a loving and committed couple, this didn't happen magically without effort—sometimes considerable—along the way.

You'll also need to continuously rebuild that circle as some connections drop away through time and circumstance. People who were once down the hall or across the street may move across the country. Their lives may move in directions that no longer sync with ours. Bob was more likely to leave friends behind as he moved from job to job or one neighborhood and life stage to another, while Sarah has a selected collection of people representing all of those life experiences.

You may find that you need to create distance from some people as you grow your own inner life. Louise was once best friends with a woman named Kathleen, but as Kathleen's depression deepened her addiction to alcohol it created more and more issues. When she stubbornly refused to seek treatment, Louise felt she needed to let go of the friendship for her own health. As we age, some people inevitably will be lost, though not necessarily forgotten. Louise still thinks of her mother in the evening, when they often shared a phone call to review the day.

We'll meet Bob, Sarah, Louise, and their circles again later in this chapter.

Whatever the number or shape of our relationships, one constant emerges: that we are innately and intensely social beings. We are wired to form positive connections with others and suffer serious consequences when we don't. Infants, for example, can literally die if they go too long without being held, nuzzled, and hugged enough, despite receiving proper nutrition.[51] The elderly, too, experience an increased risk of mortality without enough social connection, as social isolation and loneliness are major factors in depression and negatively impact physical, mental, and cognitive health. The fact is that connection, love, and touch are essential to our nature and thus our well-being. Therefore, the better we are at making and keeping healthy connections, the happier and healthier we will be. Even though both genetics and early life experiences strongly influence our abilities in the social realm, our capacity for change in this area—at any age—is great.

Born and raised in one sort of family or another, we move through life as the pulsing dot at the center of a circle that grows and shrinks over time. Sometimes it may be vibrant with color, at others brittle and gray. But if we think about our happiness—and even our health—over the years, we'll probably be able to connect it to the success of our links with others. The deepest pains in life tend to involve breaches within our interactions with others. Conversely, our greatest healing and joy come in having close, harmonious bonds.

This need for connection may become even more crucial in our older years, and more rewarding as we are able to become more and more authentic within ourselves and in all of our relationships. It is essential to understand that the relationship we have with ourselves is the key to success for all of the relationships we build with others: when we are happy and fulfilled independent of others, we are most attractive to other healthy, happy people who are living in the same manner. We can actually be uplifted by sharing our lives with each other.

The goal of this book's previous chapters was to help you make more powerful connections with your own inner world—to learn how to incorporate realistic positivity into your own life, to uncover and dispel untrue and limiting notions you may have held about yourself or others, and to get in touch with what it is that you would truly love this last leg of your life journey to be about. After working through those chapters, you are ready to move forward without those burdens and restraints to form and renew the relationships that make up your key circle of support.

In this chapter, we look at where you may need to do a bit of work to create the loving relationships that will nourish and enrich your life as you age. Here are the themes we will explore: (1) how you can nurture in yourself the qualities that will help you build strong relationships, (2) how you can reach out to start new relationships with friends as well as build on existing family and friendship ties, and (3) how to start or invigorate your intimate partnerships.

becoming the kind of
friend you'd like to have

Our ability to have successful relationships with others starts with having a healthy relationship with ourselves: when we're grounded, in our body and in the present, mindfully aware of what's going on inside us—even if we don't like it, even if it's uncomfortable—we feel much safer than when we're not in a grounded, embodied state. As we explore our thoughts and emotions, a magical thing happens: the better we know ourselves, the more we love ourselves. Everything else will follow. Here are some directions you can take as you prepare yourself to reach out and forge new relationships—or evaluate and modify the relationships you already have, ones that may not be meeting your desires or needs.

strategies for becoming
the friend you'd like to be

Read, Experiment, Learn, and Course-Correct

In this chapter, I've highlighted the strategies I have found to be the most useful in forging meaningful connections with others. Because this arena of life is so vital to our happiness and well-being, I invite you to explore the subject much more deeply (hundreds of books have been written) and as experientially as possible. Take what you learn from a book or a course and go test it "in the field." In this area of life more than some others, we get instant feedback in the form of how others respond to us and how our interactions make us feel. Additionally, I encourage you to treat this as an area of continual curiosity, focus, learning, and growth. I guarantee that you'll be very happy you did!

Develop Your Emotional Intelligence

You probably know what IQ is, and you may even have a sense of where you might fall on that scale. But how about emotional intelligence? Perhaps unlike IQ, it's absolutely something we can develop, with rewarding results.

Defined by OxfordDictionaries.com as "the capacity to be aware of, control, and express one's emotions, and to handle interpersonal relationships judiciously and empathetically,"[52] emotional intelligence was first described by two psychology professors. Peter Salovey of Yale University and John D. Mayer of the University of New Hampshire introduced the idea to the academic world, and they continue to be leading researchers. Those of us outside the university might not have heard about the concept if it weren't for Daniel Goleman, who brought the subject into our living rooms with his best-selling 1995 book *Emotional Intelligence: Why It Can Matter More Than IQ.*[53] Goleman suggested five components:

- self-awareness
- self-regulation
- internal motivation
- empathy
- social skills

The connections are fairly easy to see. In order to manage our emotions, we need to be aware of them—as they are, not as we imagine they should be. Once we're aware, we anticipate that others have similar feelings, and we develop empathy. Building this connection between ourselves and others creates an internal motivation: we want to treat others as we would like to be treated—and so we're motivated to enhance our own social skills.

I highly recommend making "becoming more emotionally intelligent" a personal project. Few efforts in life will have a more significant impact on our vitality and happiness or on the legacy we will leave from our time on earth. As Carl W. Buehner said so eloquently, "They may forget what you said, but they will never forget how you made them feel."[54]

Be Yourself—Your True Self

Courage starts with showing up and letting ourselves be seen. That's the core belief of Brené Brown, a researcher at the University of Houston who wrote the best-seller *Daring Greatly: How the Courage to Be Vulnerable Transforms the Way We Live, Love, Parent, and Lead.*[55] "It's tough to [be vulnerable] when we're terrified about what people might see or think. When we're fueled by the fear of what other people think or that gremlin that's constantly whispering 'You're not good enough' in our ear, it's tough to show up. We end up hustling for our worthiness rather than standing in it." While it's fine to work toward self-improvement, it's not okay to become obsessed with the fear of failing or making mistakes or not meeting someone's expectations.[56] Journalist Maria Shriver points out in her blog that "playing it cool is overrated." While others may warn against the danger of "wearing your heart on your sleeve," it's the only way people will know what you want.[57]

One important side effect of being vulnerable ourselves is that it issues an invitation to others to join us in sharing their authentic selves. More than one person has found that a gift presented by getting older is the ability to speak their mind and to be honest about what they want—and don't want. This doesn't have to involve rudeness or thoughtlessness. In fact, part of becoming our authentic selves is developing a compassion for others—mirroring our compassion for self—that increases our sensitivity to the thoughts and feelings of others.

Foster the Intent to Love Others

Creating deep and lasting connections with others means conveying to them our best wishes—in the most profound sense—for their well-being. My collaborator, Brookes, calls this having "the intent to love," which means giving people the dignity of their process to feel how they feel as well as honoring their right to freely make a choice that is right for them. It involves having trust that when you honor everyone's right to choose, what is true for each person will emerge, and this, ultimately, will result in the highest good for all concerned. As you can probably sense, this entire dynamic requires wanting and intending the best for everyone involved. It requires that we come to the situation with the intent to "love"—to mean well for—everyone, including ourselves.

Mindfulness can help you to center yourself before an encounter and to bring to awareness your loving intent for the person you will meet. Another way to express that is in the idea of kindness. Researchers have found kindness is good for us: psychologist Martin Seligman, summing up a large body of research, says, "We scientists have found that doing a kindness produces the single most reliable momentary increase in well-being of any exercise we have tested."[58]

James R. Doty, founder of the Center for Compassion and Altruism Research and Education (CCARE) at Stanford University School of Medicine, noted that if the doctor treated them kindly, volunteers exposed to a cold virus were less likely to actually get a cold and those who got it recovered more quickly.[59] Compassion reduces anxiety and enhances responses of the immune system. Scientists aren't sure yet why this happens, but they've seen plenty of evidence that it does.

So, set the intention to support the people in your life.

exercises

Things I Like About Me

In order to attract the kinds of relationships we want in life, we have to like ourselves. We need to know the value we bring as a friend, family member, or mate—the favorable traits and qualities we have that make us likable and a valuable person for others to engage with.

1. Simply list what you like and/or appreciate about yourself. You can list anything, except your list must contain things about you that genuinely come from the true you, and not things you do because you think others expect you to.

2. See if you can list 25–50 things. If that's hard to do, carry your list around with you over the course of several days and add to it as things occur to you.

3. Review your list. Take a moment to appreciate what's on it and to feel good about the person you are!

Evaluate Your Friendship IQ

Your answers to the following questions will tell you whether you're ready to form the kind of friendship you want and whether you're a person others will want to make that connection with. The more times you answer "yes," the more likely you are to be ready.

1. Am I ready?

   - Do I have life balance and therefore room in my life for the kind of relationship I seek? Can I say no and not take on things that are not true to me, leaving room for what is important?

   - Do I prioritize taking care of myself, which gives me energy to participate fully with others?

   - Am I able to be authentic and honest with others, where my thoughts, words, and actions match?

   - Do I approach life with realistic positivity, facing "what is" openly and with courage and focused on what I want to create?

2. What kind of friend can I be?

   - Do I have a sense of humor about myself and life that makes me good company and allows me to take challenges in stride?

   - Do I take responsibility for my thoughts, emotions, and behaviors and how they contribute to my interactions with others? Can I look at my own behavior as well as what others do if there's a conflict?

   - Am I in touch with my own inner resources for soothing myself rather than always expecting others to make me feel better?

   - Do I communicate in ways that are positive and constructive?

   - Do I mean others well?

   - Do I show up as present and emotionally available when I interact with others, knowing these are keys to connection?

Of course, many other questions could be on this list. Think about what qualities and characteristics are most important to you in your relationships and make sure to develop them in yourself. We often have a laundry list of items we want others to give to us and less often ask ourselves what *we* bring to the relationship. To attract the kind of people we want and to keep them in our lives, we need to be that kind of person.

What Kind of Friend Are You?

1. First, imagine an interviewer is asking someone you know—friend, relative, colleague—to describe you. What are the first three words you'd like them to say?

2. Using mindfulness, focus on one of these three words. See what images present themselves that show how you display this quality in your interactions. Or how you display the opposite.

3. As you conclude your mindfulness session, take your journal and write down what you experienced. If you are not meeting your goal for this quality, what can you do or say that would authentically embody it more? Make a to-do list.

4. Repeat this process for all three words.

5. Then establish some checkpoints for yourself to see how you're doing: once a week, perhaps. In mindfulness practice, let images from the previous days come to mind and evaluate your progress.

6. Another way to approach this is to think of someone you consider a good friend. What qualities do you value? How do they respond when you're feeling upbeat? How do they respond when you face problems? What can you learn from this? Make some notes in your journal.

Timeline Review: Relationships

1. Take a clean piece of paper or new digital file and divide the page into decades.

2. Under each decade, list two or three people—not relatives—who were your closest friends or "BFFs" at the time. Take a look at the list.

3. How many people moved forward from one decade to another? Are any relationships constant through most of your life?

4. What were the characteristics of these lasting friendships? How have they changed over time? Were there rough spots? How did you get past them?

5. How about the once-significant people who were left behind? Why did these relationships end?

6. What can you learn from this?

forging your essential connections

Our most important relationships provide an invaluable foundation for our lives; through significant others, we come to realize that, no matter what happens to us, we are still the same person, worthy of love and support. Whether they are family, friends, or intimate partners, these people show us that we are not alone. At the same time, we can do the same for them.

In her book *Remodel Your Reality*, Kimberly Fulcher sorts relationships into five categories—six if you include the all-important relationship with yourself,[60] which we've already discussed. Intimate partnerships—with husbands or wives or significant others—have a special quality that deserves its own dedicated section later in this chapter. And a relationship with a higher power also has a special quality; we will look at that in Chapter 6. For now, let's focus on the remaining three: parents or authority figures, children and dependents, and friends.

relationships with parents and other authority figures

How you related to your parents when you were a child has a profound effect on all the relationships that come after, perhaps the most important of which is the relationship with yourself. Reevaluating that tie and reconsidering its impact on your own notions of self-worth and self-love is important work for all times of life, and it's never too late to undo the damage that may have resulted.

If you were lucky enough to have loving and supportive parents, you may have grown up with few childhood wounds. One crucial passage that growing older presents is the loss of these key figures in your life. Even if you had relatively young parents, they are likely to die before you do, and most likely during this passage of time from late middle age to your own older age. It's a critical loss.

Louise, for example, was very attached to her mother. Her mother had built the relationship when Louise was small. Although Mom probably didn't understand it that way, in her conversations and interactions with Louise, she was in many ways modeling how adult friends might interact. Because of this, Louise and her mother had a relatively smooth transition from Louise's childhood to her adult life. They had always been good friends in many ways. As her mother aged, Louise began to take on some of the responsibilities for her care—in a very real sense she "mothered" her mother—but they were friends to the end.

Whether you share Louise's experience or you have suffered the ongoing wounds of bad parenting, finding a new "authority figure" or elder to be in a relationship with can provide important benefits. If you came out of childhood with a negative self-image, a supportive pastor, therapist, or personal coach can give you the validation you need. If you're facing the loss of loving parents, the same folks can offer you the unconditional acceptance you'll miss. Louise found a therapist who could be the person to lean on that her mother had always been. If professional relationships turn you off, consider relying on another relative or an older person among your connections who might be happy to play this role.

relationships with children and dependents

If you're past 50, chances are your children are grown-ups—although you may think they're not behaving that way! Even if they remain in your household, your relationship with them will change. "Emerging adults need a different kind of closeness than when they were young," according to Elizabeth Fishel and Dr. Jeffrey Jensen Arnett, authors of *When Will My Grown-Up Kid Grow Up?*[61] "They need emotional support that helps boost, not stifle, their confidence in their own coping skills, and they need parents to bear witness to their increasing capacity to take on responsibilities, even if there are setbacks or mishaps along the way." The authors offer five useful checkpoints:

1. *Observe respectful boundaries.* Both of you need and deserve private space. The same is true of all relationships, but we're not used to extending it to our children.

2. *Listen more than you talk.* This isn't a bad piece of advice for all friendships, and that's where your connection to the kids is headed.

3. *Do what you love together.* Whether it's a football game or a friendly Scrabble competition at home, intimacy tends to flow when everyone is relaxed and enjoying themselves.

4. *Set ground rules for how to disagree.* Again, this is a good point for all friendships, and especially for your interaction with your kids, who at one time you could simply tell what to do rather than having to negotiate differences of opinion.

5. *Make room for significant others in their lives.* If you make children choose between you and their new partners, you're probably headed for disappointment.

It may be tough to see children pass into adulthood—and, before you know it, into middle age. That's life. Bob was having a difficult time accepting his daughter Alice's adult self, in particular her sexual maturing. One day, he and a male business friend ran into Alice in a restaurant, and the friend invited Alice to join them. Bob was surprised at how easily she fitted into the conversation and at the maturity of the insights she offered on some of the issues they discussed. On their way back to his office, the business friend remarked that Alice was "very much like her dad. It must be a special gift to have a daughter you can relate to so easily." Bob realized what he had been missing and resolved to fix it. Their grown-up relationship is one of the lights of his life, even if the dependence and independence are now mutual.

Life is full of other opportunities—less taxing, on the whole—to experience the joys of having someone depend on you. Volunteer organizations are always looking for experienced and loving people to work with children. And many older people enjoy the companionship of cats and dogs, particularly if they live alone. Research among older people has shown that pets are good for your heart—they reduce both heart disease and cholesterol levels, while evoking positive emotions.[62]

Louise's brother, Mike, believed that children should have pets—probably because he and Louise had not been allowed to have them. As each of his children grew to seven or eight years old—an age where he or she could take some responsibility for a pet—Mike took the child to the local rescue center to pick out a special cat or dog. If the first animal passed on, it was replaced. While one of his four children took a pet with him when he left home, the other kids' pets—a dog and two cats—were left with Mike.

Although he told himself he should feel "burdened" by the animals, Mike knew in his heart that he was glad to have them around, especially after his wife died. The menagerie was never smaller than three and sometimes grew to four or five, depending on whether or not Mike passed an animal adoption site with an appealing critter he had to bring home.

Mike learned over time that each dog or cat had its own personality and quirks. Some, he told Louise, had gone back to the beauty line for seconds and missed out on the brains. He loved each one in its special way. While some people find that their grief for a lost pet prohibits them from adopting another, Mike saw each pet as a new relationship opportunity. Nevertheless, he kept ashes and pictures of all that had passed through his home and heart.

Having a pet while growing older is like having a contract to grow old together. Pets offer a love and affection that is nearly impossible to describe. The responsibility for the well-being of the pet—especially a dog—makes you get up and out no matter what. The added love is an emotional, physical, and spiritual advantage to anyone who can manage a pet's care.

relationships with friends

If you held an outside job while raising a family—or if you still have a full-time job—you may think you have too little time for the effort to meet potential friends and develop those connections. As family and work take less of your time, though, you may find yourself missing people, both to play with and for mutual support. In the next Exercises section, I'll offer some suggestions for starting and building new friendships.

Many people enjoy having a large social circle and a busy calendar of events. Others are content to spend more time by themselves or with their partner. Either way, most of us rely on two or three people who form our inner circle. It's important to enjoy their company—as with children, doing things you love together builds intimacy—but deeper connections are especially rewarding as we get older. To make these connections, you need to be brave enough to show your truest self.

Relationships come and go as they serve us. Don't be afraid to outgrow what has been comfortable in the past if it is no longer true for you today. But, in mindfulness practice, do reflect on why these relationships are no longer satisfying. Developing a personal notion—it doesn't have to be a formal list—of what you want or don't want in a friend is useful as you set out to make new ones and to improve those already part of your life.

strategies for forging healthy connections with others

Keep in Contact . . . through Touch

Because we are bodies, not just intellects and emotions, we need to include a sensory element—touch—in our supportive connections. I know a woman who is, shall we say, a bit on the cushiony side. But that's only part of the reason she gives such great hugs—open armed, chests touching, back patting, just short enough to be hugs instead of embraces. Her full-body touch makes people feel both connected and, if they need it, comforted. When she's connecting by phone or email, she often signs off, "feel hugged." If she's ever hugged you in person, you can feel the comfort, even if the hug is virtual. As I've already mentioned, it is known that, for babies to have a normal life, touch is essential. Similarly, it is important for the elderly as well.

Create Emotional Safety

Good relationships depend on both parties feeling safe with each other, trusting that they *are there* for you as you *are there* for them. This circle of trusting and trusted others is crucial to coping with the changes and anxieties that growing older involves.

Just having people around won't do it. To feel safe, we need to feel that the person with us hears and sees us—and accepts us—as we are and that he or she wants the best for us. Our bodies need this to heal, and so do our minds and souls. Although this safety is essential in difficult times, it also provides fertile ground to interact with each other in the best of times.

We can create this safe place for ourselves—and, better still, invite other people to join us inside. As it has been so often, mindfulness is the road to a personal sense of safety: recognizing our feelings and having the intent and means to change the patterns that don't serve us. *Being judgmental* is near the top of the list of these unwanted patterns. We need to look at our thoughts and feelings without ruling on whether they're "good" or "bad." Once we learn to treat ourselves with this compassion and empathy, we can extend the same nonjudgmental attitude to others, allowing them to feel safe.

Learn to Address Conflict in a Spirit of Love

Mindfulness allows us to step back from having a knee-jerk response when conflict arises so that we can examine both our feelings and what the other person has actually said—and intended with their words. That is, we need to listen and respond in a spirit of love, keeping our good intentions for the other at the forefront.

Lowering our defenses and heightening our empathy can help us to engage with our friend effectively. Sometimes just repeating what they said in your own words—or what you heard in your heart—can begin a conversation that will lead to productive sharing. As you work together to unravel the conflict, it's important to listen at least as much and maybe more than you talk. Look for common threads instead of just focusing on your differences. If you can identify what you *both* want, you can use that to build a resolution that pleases everyone.

A caution here: this is not the same as a compromise. In a compromise, everyone gives up some of what they want to meet the other person in the middle. The end result is lose-lose, because no one actually gets what they want. Rather, by focusing on a win-win as the only acceptable end result, and understanding what that "win" looks like uniquely for each participant, we are able to come up with solutions that provide exactly that, solutions that may have never occurred to anyone before. By entering every interaction with the intention to love yourself and the other, miracles occur.

Learn the skills of positive communication. Self-talk counts here, too. What you say to yourself—and don't we all have a steady commentary running through our daily affairs?—has a big influence on your self-worth and sense of empowerment. I'll focus, however, on communication with others, skills that will bring people closer instead of sending them running.

The way we communicate is so important because what we say affects how others feel, and emotions drive behavior. If what we communicate makes another feel good, they will likely feel good about us. If what we say makes them feel bad, they may have those same feelings toward us. Here are some key ideas:

1. *Avoid negative language; instead, paint positive pictures.* Words such as *no* and *don't* invoke our natural resistance to being controlled, called counterwill. A much more positive approach is to communicate what we do want in a situation rather than what we don't want. "I would like to spend the day alone with you— we have so little time for that" instead of "I don't want to go to a ballgame with your coworkers. I hate baseball."

2. *Avoid criticism; instead, use empowering feedback.* The message inherent in criticism is that what someone is doing is wrong or, at the very least, not good enough. To empower someone, we can focus first on what they do well and bridge that to what they need to improve on. "It's so nice to have you make dinner. Maybe I'll buy you a cookbook for your birthday." This practice builds on the principle that success builds success.

3. Hand in hand with the above is to *extend appreciation often—daily.* Point out what you like and what the other does well. Sincerely thank them for it. Don't take the positive for granted. This will make a huge, immediate difference in your relationships. In doing this, give specific acknowledgment rather than general praise that expresses your approval. So, for example, rather than "You're great"

or "I'm proud of you," which can seem condescending, comment with appreciation on what the other expressed or did. "I really admire you for taking the time to help out at the museum" or "I've seen how good you are with your own grandkids. You'll have to come meet mine." The difference is subtle, but its felt experience on the receiving end is big.

4. *Give your undivided attention—don't multitask.* Nothing says "I care about you" more clearly than looking at someone when they talk and giving them your undivided attention. Conversely, nothing says "I don't care" more than not giving someone this small courtesy. This seemingly small behavior choice has a huge impact on how we make another person feel, and plays a large role in the health of our relationships. I urge you to be disciplined enough to stop what you're doing—whether it's looking at your phone or washing the dishes—and give someone the focus they deserve. It's one of those key behaviors that builds safety and attunement. Not only will they feel cared for but you will also gain much more insight into what's up with them by observing their words, facial expressions, body language, and tone of voice. Try it and just watch the difference it makes.

While we are being considerate of others, we also need to provide honest feedback if we want to build authentic relationships. I've looked at ways to combine positive and constructive communication in my book *Mindful Anger.* Here are a couple of ideas:

1. *Prepare yourself.* It isn't always easy to be honest with someone else. Who hasn't used an excuse instead of the truth because it was easier? Instead of "My husband made another date for us so I can't come," try "My schedule is so full that week, I just need an evening to be quiet."

2. *Take some deep breaths and put yourself in a place of confidence before you speak.* And remind yourself of your intent to love this person.

3. *Use "I" statements and "feeling" messages, while avoiding "you" accusations and the universal "never" and "always."* Use "It makes me think I'm not important" instead of "You never really listen to me!"

4. *Know when to stop.* State your feelings clearly and then give the other person a chance to respond.

Finally, I'd like to share something I saw next to the phone in a nurses' lounge at a Los Angeles hospital. It was a small poster that said:
Before you speak, THINK.

> *T: Is it true?*
> *H: Is it helpful?*
> *I: Is it inspiring?*
> *N: Is it necessary?*
> *K: Is it kind?*

Being real doesn't mean being uncaring, unkind, unconscious, or reckless in how we communicate. If what you have to say *is* necessary for your own or the other person's well-being, use the tools offered in this chapter to communicate it in a way that meets the other THINK criteria.

Embrace Differences as Opportunities to Grow

Having only friends who think exactly like you—or who come from the same background—limits your learning opportunities. If you've had a long marriage, don't walk away from friendships with people who have gotten divorced or who've remained single, figuring you have nothing in common. There's *one* thing you don't have in common—that's true—but you may share many others, or you may find joy in learning from each other how people have experienced different life courses and what possibly different but valuable lessons they might have to share.

I even know someone who has gone so far as to edit books for a conservative organization, even though she's a lifelong Democrat on the liberal end of the scale. She jokes that "they pay well and they pay promptly," but she's also acknowledged over time that it's interesting to see how "the other side" views the world.

Allow Others to Help You

Too many people are shy about reaching out to others for help in dark times. Most of the time, people want to help and are just looking for a way. When a friend of mine was diagnosed with breast cancer—for the second time in 15 years—a circle of casual friends asked whether they could do anything to help. Instead of giving them a brave no, my friend shared with them that she hated the day before a chemotherapy treatment. So, the members of the group took turns taking her out to lunch the day before her treatments and making sure she had some fun memories to take with her. The point here is that she assumed they meant it when they asked, and she gave them something to do— something she needed that helped her feel supported through a hard time.

Seek Out New Friends

By our 50s and 60s, some of us have forgotten how we made friends— the skills that were so natural to our childhood and early adult years may have rusted with disuse. People looking for new partners in midlife and beyond often complain that they have "forgotten" how to date. In the same way, we may forget how to find friends. A strategy with a high return rate is to go places and/or do things you enjoy and see who you meet there. If you like to read, join a book club. If you're more physically oriented, join a gym or take a class in a new sport: golf, tennis, swimming, tai chi. We'll explore these opportunities in Chapter 5.

---

exercises

Practice Positive Communication

We can all benefit tremendously from mastering the art of positive communication. People who care about building successful connections know how important this is. The all-time classic book on this subject, *How to Win Friends and Influence People* by Dale Carnegie, first published in 1936, still tops the Amazon best-seller lists today.[63] Read it and other books on this vital subject. Here's a way to practice your positive communication skills, one conversation at a time:

1. Keep a journal and make an entry after each conversation, detailing how the exchange went and how it made you feel.

2. Which strategies created greater connection and which did not? Where do you feel you need more education, practice, etc., to help you create the relationships you want?

Make it a project to become world class at communication, and watch how your relationships and your feelings about yourself and others improve.

Set a New Relationship Goal and Take Action

1. Think about a new relationship goal you'd like to manifest in your life. Write a descriptor of it as a simple phrase. Maybe it's a particular relationship mentioned in this chapter: a close friendship or a circle of new friends to do a particular activity with. Maybe you have one or more specific relationships you'd like to improve.

2. Whatever your goal, write down three bite-sized action steps you can take right now to achieve it.

3. Take those steps.

4. Track your activity and results in your journal, as if this were a project (which it is!).

5. Make the needed course-corrections until you reach your goal.

intimate partners

Intimate partners share a sexual connection, and often a history of building a family together, which makes the tie special in a number of ways. Authenticity and vulnerability come to the forefront. The intense connection—and reward—is available only when we are able to reveal ourselves completely and give our partner a safe, nonjudgmental space to do the same with us.

The melding of souls that can result from the electricity of falling in love is still another level of connection. We experience the mutual feeling that our bond is at some level sacred—an amazing gift that it is very rare to find in this world.

One of my favorite greeting cards, created by Kathy Davis and given to me by my husband, JP, reads:

> LOVE: *Birds sing about it. Poets write about it.*
> *Everybody searches for it. And you and I are so very*
> *lucky to have found it.*[64]

Those magical moments can be just the beginning of a lifetime bond, which is also a rare gift. Sharing a life together, whether or not it involves raising a family, can bring you into older age with a level of connection that is profound. This may explain why so often longtime partners die within months or weeks or days—even hours—of each other. In many respects, they are one soul.

And, it's never too late to make this kind of profound connection. It remains possible to form powerful, intimate relationships at any age, as long as we have the courage to embrace and fully acknowledge the difficult parts of life: emotions, our own limitations and weaknesses, life situations, relationship issues, and so on.

Judith Claire and Frank Wiegers offer an inspiring example. When they were at opposite ends of their 60s, Judith and Frank "fell in love at first sight" when they met at a friend's memorial service. On the third or fourth date, Judith told Frank she wanted a husband and that he could move on if he wasn't looking for the same kind of relationship. He replied that he was willing to go "as deep as we can as fast as we can" to see if they could build a relationship that worked.

More than a decade later, that's exactly what they have. "As long as a relationship is what you want," Judith says, "being older simply gives you better tools to find the right partner." Both Frank and Judith were determined to find a partner; they knew what they were looking for and they were committed to the sometimes challenging process of building that connection.

strategies for developing and nurturing intimate relationships

Extend Your Love Unconditionally

With intimate partners, we need to communicate the sense that "I've got you (got your back), no matter what." Differences and disappointments will happen, and we should discuss them with compassion and loving-kindness as much as possible. Respect is a valued standard at all times.

Open Your Heart Fearlessly

Total honesty and transparency are required for this kind of closeness. We must not be afraid to be ourselves and share ourselves, no matter how difficult the subject or issue. Total commitment to reality and honesty supports the integrity of the relationship. We need to be open and willing to share, listen, and understand. With that intention, we will always keep learning and growing; we will live a full life.

Tell Them What They Mean to You

Sometimes, because we feel so close, we start to think that these intimate partners can read our hearts and don't need words to confirm what we feel. Words are still good, whether it's telling someone how you saw something they would love and wished they were with you or simply saying how important they are in your life. Consciously choose to actively show appreciation—finding things to appreciate in each other for the purpose of enhancing "good feelings" between you—but be sure it is only honest appreciation (i.e., must be something we truly do see, value, and appreciate), of course.

Support the Other's Independence

No matter how close we are, we remain individuals with our own needs. Mutual respect for each other's independence and time alone makes the relationship stronger. We can also advocate for each other in fulfilling each of our life purposes, as part of living fully and being true to ourselves. Accepting and being supportive of each other's projects can lead to feedback that is enjoyable, helpful, and beneficial.

Your intimate partner may come with meaningful and nurturing relationships among their own family and friends that can enrich your life, too—but acknowledge that they might want private time with these people.

Enjoy Special Time Together

Don't forget to have fun together. Especially for mates and intimate partners, it can be important to investigate new adventures you can undertake together. Don't always have dinner and a movie as your "date night." Special time can include problem-solving sessions, whether one or both of you are experiencing the problem. As we grow older and face our mutual mortality, close relationships provide an opportunity to explore our humanity and seek an understanding of life.

Keep Sex Vibrant

A stimulating, intoxicating, fun, meaningful, and yet considerate and well-meaning sex life is at the heart of many intimate partnerships. Combine sex with love. As years go by, we need to remain willing to do whatever is needed to grow and expand, to keep the satisfaction and romance alive and thriving, knowing that this keeps our love and connection strong.

Judith Claire and Frank Wiegers' book *So THAT'S Why They Do That!: Men, Women and Their Hormones* [65] offers lots of concrete advice on how to have the best relationship and the best sex of your life, no matter how old you are. The authors advise that, because the hormone-related drive for sex decreases with age, having sex requires more planning, creativity, and the open discussion that comes from a loving and authentic relationship. With testosterone—the hormone responsible for desire in both sexes—greatly diminished, and estrogen—the hormone responsible for women's heightened sensitivity, sexual pleasure, and increased strength of orgasm—bottoming out at menopause, postmenopausal and andropausal passion is ignited by oxytocin, the love and bonding hormone. As a couple, Judith and Frank set aside two or three hours every Sunday to create the erotic setting that leads to what they call "transcendent sex." Now in their early 70s and 80s, respectively, they say it's the best sex, by far, they've had in their lives.

Frank and Judith offer a good model of the need for creativity and resourcefulness in your sexual life as the pure libido of youth begins to ebb. If you want sizzling sex, they say, you first need to create the basics for a strong relationship—good communication and a loving, intimate connection to each other. Then anything else that turns you on, like sex toys, shared porn, romantic bondage, etc., adds spice, fun, and variety.

To me, foreplay begins as the previous sexual encounter ends, with tender words and gestures that are followed up by love notes, flowers, and the hugging, touching, and flirting that increase the flow of oxytocin until you're ready for the next encounter. In sex, as in all things, liberating yourself from past rules and behaviors can contribute immeasurably to life. And sex needn't be the limit of our physical interaction. With partners, there is a whole encyclopedia of loving touch that we can learn to give and receive over the years.

If this all sounds too much like work, consider the benefits that flow from sex at any age: closer bonding in your relationship, pleasure derived from bodies that may otherwise be in physical decline, and improvements in everything from blood pressure to depression, along with less pain and better sleep.

Be Proactive in Replacing Losses in Important Relationships

As I've mentioned in other chapters, an important way to gain resilience is by being proactive in replacing our losses—whether the loss is of a sense of purpose after a career has ended, for example, or when children become independent and no longer need us the same way, or it's a loss in something or someone that was precious to us—a person; a pet; a limb, organ, or other ability or function; a way of life. Often when a loved one dies, we lose several things at once: the person, our relationship with them, our way of living if they were our mate, their help around the house, our future plans, and so on. Replacing what was lost in a situation of this magnitude isn't easy, but still, we must try—because our own life is still worth being the best it can be, despite someone we love no longer being with us.

This requires allowing yourself to fully grieve the loss and to let go of expectations of filling the lost person's shoes in exactly the same way. It requires a self-awareness of your needs and the willingness to reach out toward others to take part in fulfilling them. It requires self-compassion and patience as you find your new way forward.

We've already talked about Louise's attachment to her mother. She felt her grief most keenly around suppertime, when they would often talk by phone while sipping a cocktail. Instead of replacing her mother with a second cocktail—which frequently happened at the beginning of her grief—Louise decided to fill those hours with other activities. She took a twice-weekly exercise class that ran from 6 to 7 p.m. Occasionally, she and one or more of the other participants would go out for a quick dinner afterward. Little by little, Louise's grief detached itself from that time of day and, most importantly, from alcohol as a treatment.

Sarah experienced a loss involving her identity as a mother. By the time her third child entered high school, the other two were already independent—Alice starting a career and Bob, Jr., away at college. As commonly happens, Sarah had been most attached to her youngest, "Sweet Boy" (aka Thomas), and now that he was busy forming other connections, she was lost.

It made for a rocky time in her marriage with Bob, and they sought help from a therapist. One of the doctor's recommendations was for Sarah to complete the bachelor's degree she had not quite finished when she married. Looking at her local college's list of courses, she found herself attracted to a whole new field, English literature, instead of marketing. By the time she completed her degree, her grief had been replaced by excitement and new enthusiasms. As graduation approached at last, she saw that her combination of coursework had prepared her for entrepreneurial work she would love—helping independent bookstores to promote their businesses.

---

exercises

Craft an Intimate Relationship Vision

Knowing what we want is fundamental to finding or creating it in our lives. This is also true for relationships. While we certainly don't want to dictate what others should do or set rigid expectations about how a relationship should be, it can be helpful to know the qualities of a relationship that would be satisfying to us. What do you want from a best friend or partner? Make a list of qualities you'd like the relationship to have.

Look for Love or Friendship Online

If you're looking for a partner, consider online dating. Thanks to the baby boom, online dating has increased substantially among people in the 55 to 64 age group.

1. To get started, go to www.over50datingsites.org for a review of websites specifically for people over 50, and look them over to see which ones you might want to sign up for.

2. When you complete your profile, be honest and authentic. What's the point of sounding like someone other than who you are and finding a person interested in someone you're not? Trust that you are lovable the way you are and that you only want to attract people who are attracted to the real you.

3. Follow through. Use common sense about safety when meeting someone in person, but be open, curious, and willing to see what this other person is all about. Give them a chance!

Incorporate the Giving and Receiving of Touch

1. Evaluate how much touch you give and receive. Is it daily? Is it enough?

2. Think about what you'd like and would feel comfortable with. Do you want to give more hugs? Do you need a pet? Would you like to get massages as a regular routine? Do you want to fan the flame of sex in your intimate relationship?

3. Make giving and receiving more touch a new project. Come up with the specifics of what form it will take and how you'll make it happen.

4. Execute!

***

Over the course of this chapter, we've gone from preparing ourselves to be good friends to learning the useful behaviors and communication skills for new friendships. Intimate partnerships are especially challenging, but the rewards are also great. As we have seen, all of our relationships need nurturing—which begins with our mindset and intentions and extends into our priorities, choices, and daily interactions. We build our relationships with everything we think and do, and their success depends on our level of mindfulness.

Moving beyond ourselves into connection with others is a crucial step in living the life we will love through our older years. While intimate partners can play a special role, friends and family provide vital supports during this time. It is never too late to build or repair your social circle.

In the next chapter, we will explore a number of settings where making social connections can be a happy side effect of taking on activities that will enhance our personal lives: exercising our bodies, enriching our minds, and engaging in creative efforts.

chapter | 5

enhancing your body, engaging your mind, & expressing your creativity

Fauja Singh started life as a sickly child in rural India, not learning to walk until he was five. Eighty-four years later, he completed his first marathon. His coach shook his head in disbelief when Fauja asked him for training, but Fauja was determined to do this. And it was just the beginning. On his 100th birthday, he set five world records in different running races for his age group—and he completed the Toronto Waterfront Marathon in 8 hours 11 minutes 6 seconds.[66] Early in 2015, at 104, he ran in the Mumbai Marathon.

Running in marathons became Fauja's dream after he saw an advertisement on TV, and it has been his joy ever since. Fauja has never let other people's assessments stand in the way of his dreams—a theme we explored in the previous chapter.

The same is true of Elizabeth Layton, who took her first art class at the age of 68. She used her focus on art to overcome a long history of chronic debilitating depression, beginning with a series of self-portraits that reflected her response to current events. A local journalist was the first to spread the word of her talent, and although she never sold her work—she saw it as a lifesaving gift—it has arrived in museums across the country via the charitable groups she, in turn, "gifted." Besides describing her life and art, her website includes some basic lessons on how you can get started as an artist.[67]

While Fauja and Elizabeth enjoyed a certain amount of worldly success along with the personal rewards of their new activities, you don't have to become a world champion for a new activity to be meaningful. You don't even have to be good at it—you can do it just because you enjoy it or because you enjoy spending time with the people who are your companions in exploring. And who knows what else will come of it. Fauja was looking for a way out of grief after his wife died; Elizabeth wanted to conquer her depression. While you can set continuous-growth goals for yourself, the big-picture goal is physical, mental, and emotional health.

Our potential is so vast; there is always more room to grow than years in which to do it—but it's never too late to start. To remain our healthiest and most vibrant physically, emotionally, and cognitively, we must continue to learn and do new things—to keep stepping into the territory of the new and unknown. Though it feels counterintuitive, security and inner strength come from expansion and the agility it gives us, not from clinging to what we already know.

In the previous chapters, you have learned how to approach life with *realistic positivity*, to shed the false self that may have limited your enjoyment of life, and to find your joy and use it to build a life you love around it. Now we will look at a variety of ways to create this kind of life, with outcomes that improve your health and well-being at the same time they bring you joy. In each case, I'll offer scientific evidence of the positive results you can achieve, and introduce you to some people who have paved the way.

First, we'll look at ways to enhance your physical health. We've talked about self-compassion: part of that is having compassion for a body that may no longer look as handsome or beautiful as it once did and may not do everything you would like it to do. Still, it's taken you through a long life, and it deserves your gratitude. In this regard, *show me* trumps *tell me*. The best way to give thanks is to provide your body with the diet and exercise it needs to thrive. Next, we turn to giving your mind new adventures and stimulation. Growing older doesn't have to mean loss: you can improve your cognitive powers, too.

And finally, many older people discover creative talents that they never explored in their early and middle years while they were busily raising families and promoting careers. Creativity can take a special role in your later life, helping you to connect with your authentic self and the spiritual destiny that may lie ahead.

enhance your body

While no one can deny that illness and disability often come with advancing years, we also can't deny that attitude and lifestyle affect the body—and that even for those who suffer these maladies, attention to your body can improve your condition, dissipate the pain, and increase your energy.

What You Eat

The best place to start may be with what you put inside. Dozens—or perhaps hundreds—of diet recommendations are available for people over 50.[68] The common threads are relatively few:

- lots of fruits and vegetables in a rainbow of colors
- fewer saturated fats and more good fats such as olive oil, avocados, and nuts;
- less meat and more seafood;
- few sweets and other sugar-bearing items—you'd be amazed how many there are, particularly in prepared foods.

While this may sound like a lot of sacrifice, it doesn't have to feel that way. A friend who recently crossed into her 70s has substituted almonds, cheese, and fruit in place of cookies, cake, and pita chips—and has found she can be addicted to healthy foods, too. Instead of a vodka martini and snack food, she has a glass of white wine and carrot sticks.

You might want to pay particular attention to the Blue Zone Diet, which is based on a survey of what people eat—and don't eat—in the places where people have the longest life spans.[69] The Blue Zones Project began as a journalistic expedition to find the longest-living cultures—many of them in places such as Ikaria, Greece; Okinawa, Japan; the Ogliastra region of Sardinia; and the Nicoya Peninsula, Costa Rica. One of the original sites was Loma Linda, California, but the project is now promoting the diet across the United States, from Hermosa Beach, California, to several towns in Iowa, to Naples, Florida.

For most of us, the regimen will require some discipline. According to the findings, about 95 percent of our diet should come from fruits, vegetables, grains, and beans. Meat—in portions the size of a deck of cards—should be a rare addition, while fish and seafood are okay up to three times a week. Perhaps the biggest change is to slash our sugar intake, replacing sweet treats with nuts. Water becomes the staple beverage, replacing just about everything we typically drink.[70]

When we consume the best fuel available, our energy level increases, and we can find plenty of ways to enjoy this heightened energy in physical exercise.

Physical Exercise: Making a Start

About two years ago, Brookes, my longtime writing collaborator, lost her partner to cancer. From diagnosis to death was a short passage in Frank's case, and it left Brookes dizzy with disorientation and loss of control. Newly widowed at 42, part of her vision for picking up the pieces and starting a "new life" was to exercise and, she hoped, even become athletic again.

In her youth, she was a gymnast and dancer, but Brookes all but quit regular physical activity and exercise when she entered the working world at age 21. Over the next two decades as a self-employed writer and editor with a sometimes mountainous workload, she often spent the day in front of a computer and then relaxed at night by watching TV. Though she was always busy, she spent a lot of time in one chair or another.

After so many years of non-activity, Brookes was concerned about injuring herself by trying to do too much too soon, and yet she really wanted to get "in shape." Her solution: she recruited her mother, aged 70, to be her partner in joining a gym and going to an aqua aerobics class together. Every morning at 8 a.m. they were in the pool—gradually, safely getting in shape. Because the exercise allows you to exert the amount of effort you feel confident with, both got a great workout, even though they were different ages and in different condition. And, they both loved it!

Just as important, Brookes and her mother were uplifted by the other participants, sharing a sense of tremendous joy and benefit from the class, whether that benefit was keeping them more agile, reducing pain from rheumatoid arthritis, helping them recover from knee replacement or spinal surgery, or moving ahead after the loss of a loved one.

Gradually, as her own conditioning improved, Brookes began to "venture onto land," as she says. She started taking a level-one yoga class as well as beginner dance classes. In the 18 months since she started at the gym, she has graduated to level-two yoga and intermediate dance classes. Her body composition has changed, she's lost weight, and she has regained a lot more of the strength and ability she had in her youth than she ever expected.

It's amazing what the body can do when we give it what it needs. And you don't have to still be in your 40s like Brookes—it's *never* too late. An episode of *Oprah* many years ago provided the pictures that are worth a thousand words on this subject. Oprah's guests were people who had *started* weight training in their 70s! Their activity proved to me that it is never too late to begin a sensible exercise regimen, and it underscores the dramatic benefits we may enjoy.

Let Me Count the Benefits

Perhaps you've noticed that, these days, it's harder to get out of a chair—literally—or up from the floor. Scientists attribute this to something called *sarcopenia* (loss of muscle mass and strength), which can reduce muscle mass by as much as 15 percent between the ages of 30 and 80, unless you do something to counteract it. The something you can do is called weight training or strength training—lifting weights to put some muscle back in that flab![71] Studies have shown that weight training has several benefits: [72]

- Greatly improved leg strength and endurance. After you get out of your chair easily and gracefully, in time you'll find the distance you can walk will improve by up to 50 percent over what you could do before you started weight training. You'll also get your chores done more easily—the grocery bags and luggage won't feel quite so heavy.[73]

- Reduced risk of falls. A study that involved women aged 75 to 85 who were suffering from lowered bone density or full-fledged osteoporosis showed that their scores on a test that measures proneness to falls improved by more than half after they started weight lifting.[74]

- Less joint pain and more range of motion. Making the muscles around your joints stronger takes the pressure off them. They won't hurt as much, and you'll be able to move more easily.[75]

Exercises that involve balance, stretching, and endurance will also help you become more active and engaged. Although you may want to check with your doctor if you have acute or chronic issues you're concerned about, some kind of exercise is possible for everyone, even if you're in your 90s and even if you've never exercised before (isn't it about time?).[76]

Study after study has shown that "sitting is the new smoking" and is a dangerous *in*activity that leads to illness and disability.[77] "Sitting is more dangerous than smoking, kills more people than HIV and is more treacherous than parachuting. We are sitting ourselves to death," says James Levine, director of the Mayo Clinic–Arizona State University Obesity Solutions Initiative and inventor of the treadmill desk.[78]

While exercise improves the muscles you're working, it also has a positive effect on an important organ that seems to just sit and watch. Researchers at the University of Illinois have shown a strong correlation between fitness levels and better performance on tests of mental activity. In fact, MRIs revealed that improved fitness also increased brain volume in important areas connected to cognitive skills such as memory. Although the biggest cause of dementia is genetic, there's scientific evidence that exercise slows its progress, too.[79]

While much of the research on the brain has involved aerobic exercise, recent studies have also looked at tai chi and qigong. For example, researchers found that elderly Chinese people who participated in tai chi three times a week for eight months performed better on memory tests. Their brain volume had actually grown.[80] An overview of 77 articles involving more than 6,000 people found positive results related to these practices—physical outcomes such as improved cardiovascular health, bone density, physical dexterity, and immune health. Focusing on quality of life, several studies found improvements related to tai chi or qigong, along with enhanced self-confidence.[81]

Some kind of physical exercise suits just about every level of fitness, and one of them is bound to spark your interest. If you started a regime of physical exercise early in life and continue to love every minute, you can skip ahead a couple of paragraphs here. For many of us, though, exercise has fallen under the category of *chores*, and inevitably it has fallen to the bottom of our to-do list, perhaps even beneath the dreaded *housecleaning*. If you're going to build exercise into your senior moments—and you'll be so glad if you do—you need to view it through new lenses. There are so many possibilities and many ways to pursue them—alone or with others, strenuously or cautiously, reprising the old or exploring the new.

Rethinking the Limits

Until she was 40, Candace was a bona fide athlete. Then a back injury left her with what became chronic pain, ending her daily exercise routine. For the first time in her life, she did no exercise, gained weight, and became depressed. After several years of frustration—and getting no help from the traditional medical resources she consulted—Nancy discovered Pilates and decided to give it a try. She noticed some improvement right away. Over the next three years of doing Pilates regularly, she regained full pain-free mobility. At 50—that was the year she went back to college—she was chosen and featured on posters as an example of exceptional fitness by her school.

My husband, JP, also had an inspiring comeback through exercise, far exceeding the hopes of the doctors who had left him a virtual quadriplegic after surgery. Thinking back on how he achieved his recovery, JP credits visualizing himself doing tai chi while he lay in his hospital bed, then performing the exercises once he was out of bed and in a wheelchair. He was also committed to the physical therapy regimen his doctors prescribed. When he went home after 28 days in the hospital, he continued moving as much as he could, both within and outside of his physical therapy program. He had his family's full-throated support, as they insisted he keep working and never give up. Thanks to them and to his own determination and persistence, JP is walking today, with only a cane for reassurance. Eight years after the surgery accident, he still does physical therapy several days a week.

Exercising for Fun

A few pages back, you learned how my writing partner, Brookes, used physical exercise to help her recover from the loss of her partner. One of the things she pursued after she "got out of the water" was pole dancing for exercise and fun, and to develop her "sexy side." As I listened to her talk about it, a feeling of excitement rose up in me. It sounded intriguing and something I too would like to try. Now, I'm a few decades older than Brookes, so I asked her how feasible it would be for a person my age. Women in their 50s and 60s were doing amazingly athletic things on the pole, she assured me, but she also noted the risks of attempting activity the body isn't ready for.

She suggested I take private lessons from a teacher who would craft the classes specifically for me. I decided to give it a try. I found a local studio and took my first lesson. I loved it! The first half of the lesson was a rigorous conditioning class for strength and flexibility, and the second half was a very basic beginner's version of a pole-dancing class. I've since had many lessons, and find it both satisfying and fun to do a workout like this. (And it does develop your sexy side!)

Here are some ideas to keep in mind as you explore your own exercise options, both conventional and offbeat.

Strategies for Getting More Physical Exercise
Find an exercise starting point that's right for you

Gyms often have multiple levels of classes to cater to clients of different ages, condition levels, and goals, and a number of them specialize in an older demographic. In gyms with a high population of seniors, for example, you might find chair yoga and gentle yoga offered in addition to the typical level-one and level-two yoga classes for those with a more advanced ability and practice. A few brand-name fitness classes are also offered in multiple versions, with some especially designed for seniors, where the original moves are modified to be lower in impact and intensity. Zumba Gold is one such class. Following is a chart of just a few options that are particularly suitable for people aged 50 or over, including a partial list of each exercise's health benefits.

Aqua aerobics	Can be done at all levels of fitness; low-impact, non-weight-bearing exercise; increases muscle strength, flexibility, and endurance.[82]
Cycling	Indoors or outdoors; good for knees, osteoporosis, and heart health.[83]
Dancing	All types—ballroom, tap, jazz, ballet; good for coordination, rhythm, balance, and conditioning.
General fitness	classes designed for seniors at gyms and wellness centers; increase cardiovascular endurance, muscular strength, flexibility, balance, coordination, agility, and joint stability.
Golf	For the more active senior; combines movement, hand–eye coordination, and walking in the outdoors.
Gym workouts	Can be customized for individual needs and abilities.
Hiking	More strenuous walking, including hills and rough terrain; good for stamina, lung and heart health, and muscular fitness, and can reduce depression.[84]
Jogging/ running	For the highly fit senior, some of whom have started in their 60s and 70s and run marathons; good for balance, strengthening bones, and cardiovascular endurance and strength.[85]
Pilates	Originally designed as a rehabilitation technique for dancers with injuries; eases back pain, is easy on the joints, increases flexibility, and strengthens core muscles.[86]
Qigong	An ancient Chinese system of movement, breathing, and meditation; suitable for anyone, and can even be done in a chair; good for balance, lowers blood pressure, and eases depression.[87]
Swimming	Gentle, non-weight-bearing exercise, suitable for all, especially those with restricted movement; improves heart health, increases flexibility, and strengthens muscles.
Tai chi	An ancient Eastern practice of flowing movements that led to martial arts; improves balance, groundedness, and flexibility; helps with pain from arthritis.[88]

Tennis	For the active senior; improves cardiovascular health, hand-eye coordination, tactical brain development, and muscle strength.[89]
Walking	Can be done at every age; reduces the chance of heart disease and diabetes, reduces stress and anxiety, and relieves back pain.[90]
Weight or strength training	Can be done sitting or standing; start with very light weights; improves strength and flexibility, increases bone mass and density, and reduces pain from arthritis.[91]
Yoga	An old tradition practiced in Eastern countries, very popular around the world; individuals can begin at any time in life and benefit; reduces stress and hypertension, strengthens bones, and enhances concentration and determination in all areas of life.[92]

Listen to your body

"If it hurts, don't do it" is a motto heard daily by residents at Carlsbad By The Sea Retirement Community, from their director of Fitness and Wellness, Sue Feehan. She's been sharing that message for years in the delightful yet challenging aqua fitness classes she teaches for seniors. As Sue and other great teachers will point out, there are almost always variations you can do on an exercise to modify the level of difficulty and activity to keep yourself injury free. So, modify when you need to and just keep progressing safely. You will gain positive momentum if you keep building success upon incremental success.

Think of exercise as a social event

This connection explains why fitness classes at a range of intensities, from spin classes to aqua aerobics and group hikes, have become so popular. Local schools, community centers, and various organizations offer lots of opportunities.

A local YMCA in a beach town in Southern California set up a senior cycling group, and 30 or so men and women who enjoy road cycling joined. The eldest member of the group is 84! They meet every Wednesday morning at the "Y" and ride for 25–30 miles. Afterward, they stop at a local coffee hangout and socialize.

And, for a less conventional vehicle, consider members of the Oakland Women's Rowing Club in California. Local women have been putting on their boating uniforms and picking up their oars on Wednesday mornings for a hundred years, making this the oldest women's rowing club in the country. This is not a sport for sissies. The boats are more than 25 feet long and weigh up to a ton, each of them crewed by eight women at a spectrum of ages into the 70s and beyond. Just seeing their red-white-and-blue colors on Lake Merritt lifts your heart—imagine the pleasure of participation!

Realize that exercise doesn't have to be formal to get benefits

Exercise can also be done in pairs or solo. The goal is to move your body, as much as possible, in a non-injurious way. Victor, 92, is a great example. He lives in a retirement community in Portland, Oregon, and rides his three-wheeled bicycle to get around. He goes everywhere on his bike—shopping, to the library, to his daughter-in-law's house, and on excursions up to 15 miles from home two to three times per week. Recently, when the uphill climbs became a bit too challenging, Victor added an electric motor to the bike, which aids his peddling when needed.

Even a quiet stroll in your neighborhood counts as physical exercise. The world-famous Mayo Clinic celebrates the benefits of walking for managing heart disease, high blood pressure, and Type 2 diabetes while strengthening your bones and muscles.[93] Walking also improves your mood, balance, and coordination. The Mayo Clinic website (www.mayoclinic.org) offers some guidelines for setting up a routine. While the clinic recommends a brisk walk lasting 30 minutes a day, almost any level—even getting up and walking around the house for two minutes every hour[94]—has benefits compared to nothing at all. To read more, just search for "walking health benefits" in your Internet search engine.

Use gadgets to help push you and keep you on track

One advantage of group activities or classes where a teacher is setting the pace is that they help you to push yourself beyond what you think is your comfort zone. That's where toys and gadgets can help you motivate yourself and keep you engaged.

Raj, 62, is an entrepreneur and venture capitalist who runs three businesses out of a multi-building complex. Raj's day is packed with work activity, and he doesn't take time for formal exercise. He does, however, make sure he actively walks every day. One strategy toward his goal is his commitment to walk whenever he is on his (hands-free) phone. Another is that he intentionally parks at a distance from his destination, ensuring that he gets some exercise on his way. Between going from building to building to meet with or coach his staff, walking to pick up or eat out for lunch, making a trip to the local post office, and his routine commitments, Raj averages 20,000 steps per day—about four miles—which he monitors using a step-counter device on his smartphone. That's another habit he's committed to.

There are all kinds of fitness trackers available today, and they track everything from your sleep patterns to the number of steps you take to several other activities. They can give us a sense of challenge, fun, and accountability for developing and maintaining the habits and goals that are crucial building blocks for us to have the life of our dreams.

Don't compete with others, or even with your former self

It's fine to get inspired by others, but competition can also spoil the fun. If you're a Type A personality, not being the "best" may deplete your motivation. Instead, focus on enjoyment, how you feel, and your continuous improvement. And don't compete against your old self—the kid who could play 36 holes and beat par on both rounds. Remember that you're doing this solely for yourself and your quality of life. There is nothing to prove, only life to live and enjoy each step of the way.

exercises

Timeline Review: Physical Activity/Exercise

1. Dividing your life into decades, list your physical activities during each period, noting separately team sports, exercise classes, and individual activities.

Example: Maryann, age 78

0–10: Dance, swimming, bicycle

10–20: Basketball, football, baseball, tennis, archery, badminton, swimming, water-skiing

20–30: Tennis, basketball (college), swimming

30–40: Tennis, golf, running

40–50: Tennis, dance, Pilates, tai chi

50–60: Tennis, tai chi

60–70: Tennis, tai chi, qigong

70–80: Tennis, tai chi, qigong

2. What have you enjoyed in the past? Would it be uplifting to return to one or more of those activities?

Explore Something New

Now that you've reviewed what you did in the past, open your eyes to what you haven't yet tried.

1. Review the chart of exercise options particularly suited to people over 50, offered earlier in this chapter.

2. Looking at the list, see what jumps out at you as something you might like to explore—or think of other things you'd be willing to try. If you're looking for ways to increase your circle of relationships, choose group classes or activities that have a social dimension, such as golf.

3. Inquire with your local fitness centers about their offerings. Can you find something you will commit to giving a try?

4. Do it! It's never too late to start and never too soon to begin. Start today.

engage your mind

Another element crucial to a rewarding older age is to feed your mind and soul. We humans can—and should—keep learning as long as possible. What applies to our muscles applies to our brain: if we don't use it, we lose it. As Bob Dylan sang, "He not busy being born is busy dying."[95] Why not continue being born—i.e., learning and growing into something expanded and new—all of our lives? There are thousands of ways to do this.

"Your brain doesn't know how old it is," says Paul Nussbaum, president of the Brain Health Center at the University of Pittsburgh School of Medicine, which helped design a program of brain exercises for senior communities. "And what it wants to do is learn." All kinds of concentrated activities, such as learning a foreign language or how to play a musical instrument, can be fulfilling for older people, Nussbaum says. A brain that is fully engaged socially, mentally, and spiritually is more resilient.[96]

The science of brain plasticity reveals our ability for, and inherent tendency toward, continual growth. Most studies focus on the contributions of learning activities to cognitive and emotional well-being. A study sponsored by the European Commission's Lifelong Learning Programme found that quality of life improved significantly among participants in educational projects—once basic needs such as physical health and financial security were met.[97]

Today, there are new and interesting innovative ways to exercise the brain. Becoming more prevalent are centers offering neurofeedback—a computer-aided training method that gives us a look at what's happening in our brain in real time—to help clients improve their brain's function. One study showed that participants between 70 and 78 could speed up information processing and increase their attention focus, while another showed improvements in memory.[98]

A physical impact is supported by an inspiring story that comes from the research of epidemiologist David Snowdon in his book *Aging with Grace*. In 1986, Snowdon began a longitudinal study with 600 members of the School Sisters of Notre Dame, who made a habit of engaging in mental challenges—quizzes, puzzles, and debates on public issues. Many lived to be 100 or more, and Snowdon was curious about why. As part of the study, the nuns participated in cognitive tests from time to time. When they died, they donated their brains for postmortem study.

Among them was Sister Bernadette, who was scoring in the 90th percentile on cognitive tests until the very end of her life. And yet the autopsy showed massive inroads by Alzheimer's disease. Snowdon believes her brain—responding to her mental activity—found ways to overcome the genetic hand she'd been dealt.[99] And Sister Bernadette wasn't the only nun who demonstrated this result. So far, researchers have found that 15 sisters suffered Alzheimer's damage but showed no symptoms during their lifetime.[100]

Scientists aren't sure exactly how this might happen, but they have plenty of evidence that it does. Epidemiologists at Johns Hopkins University found that women who were trained how to teach children basic reading, library, and other skills and then worked as volunteers in a local grade school felt physically stronger and enlarged their social support network.[101]

While there are plenty of health-oriented rewards to inspire you to stay mentally engaged, the biggest bonus is the fun. All kinds of thinking activity—learning new languages, doing puzzles, playing cards or computer games, and reading books—promote positive brain activity that keeps you young both literally and metaphorically. Many of these activities also involve engaging socially with people who share your interests. With one simple activity, you can enhance your life immeasurably—why not try three or four?

Here are some strategies that offer ideas and suggestions.

Strategies for Engaging Your Mind

Learn the language of your next travel destination

Say you're planning a trip to Italy and would like to communicate at least at a basic level with the people there. Even a few words—*hello, please, thank you, where is . . . ?*—will help you connect and make travel less stressful. Besides the social benefits of learning the new language, the process of doing so may slow the cognitive decline that comes with age and may even delay the onset of Alzheimer's disease.[102]

Go back to school

Whether or not there are physical benefits, many members of the aging cohort are returning to formal education as they get older and have more time to select their own activities. Maybe you never got your high school degree—or you were working on a master's degree when raising a family got in the way of your studies. By 2030, 70 million Americans will be aged 65 or older, over 20 percent of the population.[103] Researchers find that older adults return to school for a variety of reasons, from learning new skills they can apply in the job market to indulging longtime interests and simply meeting peers who are interested in similar subjects. Colleges and universities are working to respond to the needs of people aged between 55 and 79 who have new ideas about how they want to spend their older age. Only 17 percent aspire to "not work at all," about the same percentage who hope to "never retire."[104]

Play more, using your brain

As we grow older we tend to forget how to play: the dictionary tells us that *play* is an activity we engage in for en-joy-ment and re-creat(e)-ion, rather than for a serious purpose. Think of childhood games—and don't necessarily rule them out. Chess and checkers, bridge and gin rummy—yes, even bingo—are all games we learn as youngsters and can enjoy throughout life. While many games are competitive, some are pure fun. One contribution of the Internet has been a plethora of strategy games, where you find hidden objects and attempt strategic challenges. Plain old puzzles—whether jigsaw or crossword—are also enhanced by digital adaptations.

We call it *play*, but researchers call it brain training. Different kinds of games have different cognitive benefits—they can actually change your brain and certainly enhance its function. Competitive games also have a social component that connects you to dozens of people with similar interests. This is true, by the way, of online games, where your playmates may live half a world away.

Write about something that interests or intrigues you

As we saw in Chapter 3 with Priscilla Moulton's work to curate the art of JOJ Frost, taking an interest in a person or subject can lead you into a whole range of activities that end up in the creative and synthetic activity of writing. Research alone can be an endless joy as one piece of information inevitably leads to another. It can also lead to social connections with other people who want to know about the same subject—or, if they know more than you, who might be willing to share.

In these days of digital media, writing and publishing are not as arduous as they used to be. Writing on a computer allows for easy editing and manipulation. It's not so hard or expensive to establish a blog that shares what you know with the digital universe,[105] and Amazon is one of many outlets that facilitate publishing your own book, either digitally or in old-fashioned paper and ink.[106]

If you don't know where to begin, you might start with your own life. Many people in their older years write a memoir—Amazon shows almost 140,000 published memoirs, ranging from best sellers such as J. D. Vance's *Hillbilly Elegy: A Memoir of a Family and Culture in Crisis* to the book of Betty Chiang, an 83-year-old non-professional writer who wrote her memoir for her family and sold 50 copies to fellow residents at Channing House in Palo Alto. "I want the world to know my story," Chiang says. "My father's death was a rock in my heart. I want my grandkids to know what happened." Her son, Arthur, sees its rationale: "I learned a little more about my mother's life," Arthur Chiang says, "and now it's all together in one place. This is a solid accounting of her life to be passed down, and it gave my mother a purpose in writing it."[107]

The personal benefit was important to George, who began writing after he was diagnosed with prostate cancer; the doctors said he had up to seven years to live. Feeling a great desire to write, George mapped out five books and over the next 15 years proceeded to write and publish them through a commercial self-publishing company. *Over the next 15 years.* About a year after he completed his last book, he finally succumbed to the cancer and passed away. Both he and his family believe his desire to share his life with friends and family through his books and the sheer challenge and enjoyment in writing them gave him twice the life the doctors had forecast.

---

exercises

Timeline Review: Educational Activities

1. Dividing your life into decades, list your educational activities during each period. Include items that wouldn't have a place on a conventional resume.

   Example: Sarah, age 72

   0–10: Elementary school

   10–20: Elementary school, high school, college

   20–30: Graduated with a BA in English

   30–40: Extension class in social science

   40–50: Extension classes in anthropology

   50–60: Various book clubs

   60–70: More book clubs, class in my state's history as part of museum docent training

   70–80: Research for docent newsletter

2. Which did you most enjoy? Would it be uplifting to return to one or more of these activities?

3. Use an online resource to find out what's happening in the evening and weekend programs at your area high school or community college. See whether anything calls to you.

4. Check it out—and be persistent. You might want to stop by during sessions. The excitement of others may turn on your own interests, and most schools have counselors available to help you decide what you might like to dip into.

Colleges and universities at various levels are seeing the potential resource in seniors. They will often adjust course load and deadlines to make them easier for seniors to accommodate—and sometimes they'll provide financial support. And many state universities allow you to sit in on classes for a small fee or none at all.

Create a Learning Bucket List

We all know what a traditional bucket list typically entails: the places we'd like to go and the things we'd like to see and do before we die. Well, how about also including what we'd like to explore and learn about in the time we have left?

1. Brainstorm potential ideas to add to your learning bucket list. Come up with 5–10 things you feel it would be really enriching to learn more about.

2. Giving yourself quiet time and space, evaluate your list, one item at a time.

3. As you envision what the experience of learning about this item would feel like and mean, decide whether it's really something you'd like to invest your time in. Put a check next to items you want to continue to consider and strike through any you want to omit from the list.

4. Continue going through your list until you can narrow it down to just three things, and commit to beginning the one you feel the strongest about.

5. Come up with the first three bite-sized action steps that will get you started.

express your creativity

The stories of a small group of friends—Jackie, Hester, Merijane, and Pamela—show us it's never too late to get creative, either for its own sake or for the social opportunities that can come with it.

Jackie was in her mid-50s when she got a strong whiff of her childhood in a home she was planning to rent. Just inside the front door was her old piano—well, it wasn't the one her parents bought for her in 1953, when her interest in playing piano had lasted through a few months of practicing at a local school. But it was the same brand, the same model, the same wood finish. It even sounded the same. The discovery made her rental decision for her, and in the six years she lived in that house, she played the piano regularly—even took lessons for a while. When she moved into a condo, one of her first actions was to buy her own piano.

About the same time, Hester took up the viola, then switched to the violin, then went back to the viola. Despite many lessons, two instruments, and more than one teacher, however, she decided after several years that playing wasn't her thing. In the meantime, though, she'd fallen in love with the music school and the people who taught and learned there, and spending time there had become a regular feature of her retirement routine—she even had a part-time job there.

Friends of Merijane and Pamela knew the two had special gifts when it came to putting together room décor and their own wardrobes. As they moved into their 50s, both put their innate skills to broader use. Pamela began putting paper scraps and objects others would call junk—stray screws or pieces of wood—into fascinating collages. She now exhibits regularly in Bay Area galleries.

Merijane started with scraps of fabric, making at least one full-sized bed quilt and dozens of wall hangings and placemats, before she decided to try paint. She found a class on abstract expressionist works using acrylics, inviting Jackie to join her. For Jackie, painting began as a solace during a time of grief, but it evolved over time into an interesting hobby with a circle of women she came to care about deeply. For Merijane, however, one class led to a dozen others. Recently, she gave a lecture on her work before an art group at the retirement community where she lives. She has exhibited there and plans to explore gallery options soon.

One small circle of friends, these women provide some representative examples of how creativity can enhance life in older age: reviving old talents, exploring new ideas, making friends—even finding jobs.

The Benefits of Expressing Your Creativity

Participation in a wide variety of creative activities like the ones these women enjoyed has a positive effect on physical and emotional health. A review of 11 studies published between 1985 and 2006—most of them since 2004—found that elders enjoyed benefits ranging from improved health and balance to better problem-solving and memory—and an overall sense of emotional well-being. Activities included jazz dance, choral singing, instrumental music, and drama.[108]

Many creative activities also make you engage with others, and the combined impact is to reduce feelings of loneliness and isolation and help to build social networks.[109] Other research has shown the connection between these emotional impacts and physical health. A rigorous study sponsored by the National Endowment for the Arts found that people over 65 who joined in weekly arts programs reported (1) better health, as measured by fewer trips to the doctor and less use of medications; (2) better self-reported responses about depression and anxiety; and (3) an increased engagement in social activities of all kinds.[110]

The research has been so persuasive that creative activities have become a common offering of community centers and senior residences. A nonprofit organization called EngAGE has converted existing resident facilities into centers where residents share a common interest in one or more of the arts. These are ordinary folks, too—people with modest incomes and an average age of 77 or more.[111]

One of the interesting things about the EngAGE homes is that they list gardening and cooking among the creative activities, along with more traditionally "cultural" interests such as music, dance, and drama.

Here are some guidelines as you seek to connect with your creative soul.

Strategies for Being More Creative
Broaden your definition of "creative"

Some people have a narrow view of what it is to be creative, so they decide this doesn't apply to them—and then they don't try. The truth is that no one is uncreative. By definition, to create means to bring into existence something new. That can be anything! The more we broaden the definition of what it means to be creative, the easier it will be to participate in creative activities that will stimulate the mind as well as bring us greater joy. People forget that the imagination is an important key to creativity. You can be imaginative about anything—from the way you dress to how you decorate a room or home to how you place ingredients on a plate of food to art, music, and dance. Creative storytelling and improvisation—such as grandparents expressively reading to children—are good ways to dip your toe in.

Step into the unknown

In earlier chapters, we talked about things like beginner's mind, wonder, and innocence. This state of mind is about stepping into the unknown—stepping into a blank space or void and totally relinquishing the need to know. That's where new ideas and inspirations emerge. A great way to step into the unknown is to engage in creative activities. People fear that if they risk stepping into the unknown, nothing will happen, but if we can truly let go of our need to know, something *will* come forth. Try it!

Pick up activities you've always loved, in a new way

A college biology professor, Steve always had a passion for classical music. After he and his first wife divorced, he met and married Florence. As part of starting a new life together in their mid-60s, Steve and Florence joined a local church. Despite the fact that Florence had never sung in a choir before, and that Steve had not since his high school church choir, both were drawn to enter the church's choir, which had a well-developed program and concert schedule. As it turns out, they both love it. The twice-weekly rehearsals have become a joyful part of their routine and life. Steve finds it rewarding to actually participate in making the music of some of his favorite classical composers, rather than just listening. And it's something they now have in common and do together, which has strengthened and deepened their relationship.

Think about art as therapy

Creativity can have dramatic positive effects on elders. For William Carlos Williams, a pediatric practice was his day job until he suffered a stroke in his early 60s that prevented him from practicing medicine and sent him into a severe depression. He turned to the writing that had been a creative outlet for him for many years, and he pulled out of the depression one poem at a time. In many ways that was the important thing, but there's also this: ten years later, he won a Pulitzer Prize for *Pictures from Brueghel and Other Poems.*[112]

Music, art, and writing are the "big three" we think of when we talk about creativity. Neither age nor your preconception about your talent should stand as a barrier to your involvement. Remember that you can celebrate creativity by listening, looking, and learning. But don't settle for that until you've tried *doing*. Art and writing are easy areas to try on as hobbies—the materials are relatively inexpensive, and the basic mechanics are not difficult.

Today, you can get coloring books for grown-ups. Pick one up, along with colored pens or pencils. After you've experienced the sensory pleasure of pen moving against paper, put the book aside and get a plain sketchbook so that you can color outside the lines.

So many activities can fall under the banner of creativity that there's almost certainly one in your current routine: think about gardening, setting the table, arranging furniture. Identify it and then build more imagination into what you do. The feeling of seeing your imagination embodied in a concrete shape is almost magical. Everyone should experience it at least once (a day)!

---

exercises

Timeline Review: Creative Activities

Create a timeline review of your more formal experience with creativity and the arts. Here are a couple of examples to get you started:

Example: Catherine, 74
Childhood and youth: Dance
Youth and teenage: Piano and singing
College – PhD: Music and singing, choral directing
40s: Dance and singing
50s and 60s: Dance and singing
70s: Drawing and painting

Example: John, 63
Childhood and youth: Crafting and art projects in school
High school / college: Belonged to a garage band for a while

30s and 40s: Too busy with career and family

50s and 60s: Began to work with wood leftover from household chores; bought a cookbook and began to explore foreign flavors

Start with Yourself: Write about Your Life

Many people turn to writing as a way to record the memories they've accumulated over a rich lifetime. Certainly, children and grandchildren will appreciate these written memories, and with all the opportunities offered by the web, you may find a wider audience. You might start with a "diary" but one that's dated in the past. What were you doing in 1968? Who was in your social circle then? What did you eat and drink? What were your favorite things to do? What were your hopes and dreams? What did you learn? As a place to start, choose a time that was especially meaningful and memorable to you.

Do Something Small That Uses Your Creativity

1. Think up a really small project such as rearranging a room, dressing yourself differently for the day, or arranging flowers.

2. Start with a vision—not of how it will look or be, per se, but of how it will *make you feel* when you're done.

3. Don't let there be a "right" or "wrong" way of doing it. Just go with the flow of ideas that come as you hold in your mind your desired end result.

4. Reflect on how this experiment went for you. Was it challenging, or easy and filled with joy? If it was a struggle, don't be concerned— you're just not used to allowing yourself to access your creativity.

5. Give yourself a goal of doing something small that uses your creativity at least twice a week. You will be amazed at how easy it becomes, and what it opens up in other areas of your life.

chapter 6

developing your spiritual side

When Caroline thinks about *spirituality*, she revisits the almost mystical emotions and sensations she experienced during services at the Catholic church she attended as a child. The smell of incense, the sound of the choir and ringing bells, the connection she felt to the people who surrounded her—all of these evoked a world beyond the everyday. Although she had no connection to Catholicism after college, she turned as a seeker in her 40s to the Episcopal Church. For a time, she found that the similar rituals evoked the same feelings, but her most important connection in this phase of her life was the social support she could give and receive within the congregation.

Caroline's experience has some similarities to mine and some substantial differences. Although I was Jewish by heritage, after the death of my grandfather my family's orthodox practice of Judaism dissipated. While I did go to Sunday School, our household was not religious and neither was I. I have since, however, found a wonderful social connection in the spiritual group JP and I became part of nearly two decades ago.

Although we have no specific ritual, and a different leader is chosen from within the group for each meeting, we always create a place that fosters spirituality. Our talks sometimes digress sometimes—to the personal issues of a member, to the general challenges of aging, or to what we want to do with the years we have left. There is movement and music. And the session always begins with meditation.

As a psychologist, I have come to understand that we view existence and live in the world from two very different perspectives. In the first, we are fully embroiled in the "drama" of our life, believing that the events we experience and our thoughts and feelings about them are "real." The second perspective is one we get to through mindfulness and meditation, which give us enough space beyond our drama to realize that it is not the real us—or the real anyone else. Who we are is outside of our drama. Through mindfulness, we can observe this truth.

To me, the part of us that is the observer is an aspect of our spiritual self. And as anyone can attest who has experienced the detachment from drama that mindfulness provides, this is a happier, more peaceful approach to life. While our meditation periods promote spiritual feelings, for me the group's most valuable aspect is the social bonds we have formed. I have met some really great people who I can count on and I can reach out to so that I don't feel alone.

The power of social support and a spiritual routine—whether or not the group is formal and historical and steeped in tradition—provides an important link to the spiritual for people at every age, but particularly in older years. Since the beginnings of human life, people have gathered in ceremonies reflecting spirituality. Many of these rituals took place in beautiful outdoor settings at significant passages in natural life—sunrise or sunset or an eclipse of the moon.

Nature may also stimulate solitary and evocative moments that seem to carry us beyond the everyday world. Caroline, for example, realized that many of the same childhood feelings she recalled from church were also tied in her early years to the natural world. She had always been moved by settings where the beauty and power of nature were displayed. Traveling to Niagara Falls in her 60s, for example, she took a boat ride through the gorge and into the mist and falling water. Engulfed in sound and sensation, she experienced her most profound spiritual joy.

Spirituality is subjective, and our approach is personal to each of us. For many, it includes a belief in and an engagement with the part of our own nature that is spirit or soul—the part that is an intelligent energy or consciousness separate from the body. Those who are spiritual may further feel a connection to the universe, which they consider to be an intelligent life force. Some people believe that everything in our lives is happening for our greatest benefit, as a mechanism for learning and growth—that the universe is always helping us live to our highest potential.

As we age, many of us begin to ponder the world of the spirit and what it means to us personally. What is my "spirit" and how am I connected with it—or *am* I connected with it at all? What will it be like to move from life to spirit? Where can I find support for this journey?

Spirituality can be the road map we travel along this path, whether we are following the steps of Abraham or the Buddha or Jesus or Mohammed or our friends, and whether or not we pass through one or more formal institutions—organized religions—on our way. It's a journey that's especially suited to life after 55 or 60, as we approach a crucial milestone: the separation of our physical body from the soul or spirit or personality we identify as "me." Spirituality supports us by helping us forge connections to like-minded fellow travelers, to the universe of other beings that embrace us, and to whatever we find beyond the moment of our death. In fact, both spirituality and organized religion have often assured their adherents that life extends beyond death in this world, and this is a major attraction. In other words, spirituality is like a first-class passage from this world to the next.

In this chapter we will look at the many roles spirituality can play in our lives and the benefits it provides both emotionally and physically in this more challenging life cycle.

developing your spirituality

Spiritual practice of almost any kind disengages us from our thoughts and feelings and greatly reduces stress. Physiologically, it calms the body, taking us out of the typical fight-flight-or-freeze response we have to everything going on in our life. From this more relaxed place, our mind and energy can be freed from working mostly for our safety and protection, and put to a higher use. This calmer, more objective perspective is the gateway to immense inner resources, such as insight, wisdom, resilience, creativity, and innovation, with which we can create a much more fulfilling life from our own highest vision for ourselves. Also, by connecting more consciously with the indomitable human spirit, we can more easily overcome trauma and traverse the inevitable challenges of older age.

the psychic and emotional appeal of spirituality

A particular fear that arises more strongly at this stage of life, as our own mortality comes into sharper focus, is the fear of death. Recognizing our vulnerability often leads us in one of two directions: either we shrink away from life as a reaction to our own discomfort, caused by the fear of death (which "robs the second half of life of its purpose," as Carl Jung put it),[113] or we embrace life with gusto, urgency, and appreciation, knowing that our days are finite. We finally live life like we mean it, according to our own highest vision for ourselves.

A connection to the spiritual dimension of life, whatever that means to us personally, can make us feel part of something much larger than ourselves and provide a sense of wise, loving support. It gives us an awareness of existing beyond the physical realm of the body and day-to-day drama and compels us to reach for an ever more purposeful life. Finally, connecting with our spiritual nature often paves the way for connecting with others. People who have a similar view of the spiritual side of life often gather together in common practices and observances. But beyond like-mindedness, a recognition of and identification with our own spiritual nature tends to lead us to view others as the same expression of divinity as we are.

The traditional Hindi greeting "namaste," used upon meeting or parting, speaks to this recognition of the divinity of others and our oneness with each other. Commonly heard nowadays in the United States, particularly in meditation or yoga settings, it literally translates to "I bow to you," but it is widely accepted to mean "the soul in me bows to the soul in you" or "the life force within us as individuals is the same as that in everyone and everything." It points to the idea that we are all connected in spirit—that we are all one. And, as we've all probably experienced firsthand, when we view others as the same as us, we approach them more openly, treat them more kindly, and thus connect with them more easily, leading to a more meaningful exchange.

Spirituality, then, engenders the sense of a friendly universe, allowing us to put down our defenses and focus on what we love and want in life.

physical advantages
to spirituality

Research often features evidence that spirituality is a key element that promotes well-being in older age. Introducing the concept of *positive spirituality*, which includes elements of organized religion, a 2002 study revisiting the famous Rowe-Kahn Model of Successful Aging investigates the importance of a personal relationship with the sacred in how well we age. Discussing a large number of studies that connect positive spirituality with good psychological and physical health outcomes, the authors urge people who are working with the elderly to include these considerations in their treatment.[114]

Extensive studies have linked spirituality with good health and longevity, and other research has examined the success of spirituality interventions to promote well-being in old age. A 2010 study by Helen Lavretsky provided a broad review of research on the topic, including both religion and other forms of spirituality.[115] Acknowledging the evidence-based connection between spirituality and coping or adaptation among older people, hospitals and doctors are being encouraged to consider the spiritual lives of their patients. Interventions or programs using spirituality to promote well-being have involved prayer and religious rituals, meditation, mindfulness and yoga practice. Researchers argue that the changes to our nervous systems promoted in this way are associated with decreases in heart rate, blood pressure, and respiration rate.[116]

One of the most important questions a person can ask, as Frederic W. H. Myers once noted, is, Is the universe a friendly place? It is a question that all people must answer for themselves, and the answer determines how we use our resources and see our purpose. Individuals who believe the universe is friendly will tend to look for the meaning, benefit, and opportunity for growth in everything that happens in their life. A connection to spirit helps us to answer "yes." Following are some suggestions for developing your spiritual side.

strategies for becoming more spiritual

Explore the Options

Many people find it very rewarding to devote time and attention to this particular aspect of life. Whether it is a new or old area of consideration for you, make it a project to explore spirituality and expand your view of the world. You can start by simply pondering the possibility that you have a spiritual dimension—a spirit or a soul. Ask yourself, "What does that mean to me? If it were true, how might it affect my view of and feelings about death—others' or my own? About how I live my life?"

If you already have an uplifting and enriching spiritual dimension, then I hope that some of the other suggestions in this chapter will add value to this already well-developed aspect of your life. If a spiritual or religious practice used to be part of your life but for some reason fell away, consider whether you'd like to revisit that particular practice now or explore other spiritual pathways that might become a source of upliftment and support.

We heard about Caroline, who turned from one institution (Catholicism) to another (the Episcopal Church), but opportunities also abound outside the limits of mainline religion. Many people find a spiritual feeling and expression through the practice of meditation, tai chi, qigong, and yoga—often in social groups. The bulletin board at your local coffee shop may provide some prospects to investigate. In another example, a friend of mine doing research for a book took himself to an evening in which a young woman channeled the spirit of an Indian guru. Working hard to leave his journalistic skepticism at the door, he experienced a real sense of spirituality in what took place there. While he didn't pursue it, the evening opened his mind to a whole new area of possibility.

Today, more than ever, it's easy to find like-minded people and to join or form groups based on common interests. The web offers plenty of assistance, whether you're looking for an existing spiritual group[117] or would like to start one of your own.[118]

Just "Be" to Get in Touch with Your Own Divine Nature

By forging a strong identification with our spiritual self, we can develop a more proportional connection to the physical self as it is starting to slow or falter. This also allows us to put our focus on our deepening inner development and expressing it outwardly, which can bring tremendous meaning and fulfillment at this stage.

Mindfulness and/or a more formal meditation practice are useful ways to get in touch with our spiritual selves amid the hurly-burly of daily life, and they lower our stress response at the same time. By now it should be apparent that our thoughts have a profound impact on our psychological, emotional, and physical health. When we can quiet the mind's usual chatter, which can itself induce stress, we have the opportunity to just *be* with ourselves. To be, without judgment, criticism, or worry. To be, with curiosity, openness, acceptance, and love. This practice gives us the rare feeling of unconditional self-worth—meaning that our value comes without having to *do* anything to earn it.

Some people see their lifetime as "continuing education" in who they are "in the best of all possible worlds." The opportunity is there in every moment to be the person we are capable of being. When we think this way, full of intention, aging itself becomes a spiritual practice that catapults our growth.

Intentionally Develop a "Higher-Self" Quality

How do we evolve or grow spiritually? Some believe, as I do, that an important way to define and gauge our own spiritual growth is by how much we authentically embody and express in our lives the "higher" human values and qualities—such as love, kindness, compassion, empathy, forgiveness, serenity, gratitude, joy, generosity, courage, and integrity. "Our problem isn't that we don't think love is an important thing," spiritual teacher and author Marianne Williamson has said. "It's that we don't think it's the *most* important thing."[119]

The first step is determining which qualities you admire or value most. If you're not instantly clear about this, think about people who really inspired you at some point in your life. If you isolate or distill down a few qualities about that person that you were impressed with, what are they? Your answers can be clues as to what would be most meaningful to develop in yourself.

This sentiment was famously expressed by His Holiness the Dalai Lama: "My true religion is kindness."[120] When we think this way, full of intention for engaging with others from the highest part of ourselves, living itself becomes a spiritual practice, one that both catapults our personal growth and increases the meaningfulness we experience in life.

Engage in Opportunities to Help Loved Ones

Over the course of growing older, we will surely experience the illness and death of loved ones. Many friends and family members run from death, as if it were contagious. Those in most need of the comfort of others may find their circle shrinking with the news of their situation. Make it your goal to reach out instead of walking away. We'll be talking much more about this aspect of our spiritual side—giving to others through service—in Chapter 7.

Develop Your Intuition

Where do you find your spiritual self? Think about that little voice within you that often brings important insight that seems beyond the knowing of your conscious mind. Many people believe this is one element of our spirit. By becoming more attuned to that small, still, inner voice of wise guidance, we can develop our spirituality. Almost magically, intuition seems unlimited compared to the rational, thinking mind. You develop it by becoming aware of all that is around you. Use all your senses to tune in to the various energies without filtering. Gradually, the information you receive will be more and more powerful—and you will begin to trust it as well.

Researchers—including Daniel Kahneman, a Nobel Prize winner in Economic Science—are coming to believe that intuition is a third dimension of our personality, in addition to the rational mind and the emotions, which have often been seen as the opposing poles in explaining human behavior. Kahneman's influential book *Thinking, Fast and Slow* defines intuition as "fast, automatic, frequent, emotional, stereotypic, subconscious," contrasted with what we usually consider "rational" thinking: "Slow, effortful, infrequent, logical, calculating, conscious."[121] To use a mundane example, I've often found I have the most success with puzzles when I put aside logical step-by-step activity and respond in an apparently random "thoughtless" way. Once dismissed as "hoo-hah" or a supposedly "feminine" substitute for "real thinking," intuition is now being acknowledged for its legitimacy and usefulness by everyone from corporate trainers to the U.S. military. Apple creator Steve Jobs once told an interviewer that "intuition is a very powerful thing, more powerful than intellect, in my opinion. That's had a big impact on my work."[122]

Interestingly, new research from the Institute of HeartMath is revealing that the heart has its own intelligence. This research is showing that "the heart sends us emotional and intuitive signals to help govern our lives."[123] It receives information through an energetic field even before that information can be perceived by the brain. We're continuously receiving billions of bits of invisible information in the form of energy from the outside world. When we are able to tune in to that energy, we have a tremendous inner resource for making informed decisions that are for our highest good. Receiving our intuition's messages and following its guidance *is* engaging with our spiritual nature—it *is* living a spiritual life.

A way to feel more connected spiritually, then, is to become more attuned to our small, still inner voice, whose wise guidance seems unlimited compared to what we know based on facts alone. This attunement can be achieved through the practices of meditation and prayer and through the quiet self-awareness of mindfulness. A tremendous comfort comes from asking for guidance, hearing it as a distinct inner voice, and then acting on it and seeing it bring you or others healing, peace, and happiness.

To receive information from our intuition, we have to bypass the rational mind, which will reject what it hears as not making perfect sense based on information for which we have tangible proof. Intuition doesn't have such limitations. To prevent us from limiting ourselves, we have to step into a mindset of innocence, of beginner's mind. Creating a wavelength on which intuition can reliably communicate requires openness, intention, receptiveness, and the courage to follow through.

Spend Time in Nature

Another way of simply "being" that powerfully connects us to the spiritual is spending time in nature. More than nearly anything else we can experience, nature gives us an overwhelming sense of how mystical, awe-inspiring, and wonder-filled the world is. Not surprisingly, spending time in nature has also been shown to generate tremendous psychological and physical health benefits, in part because of the way it allows us to reduce rumination, or the negative thinking we do about ourselves.[124] Health benefits linked to spending time in nature include lower blood pressure and cholesterol; reduced stress, anxiety, and depression; decreased risk of mental illness; improvements in attention-deficit/hyperactivity disorder; reduced risk of cancer; and greater longevity.[125]

Spending time in nature also helps us to remember that *we, ourselves, are nature.* We are an important, albeit tiny, part of our amazing natural world. The incomprehensible intelligent energy by which all things are born, unfold, evolve, and die is operating within us. An awareness of this fact also helps us to feel our oneness with all of life and to take a kinder, gentler, and more thoughtful approach to our interactions with the world.

Most of us have experienced the amazement of wonder in natural settings—it's the drive for these experiences that takes us to America's national parks and to inspiring settings around the world. Think of Caroline's experience at Niagara Falls on the Maid of the Mist boat tour.

It isn't necessary to get in a car or on a plane to reach inspiring geographies. In fact, beauty is right outside your window. If what you see looking down or across isn't so grand, try looking up. The sky provides constantly changing scenic wonders.

How can you increase your connection to nature? An article originally in the AARP Bulletin introduces us to Marti Erickson, who carries two folding chairs in her car—one for her grandchild—so she can stop and enjoy the view wherever she is. Time spent in nature "may be one of the best and most accessible natural stress-busters any individual or family could find," she says.[126]

Like Caroline, many of us may experience the wonder of nature—a spiritual connection to the larger world of beings—somewhat serendipitously. It catches us by surprise as a bird in flight or a change in the kaleidoscope of sunset suddenly evokes an emotional response. It's possible to make this connection intentionally by forming a commitment to spend time in nature—preferably alone—to take a few quiet moments in a favorite spot, sit down, and observe the world around you. Again, mindfulness practice can play a role here.

Explore Organized Options

If you don't already have a religious or spiritual practice, read about the basic tenets of the major world religions and see what, if anything, resonates with you and prompts you to learn more. If a spiritual or religious practice used to be part of your life but for some reason fell away, consider whether you'd like to revisit it now as a form of support and a resource for best handling the challenges of this age-stage.

I encourage you to study a variety of viewpoints in order to discover what rings true for you. For example, does the Christian belief that Jesus died on the cross to absolve those who believe in him of their sins inspire and uplift you to forgive yourself and others, let go of your view of yourself as wounded, and thereby engage more fully with people and with life? Do the Four Noble Truths of Buddhism, which address the existence, cause, and end of suffering, give you an effective way to deal with the physical and mental pain that humans endure? Do the "naturalness," non-action, simplicity, and spontaneity of Taoism appeal to you as way to live in harmony with the universe?

My personal view is that when a religious or spiritual belief is uplifting and prompts us to live a more connected, enriching, and fulfilling life, then it's good. If it causes us to see ourselves as separate and to view others with hate, then it is destructive and will not add to our health and well-being in older age. Do you agree? If so, reflect on your beliefs and hold them against this criterion. If there are those that you feel hinder, limit, or harm you in some way, consider shedding them and finding others that feel more true and empowering to you. Like everything else, our spirituality should help us live our best life and not keep us in fear and feeling small.

exercises

Timeline Review: Spirituality

1. Complete a timeline review of your experiences with religion or spirituality by decade.

   Example: Caroline, 67

   Childhood and youth: Strong Catholic upbringing, including 16 years of Catholic education. Profound experiences of spirituality and connection to a higher being.

   20s–30s: No church. Agnostic belief.

   40s: Began to explore organized religions again.

   50s: Joined a church and felt a sense of spiritual renewal.

   60s: Lacking a compatible congregation, remains churchless, but renewed in spirituality through nature.

   Example: Jolyn, 76

   14–40: Heavily involved in church, choirs, directing choirs.

   40–60s: Exploration of spirituality in many forms—meditation, Eastern philosophies and practices, forms of energy healing.

   60s–70s: Appreciation of each spiritual journey taken by individuals. Continuing and deepening spiritual practices and seeking.

2. Ask yourself the following questions:

   • Did you belong to a church, temple, or other religious or philosophical group earlier in life?
   • How often did you pray or meditate?
   • Did your belief system include a supreme being and an eternal life?
   • How did your beliefs and experience make you feel?
   • Did your religious/spiritual practice influence the life choices you made?

- If your experience was largely negative, might there be another spiritual viewpoint that resonates with you?

Answer Frederic W. H. Myers's Question "Is the Universe a Friendly Place?"

1. Ask yourself and answer this key question. What did you say?
2. If your instinct is to say no, take some time—after settling into mindfulness mode—to consider what factors support your answer.
3. Now take a few cleansing breaths, and move your vision in the other direction. What signs would suggest a positive answer?
4. Can you make it your intention to consider whether and how you might want to incorporate a view of a friendly universe into your life view?

Engage with Your Spirit More

Often, much of the discussion about spirituality is intellectual—about learning and beliefs—but we've also identified ways to connect with our own spirit so that it doesn't have to remain intangible. Over thousands of years, humanity has discovered, developed, and practiced ways to *experience* and *engage with* spirit—the divine energy within ourselves and around us—in order to strengthen our connection to it. Here are a few of the better-known methods people have used:

- worship
- prayer
- meditation
- mindfulness, including being in "innocence" and nonjudgment
- "conscious" movement that purposely incorporates the breath, such as certain forms of yoga, qigong, and tai chi
- trance or ecstatic dance, also known as movement meditation
- practicing love, compassion, empathy, and other higher-self qualities
- "being" in nature
- intuition exercises

For this exercise, choose one of these you might like to explore and give yourself the opportunity to do so. Look online for methods and instruction, join a local group or house of worship that offers the practice you have chosen, or sign up for a class. Since seeing benefits with any new activity takes time, perhaps commit to giving yourself a couple of months before deciding whether you've received benefit. If the activity you've chosen doesn't resonate, try another . . . and another. By seeking, I do believe you will find.

Develop a Higher-Self Quality

1. Choose a quality you would like to embody in a more substantial way, perhaps a quality you've admired in someone else or a quality that is opposite to one of your weaknesses. You might choose patience or serenity, for example.

2. On a blank sheet of paper or a fresh digital file, write the quality at the top of the page.

3. Next, make four columns across the page, with these headings: "Thoughts and Feelings," "Body Language," "Actions and Behavior," and "Words."

4. Then, beneath the headings, fill in ideas about how this quality would be exemplified in your life.

5. Do this with two other qualities you are inspired to develop.

6. Finally, choose one out of the three to begin cultivating and brainstorm ways of doing that.

7. Take action and bring this intention to life in the world.

embracing your mortality

Everything in the physical world changes and ages—going from birth to growth to death—but the spirit or soul, as many people understand it, is eternal and exists outside of linear time. If we are indeed spiritual beings with a physical or human experience, as so many believe, then by understanding and connecting with our spiritual nature, we can overcome the fear of aging and death and embrace life most fully. In addition, by seeing the divine within ourselves, we more likely see it in others too, bringing us closer to the truth that we are all connected, all one, all deserving of compassion and love.

The truth is that we don't and can't possibly know the full reality of our multidimensional nature. Therefore, why not create a paradigm for ourselves that helps us live our best life, right up until our dying day?

Here's my personal philosophy, in a nutshell, which I share in case it helps you:

1. I understand that I am mortal, that I will die at some point, and that my time on earth is limited.

2. I believe I have or, more accurately, *am* a spirit (or energy) being and that, when I die, I will pass on to another plane, where I'll be in for another adventure!

3. I'm not afraid that the moment of death itself will hurt, as I believe my spirit will be lifted from my body in a pain-free way, but I am concerned about the possibility of prolonged sickness or pain before I die.

4. I am sad now about leaving behind this world and all those in it whom I love. I do believe that when I cross over to the "other side" I won't feel that sadness and that I will be able to see and interact in some ways with my loved ones from my new "location."

Here are the effects these beliefs have for me:

1. I appreciate and find happiness in each and every day. I take everything as an opportunity to love and live as fully as I can.

2. Rather than being in fear about death, I set my focus on what I want for my life and approach it like a large canvas I am continuing to paint—a creation I am continuing to create, the nature of which is totally up to me as its creator.

3. I am motivated to keep myself healthy—exercising, eating right, learning continuously and expanding my brain, and keeping myself growing, stimulated, and engaged in every possible way.

4. I appreciate the people in my life and see our time together as limited and, therefore, precious. This perspective allows me to

have much more patience with myself and others, and to focus on and operate from love, understanding, compassion, and kindness.

These thoughts focus, with a broad brush, on how we can address our mortality in a way that sustains us through episodes in life in which we consider our approaching death (these episodes will probably come and go over the course of aging). Sometimes the illness or death of loved ones invokes thoughts about dying; other times it may be your own illness or increasing frailty.

Mortality—and its timing—also can have more mundane implications. When Stephanie opened the door to the laundry room in her apartment building, she had nothing on her mind besides putting wet clothes into the dryer. A neighbor was folding clothes and, while she did, they talked. The neighbor's nephews had invited the neighbor to move across the country so that they could care for her in her "old age," she said. Recently retired, Stephanie's neighbor looks like she's barely 60, and she's lived in the same condo in the same city for more than two decades. This is where her life is. And yet . . . what if she faced a lingering death from a terminal illness? Talking to Stephanie, she wondered: "Uncertainty. It's the worst thing about death, isn't it?"

It wasn't the first time Stephanie had considered the possibility. When her life might end came up regularly as she and a friend tried to calculate how many years beyond 75 they might be able to travel abroad—or even across country. Or when Stephanie was looking at what seemed to be fairly substantial savings and wondering whether they would be enough. Her financial adviser said she was good to age 90, but what if she lived longer? How do you weigh today's pleasures against tomorrow's security? That's a lifelong question, but it's easier to answer when the end is theoretically a few decades away.

Approaching these episodes with mindfulness can help us to balance our long-term and short-term material needs against our more fundamental purpose of living life to the fullest every moment that it's ours to enjoy.

what happens after death?

Scientists are using their tools to try to answer a question that has been asked as long as people have lived. For years now, we've been hearing stories about people who have seen a "bright light" or remembered hovering over their own bodies after apparent death. Now scientists at the University of Southampton are adding some scientific clout to those anecdotes. About 40 percent of patients who were surveyed about their experiences following cardiac arrest described some sort of awareness after their brains had shut down.[127]

"This is significant," said Dr. Sam Parnia, who led the study, reiterating that up until now the experiences people have reported have been viewed likely to be "hallucinations or illusions occurring either before the heart stops or after the heart has been successfully restarted." This study, however, revealed that consciousness "appeared to occur . . . when there was no heartbeat."[128]

Over the years that near-death experiences have been reported—and they've appeared widely—scientists have offered the explanation that the body releases chemicals to guard against the impact of trauma, and a side effect is hallucinations. Some point out that a similar experience can be caused by the drug ketamine. Dr. Parnia's new study challenges these explanations, and it will certainly stimulate a new round of research on what happens as someone is dying.

In addition to near-death experiences, some of us can recount what we believe are experiences of contact with loved ones after their death. When someone we love dies, perhaps more than anything except for wanting them back with us, we want to know that they are okay. And we want tangible proof, not just wishful thinking on our part. Often in our deepest grief, we ask our loved ones for a sign that they are still with us in spirit and to let us know how they're doing. We want them to reach out to us, in the physical world, with a communication that will confirm their well-being and help us shift, even if only a little, in our grief.

The following true story perfectly illustrates this idea. It comes from my collaborator, Brookes, and concerns an event that happened less than two weeks after her life partner, Frank, passed away. It is an unusual enough happening, I think, to compel us to at least entertain the possibility of the soul living on after the body dies and the idea that we might be able to interact with those we leave behind when we're gone. I share it with you in Brookes's own words.

A Special Visitor

In my grief after Frank passed, I had asked him for some tangible sign that he was around me and that he was okay. I returned from running errands on my worst day of grieving to find a pure white bird—I realized immediately that it was a dove—sitting two parking spaces away from mine in my apartment's lot.

At first, I sat very still in my car and watched it, not wanting to scare it away. When it stayed there peacefully, looking at me, I got out of my car and still, the bird didn't budge. As a passing neighbor joined me, I wondered aloud if the remarkably tranquil dove could somehow be a messenger from Frank.

To our amazement, it walked down the short sidewalk toward my apartment and waited at the landing by my door. Open to the possibility that Frank's spirit was communicating with me, I went into my apartment and invited the bird to join me. After a few minutes, it came inside, made a single circle around my living room, and then flew onto the kitchen counter. It seemed perfectly happy there—grooming itself, resting, standing on a cookbook and pecking at it gently (at a photo of pasta no less—Frank was a good Italian boy and this was his favorite food).

After several hours, a friend of mine quite easily coaxed the dove into a box, put some netting over it, and slid it under my kitchen table. I turned out the lights and went to sleep in the next room. In the morning, the dove seemed restless, so I took the box outside and opened it. The bird flew out but stayed nearby for the rest of the day, while visitors came and went.

When I left for dinner, I thanked the bird for coming. Unless it was supposed to become my pet, I said, it was okay if it left. When I got back, it was gone.

I believe the bird's visit was Frank's way of answering my request, encouraging me to have courage and faith for my future, which is incredibly hard at times because I miss him so very much.

When we've had an experience like this that validates to us the reality of the spirit, we understand death in a new, less fearful way. The question this then brings us right back to is the most important one we can have—how do we live in the most meaningful way with the time we have left? That's what this whole book has been about.

examining different views of death

Over the course of the 20th century, Western culture came to regard death as something unnatural that should be prevented at all cost, an idea promoted by the principle that doctors should continue treatment to death's door. More and more attention has been given recently to other ways that medical care can address death—and perhaps ease that transition without trying to reverse the course.

Historically in Western culture, death has become associated with images such as the Grim Reaper. It is something to be avoided strenuously and thought of as little as possible. Since the 1960s, this culture of death has been changing, with stories of near-death experiences providing more joyous images of death.[129] News accounts said computer entrepreneur Steve Jobs's last words were "Oh wow, oh wow, oh wow"[130]—as though in the midst of a beautiful and joyous experience.

In this respect, Western civilization represents a pole of belief. In Buddhism, for example, life and death are not viewed as separate parts of the whole. They happen together every minute with the inhalation and exhalation of breath. Dying becomes something ordinary, uniting us with a world of beings that come and go. As for what happens after physical death, Buddhists also see this as part of the flow, believing that the soul—or some essential part of us—exists before this material life and will continue after it is over.

Although it's called the Day of the Dead and often incorporates Halloween-style images, for Mexicans the celebration that coincides with All Souls Day is a time to reconnect with family in a joyful way, sometimes even sharing a meal over a family grave. Belief that ancestors—eventually, you too—remain a spiritual part of the family is a key feature of many African and Far Eastern cultural practices.[131]

On the practical side, the hospice movement has been providing alternative treatment regimens for the terminally ill since the 1970s. These focus on easing pain and providing comfort and peace in the closing days.[132] In a 2013 survey, the Pew Research Center found that more than half of Americans say they would choose to stop medical treatment if they were suffering the pain of an incurable illness or became totally dependent on another for care. More than half believe in a moral right to suicide under similar circumstances.[133]

strategies for accepting your mortality so you can live your fullest life

Make Preparations

More than half of Americans have no legal document making provisions for their material resources after they die. Even fewer have a living will that gives loved ones and medical personnel instructions about the care they would want if they were no longer able to communicate—including the limits they would set on life-sustaining procedures.

Of more concern to me in this book is the other preparations we make for death and the emotional and spiritual processes we go through as we look ahead. Many of us feel anxiety around this topic, and so we refuse to consider it. While excessive preoccupation with death isn't healthy, sitting with the idea in a mindful way can reduce the very anxiety we think it will cause.

A story about how my mother and my mother-in-law approached their deaths will illustrate this point. Both women were diagnosed with an illness about the same time, my mother with a stroke and dementia, my mother-in-law with cancer.

My mother had no faith or spiritual belief, and so she had no spiritual solace to hold on to. Always a high-strung person, she was a complete wreck, angry and terrified. Instead of talking *to* me about her approaching death, she talked *about* me in the third person, using *Andie*, the nickname she had given me as a child. "Andie looks happy," she would say, as though I wasn't there. She would call out for me in total desperation, but the only thing I could do for her was to rub her back, as her mother had done, in an effort to calm her. We had always had a contentious relationship, and that's how it ended, too.

My mother-in-law, on the other hand, went back to her Catholic faith. Instead of spending her last months in treatment, she decided to enjoy the company of her sons and grandchildren. In her final days, she radiated inner beauty and peace.

In his book *Aging as a Spiritual Practice*,[134] Lewis Richmond describes a range of responses to fear of death, including high denial (there's *no* problem), low denial (worrying without resolution), and compartmentalization (I'll think about it later). He suggests the *non-denial* alternative offered by Buddhism. It's "really just mindfulness," he says. "In this kind of mindful awareness, we neither take up the worry nor try to push it away. We just observe it."[135] Richmond offers a contemplative reflection that induces calmness instead of the frantic feelings of anxiety.

Others are simply sitting down to talk about it. On August 24, 2013, Laura Sweet, a former hospice volunteer in Walnut Creek, California, attended one of 300 "Death over Dinner" conversations held in churches, assisted living facilities, universities, and private homes.[136] The idea was to remove the taboo on such discussions and give people a comfortable, social place to share their ideas and concerns across the table: "It's a good place to have difficult conversations," said Michael Hebb, a Seattle-based artist who originated the idea and helped bring it to life in a small experimental graduate course at the University of Washington.[137]

Accept Death Mindfully

One case in which someone turned from fighting death to preparing for it is described on the website of the Sonima Foundation.[138] Faced with a recurrence of pancreatic cancer, Gretchen decided to reject medical treatment and turn instead to practices that would help her endure the inevitable pain leading up to her death. Her history of mindfulness exercise was an important tool. A big step was to reject the idea of "battling" cancer and instead treat it with kindness and respect. Instead of focusing only on her body's suffering, she looked to its ongoing sensory experiences: "watching the full moon rising in the starlit sky from her porch, and witnessing the cloudless blue sky over lunch in the town square."

Gretchen viewed her illness as "a portal, to get a glimpse of what's greater." As the Sonima Foundation article recounts, "From 'the crack in the ego that happens when facing something tough,' Gretchen gained insights that allowed her to see life and death with equanimity." Zen priest Robert Chodo Campbell urges people to consider their own vision of a "good death" and to accept the process that precedes it, as Gretchen did.

Make a Playlist

Not long ago, I was shocked to open my *New York Times* to the following headline: "My Death Playlist (and Yours)."[139] The author— still in his 40s, by the way—has been making preparations for death in a variety of ways, including legal documents. In this essay, he suggests putting together a "singing will," inspired by what happened at the deathbed of a friend, Lois. Recalling that she was a former volunteer at the Tanglewood music festival, the friends who were with her as she died played the music—Brahms, not Beethoven—that they thought she would enjoy. We don't know how she responded, but it was surely a comfort to them in bringing her life to a close.

The more I thought about it, the less weird it seemed. Today we have playlists for driving, for exercise, and even for labor and delivery, and more and more people are planning their funeral or memorial service. Why not make a plan for one of the most important milestones in your life? Who would you like to be there? Are there clothes you would like to wear? What objects would you want to touch or see? And what do you want to hear?

For Lois, Yo-Yo Ma was playing at the moment of her transition. For Frank, Brookes played the Beatles, Bob Dylan, and Sarah Brightman. She also found recordings by Dominic Chianese of Frank's favorite old Italian ballads.

exercises

What about Death Do I Fear?

1. Within the framework of mindfulness (being curious, open, accepting, and loving), ask yourself: "What is it about death that I fear?"

2. Make some notes in your journal.

3. Can you address some of these issues now?

4. If you need help, consider working with a therapist or a spiritual teacher or guide.

How Would I Like Death to Be?

1. Using mindfulness or meditation, reflect on your death. You shouldn't wait until the moment is upon you. Do this while you are still healthy and your mind is free of immediate concerns and fears.

2. Imagine the setting. Would you like to be at home in bed or at a place you particularly love, perhaps the ocean or a garden? For now, don't consider medical requirements but only what your heart would love.

3. Would you like to be with others or to be alone? Who would you want at your side—not only humans but perhaps also beloved pets. It's okay if you want to be alone. Some people want to say goodbye but then would prefer a solitary time to make the crossing.

4. Leaving medical necessity aside again, consider the sensory. What foods or flavors would you like to enjoy? Objects or smells that bring to mind happy moments in your life? Favorite clothing or fabric?

5. Would you like music or perhaps a favorite book being read aloud? Would prayers give you comfort?

6. How would you like your death to be marked? Do you see a formal religious service? A memorial gathering? Maybe you'd like

everyone to gather for a meal in a restaurant you loved? In your imagination, you can have anything you want.

7. Make some notes on your vision of your passing and share them with someone close. If you are unable to communicate near the moment of your death, they will provide helpful information so that loved ones can bring your vision to reality.

***

Having a strong spiritual connection can give us an understanding of our true nature—helping us grasp the great contradiction that, while we are but a tiny speck in a universe that is incomprehensibly vast, we are also valuable beyond measure. Knowing who we are and feeling that our life matters can fuel us to take ourselves and our place in the world sincerely (as opposed to seriously), and inspire us to live our best. In that pursuit, we quickly learn that living our best entails helping others to live their best, too. In the next chapter, we will explore that sense of purpose, the benefits it gives us to have it, and how to fulfill it so that we can create a life we truly love.

chapter | 7

transforming your "little corner of the world"

Let me introduce you to two people who model the concerns I want to address in this chapter. Both are contributing to their communities at the same time that they are fulfilling the life purpose that brings them joy.

For Homer Bryant, this means sharing his talents as a world-class dancer and teacher with inner-city youth in Chicago.[140] His work and the center he founded as a home for it bring little in the way of financial compensation. To him, the money isn't nearly as important as helping young people to absorb the value of discipline—at the same time they're having fun.

On the other hand, Susie (whom we met in Chapter 3) has found many ways to serve and many people to receive her gifts. She and her second husband, David, moved from the East to the West Coast so that she could contribute to the lives of her grandchildren. Once there, she began using some of her time and energy to be a volunteer, a group leader, and a friend's helpmate—activities that sustain both individuals and groups in her new home.

We will learn more about Homer and Susie later in this chapter. What strikes me right off is that both of them are focusing much of their attention on children. Although we'll be talking here about using our gifts to benefit our communities and to enact our life's purpose, the same actions build a legacy, something we may give more thought to as we grow older. What we give to children will endure beyond our years. We will not live to see all the ripples our involvement creates, but we can be reassured knowing that the youngsters will extend our impact beyond our own years.

Our older years are truly our greatest opportunity to contribute to the world. It's only at this time that we have amassed the wisdom, skills, and resilience to put ourselves into something with great clarity and energetic clout. In so many important ways, we are truly in our prime. Our gifts to others will have great value, not only to those who receive them but also to everyone their lives touch through an infinite range of time. As a result, we can now see "community service" as much more than a resumé item for our college or job application. It has profound consequences for ourselves and for society.

> *"The call to community is not a hollow protestation*
> *of universal brotherhood. It is a call to make another's pain*
> *our own and to get in touch with our true fearless self through*
> *giving. This is not the cold abstraction of giving to humanity*
> *in general and to no human being in particular.*
> *It is concrete, intimate, tangible."*
>
> —Arianna Huffington[141]

As with so many things, what we give returns to us a hundredfold. People who give support to others live longer, and the positive effects of *giving* are stronger than the (also positive) effects of *receiving*. In particular, volunteering seems to provide a sense of accomplishment, a sense of purpose, especially for those who have lost the midlife purpose of child-raising and careers. In fact, volunteering has been shown to provide more satisfaction to older people than their paying jobs did.[142]

Perhaps this is because the goal of volunteering may be closer to our heart and our values than the job we have in the workaday world. "Purpose in life seems to protect against the risk of developing Alzheimer's disease and other, milder forms of cognitive impairment, and appears to help older people maintain cognition even when they have some of the hallmark changes of Alzheimer's in their brains," says Patricia A. Boyle, a researcher at Rush University Medical Center in Chicago.[143] A study of 6,000 people over a period of 14 years found that a strong sense of purpose consistently predicted a longer lifespan, no matter what the person's age.[144]

"Service" doesn't have to be huge. We don't need to save the world, only improve our little corner of it. While creating art or promoting social justice are fine goals—Homer's gift—some people who benefit from a sense of purpose simply offer support to family and friends, as Susie does every day.

Despite its many benefits, a surprising number of Americans don't feel a sense of purpose in life. According to a Centers for Disease Control and Prevention survey conducted in 2008, 40 percent of Americans—some 120 million people—can't say what their purpose is.[145] To me, this means that too many people are running on something less than this powerful fuel that makes life much more worthwhile. If this group includes you, let this chapter help you change that.

We began this book at the innermost center of our lives, looking at our core being, our truest selves, and doing the healing and strengthening work that will help us not only to meet the challenges of our older lives but also to celebrate and enjoy the many opportunities we are offered. We learned how to live more authentically and fully from a place of freedom and choice rather than being bound to the past. Then, we turned to the next ring of our lives, the family and friends whose relationships are crucial to our well-being at every age—and more and more with every year. We explored the many ways to fully engage the energy, vitality, and support we need to function at our happiest and best: through maintaining a healthy body, nurturing our curiosity and creativity, and enhancing our spiritual connection to the universe.

In the process, we have created tremendous assets. Now it is time to consider how we want to invest those assets in the larger social world around us.

nurturing the ground where you're planted

When we have a purpose, we don't let the unimportant things in life get to us. Our focus is on something higher and more meaningful. Rather than dwell on problems, we seek to understand them and then put our focus on solutions and the vision of what we *do* want to experience or create.

Some people—and I'm one of them—believe that each of us has a unique purpose to achieve in life. When we're moving toward our goal in an earnest and focused manner, we can find ourselves suddenly "in the flow" or "in the zone," where we experience a high that makes us feel as though time has stopped and our energy abounds. Well known to those in performance, sport, and art, this flow is a powerful indicator that we're doing something we love, something that is aligned with our true nature. Phenomena like this don't discriminate against age. It's never too late to find a new purpose or reconfigure an old one or to experience the tremendous highs that come from doing so.

Betty Reid Soskin had lived a long and interesting life—as a manager of a music store and a community activist—when she was invited to help plan a park in Richmond, California, to honor the women who had worked on the home front during World War II, taking the places of men in the military. The year was 2000, and Betty was 79.

The result was the Rosie the Riveter National Historical Park, where Betty serves today as a volunteer—at age 95. She is the oldest park ranger in the United States, and she treasures a personal greeting she received from President Obama and his wife, Michelle, when she was honored for her national service. If you who think you're too old to use social media should know that she's been keeping a blog to record her activities since September of 2003.[146] Here's what she said on her blog about being interviewed for a 2015 podcast:

> *Wish I'd had that confidence when the young Betty needed it to navigate through the hazards of everyday life on the planet. But maybe I'm better able to benefit from having it now—when I have the maturity to value it and the audacity to wield it for those things held dear.*[147]

what being of service does for you

I sincerely believe that the purpose of life is to bring forth the best that is within us. Giving and being of service, when the actions come from an authentic place of what is true for us, help us to accomplish this. Doing for others also builds our own emotional well-being in a variety of ways.

It Helps Us Develop Resilience and Fearlessness

It's much easier to go through life fearlessly when we're filled with a purpose that is larger than ourselves. When we experience feelings of fear, reservation, or self-doubt, we can acknowledge them and then put them aside to refocus on what we really want, our truest goal. The passion we feel for our cause simply won't allow negative feelings to get in the way or hold us back; what is at stake is much too worthwhile.

It Helps Us Recover from Trauma

Perhaps no event is more likely to trigger isolation than a trauma. Getting out of yourself, focusing on someone else's need instead of your own trouble, is a time-tested way to recover—whether it's from the loss of a job, a partner, a parent, or a child, or perhaps from a diagnosis that abruptly brings fear and risk into your life. Helping others in need can quickly offer evidence that other people have it worse than you do—helping out in prisons, nursing homes, or soup kitchens, for example, are tasks that will put your problems in perspective. Other tasks will invite you into a joyful world. Usually these involve children. Maybe you can take the kid you're mentoring to a skating rink—where *both* of you can try your skills. Or keep score for a Little League team. Or sit in as a helper at a local school, reading books for kindergarten tots or helping third graders learn to read for themselves.

Curling up by yourself is just about the worst way to heal. You need to reach out in order to recover. In that way, you can get past the loss or the present health crisis and move ahead to a future that holds infinite other possibilities. Psychologists have found that helping others reduces your own depression,[148] and advocating for change may give meaning to a personal tragedy.

Laurie Becklund, an award-winning reporter for the *Los Angeles Times* and the author of four books, spent much of the time between her diagnosis and death from metastatic breast cancer doing what she did best: investigating the disease that was taking her life and speaking to others about what she found.[149] In her last weeks, she wrote an op-ed piece advocating for the use of donor dollars to build "a new system of data collection and an open, online, broad-range database about patient histories that will provide information invaluable to those who've been given a death sentence."[150] Laurie lived almost two months past the deadline the doctor had given her. No one who knew her was surprised.

It Helps Us Contribute to Others' Healing

In pursuing the path for our own healing, we may find that we become the guiding light for others to heal, too. We cultivate an inner strength that allows us to live life with greater vision and power, and less fear.

KT had her own healing in mind when she took to the pool in her RV park. She had survived a devastating motorcycle crash in January 2015, which had taken the life of her husband of 25 years and put her in the hospital in an induced coma that doctors used to facilitate her recovery. Returning home from the hospital as a lower-leg amputee, she intuitively understood she would have to prioritize her losses and deal with healing her body first, as it was the most immediate necessity. At age 67, KT felt she had been left alive for a reason and was determined to pursue this purpose one small step at a time.

A retired aqua fitness instructor and pioneer in that field, KT knew that the pool was the place to go for exercises that would increase her flexibility, develop her core and other muscular strength, and improve her range of motion. What she didn't know—at least right away—is that other residents of the park were watching. They began to inquire about the exercises she was doing and, before long, asked whether she would lead them in a class so they could benefit as well. A group formed quickly and grew as the news spread through the park.

Today, KT teaches her fellow residents on a donation-only basis three days a week. The positive energy she gets from the people she helps has promoted her own healing and given her the resilience to courageously face her grief and the other challenges that life might bring. In helping herself she found the opportunity to help others, and in helping them, she found the courage to go on. Service, when done with love, is a win for everyone involved.

It Helps Us Be Useful and Relevant

Leo Rosten said, "The purpose of life is not to be happy. The purpose of life is to matter, to be productive, to have it make some difference that you lived at all."[151] To be relevant and useful, we must bring together and *put to use* all the hard-won inner and outer resources we have accumulated over our lifetime. The reward of deeply engaging with life is not winning but participating. As Arianna Huffington notes about running for governor of California, a race that she lost:

> *The biggest lesson I took away from that experience is that being "in the ring," fighting the good fight, whether through running for office or speaking or writing or organizing, is always more fulfilling, more exhilarating, and more effective than watching the battle from the sideline. You may not win the contest, but that doesn't mean you don't win.*[152]

We can be useful and relevant in older age in innumerable and immeasurable ways.

It Helps Us to Self-Actualize

To reach our potential and experience the kind of fulfillment that doing so uniquely provides, there's no magical age when you can call yourself "done." As long as we live, we have an opportunity to alter and pursue our life's purpose. I tend to agree with those people who believe we are born with a unique individual purpose and that the only way to be truly fulfilled is to live that purpose. The passion and joy we experience when contemplating and doing activities related to that purpose help us to positively identify it. In the past, we may have failed to recognize that purpose—or ducked reaching for it. Yet, it's never too late to discover it and bring it to life through our actions in the world. This is the challenge and invitation I've been posing to you throughout this book. Again I'll ask: What, really, have you got to lose?

It Enables Us to Leave a Legacy

Everyone mentioned in this chapter is leaving a legacy in the way they touch others' lives. We don't have to end apartheid, sell millions of albums, find a cure for cancer, or leave priceless works of art for our contribution to live on for generations after we're gone. Every life we touch will carry a bit of us forward into new generations. Of course, it's best if we have a positive impact on others, helping them transform into a higher, more whole, and more true version of themselves by what we do here. That can be through our thoughts and words, our nurturing and care, our creativity and artistic expression, or simply our example. Identifying our gift is an important step toward this legacy.

> *"We make a living by what we get,*
> *but we make a life by what we give."*
> —Norman MacEwan[153]

Having the courage and tenacity to embrace our gifts and give them to others creates a legacy at the same time that it creates a life we love to live. If you're having trouble identifying your gifts, here are various areas of your life experience where you might look.

where your gift might come from

Your Know-How, Talents, and Skills

What are you good at that could be used to improve the lives of others in some way? For over half a century, Jill Lesly Jones used her blonde beauty, charisma, and versatile voice to build a career as a professional model, actress, and broadcaster. As an encore, she decided to work on the other side of the camera. Using a lifelong passion and talent for photography, she takes people's portraits to help them see their own uniqueness, beauty, and gifts. Having spent so much time in front of the camera herself, she is able to successfully coach others to bring out their best, most authentic self. Then she captures it and reflects it back to them in her photos. The process is fun, and the results meaningful beyond the photographer and subject. As she said in our interview, "The photoshoots give them a better sense of who they are. And because they know themselves better, they have more confidence and enjoy being themselves more. Then they express that joy and confidence outward to others, which makes the world a more authentic and happy place."

Your Values

What qualities do you prize that you can share with others to improve their lives? Jill's values of authenticity, confidence, and joy drive her work to help people see themselves more accurately and to value and love themselves more completely. Core values are also at the heart of the work of Homer Bryant, whom we met at the start of this chapter. As a young man, Homer was a principal dancer with the renowned Dance Theatre of Harlem, and he appeared around the world with some of the most illustrious dancers of his generation. He also helped create the choreography for three Cirque du Soleil productions. He was in his 40s when he founded the Chicago Multi-Cultural Dance Center for inner-city youth; it teaches prospective dancers as young as three his core slogan: "The fun is in the discipline; the discipline is in the fun."[154] Now 67, he still embodies that vision. While not all students will become professional dancers, Homer acknowledges that "a body infused with the discipline of dance is a more focused, harmonious, caring, and sharing human being with a reverence for life."[155] Ballet may be the vehicle he uses, but helping to create resilient and loving young people is his desired end result. The high value he places on character and "being a good human being" is a driving force that is making a positive difference in the world.

Your Insight, Healing, and Transformation

Our greatest insights and understandings about life often come by finding our way through our most difficult times—our metaphorical walk through the desert, our "dark night of the soul." The insight and experience we gain are treasures we have to offer others, and doing so fully integrates the learning we attained on that voyage into who we are. What we experienced has changed us forever and made us more whole.

And, now, we cannot help but have a powerful effect on those we interact with. Rather than stay stuck repeating history unconsciously, they too reap the benefits of our journey to either bypass or advance more swiftly through the trials that were ours. Standing on our shoulders, they take on challenges at greater heights. This is in part how human consciousness evolves. Looking at the most profound lessons you have learned in life, is there a particular message or process that you feel inspired to share? To help get you thinking, here are sample messages from a few of the people you've met in this book:

- Andrea (me): Security does not come from clinging to what you know, but from being able to expand. Don't settle; push the envelope. Ask yourself: "What more can I do?"

- Cynthia (Chapter 2): Curiosity and imagination will keep you young forever.

- Homer (Chapter 7): Life will be slightly uncomfortable; get used to it. It will make you grow, change, discover, experience, and learn.

- Jackie (Chapter 5): Some of the most interesting and rewarding turns in my life happened serendipitously while I was making other plans.

- Raj (Chapter 5): Treat others as you'd like to be treated. Do that, and the rest will take care of itself.

- KT (Chapter 7): To make a difference in someone's life, you don't have to be brilliant, rich, beautiful, or perfect. You just have to care.

Your Joy, Passions, and Loves

In Chapter 3, we explored what gives us joy and excites our passion at this point in our lives. The energy generated can fuel a mission or purpose. What did you discover you love to do? Which of those joys or passions feels like it might have potential beyond your own enjoyment and fulfillment? And which might be something you could now share with some particular corner of the world? Sometimes, we may find our gifts bubbling up and setting the agenda for us.

Spouses and co-authors Judith and Frank (whom we met in Chapter 4), now in their 70s and 80s, respectively, learned a lot about building successful relationships and a vital sexual connection in their 60s as they were coming together as a couple. The seemingly natural next step was to share their experience and helpful advice with others. "The older you are the more tools you have to build a relationship," they say. "It's only too late when they're closing the lid."

Some people believe that we don't actually *own* our gifts but are stewards or custodians of them. Our job is to share them with the world and make a positive difference in other people's lives. We need to ask ourselves: "Am I living my life's calling? Am I giving my particular genius to the world? Am I willing to go to any lengths to share my blessings with those who need them?" This giving is part of feeling fully ourselves and living a full life. Without it, we can't be completely fulfilled or at peace.

Giving and being of service is an extension of our true self. *What* you choose to do is not what's important—it doesn't matter because anything you do with the right intention will be of value. What's important is *how* you do what you choose to do—where it comes from, inside of you. It needs to come from love, compassion, and wanting well for others and for yourself.

You may find your own gifts in all of the sources above, or you may create that gift now as a culmination of all the "iterations" of yourself you've had up to this point in your life—this one best representing the most complete and true you. Our purpose seems to call us to this completed version of what we are—our whole selves—which is part of what makes it so satisfying and meaningful to give.

It's never too late to reinvent ourselves. Who we've been to date—who we might think we are—doesn't have to restrict who we can be today and tomorrow. Our unique contribution to the world in older age needs to come out of who we are as we continue to grow. The strategies that follow will help you in finding and giving your gifts to others.

strategies for finding and giving your gifts to the world

Discover and Name Your "Gift to Others" (What Is Uniquely Yours to Contribute?)

To discover what, at this particular stage of our lives, we feel compelled and inspired to give back to the world requires self-exploration and mindful observation. Look to your inspirations, passions, and joy, and consider: What would enrich both others and myself? The result of this introspection is yet another tremendous opportunity to live more fully as our truest self. Simply start with the desire and intention to be of service, letting go of the need to know, and observe what seems or feels obvious and available to do; it will lead you to your next step.

A caution: *don't base this on "shoulds" or moral judgments or notions of what others think.* The sole criterion needs to be what is *true for you—true to your heart*—not what society or some little voice that reflects your insecurities dictates as worthy or worthwhile.

Find the People You Want to Serve—
Your "Little Corner of the World"

The target of your energy and gifts might change over the course of your lifetime. For example, I have spent much of my career on helping people around the topic of anger. I specialized in it, wrote two books on it, and taught it for over 30 years. A couple of years ago, I began thinking about how I could help people with the challenges brought on by aging.

I'd had quite a role model in my grandmother, who showed that we can be vital and engaged potentially until our dying day and that we never have to live according to others' values or to settle for an unhappy life. She built a career at a time when this was an uncommon achievement for women. When she was 92, she divorced her second husband because the marriage wasn't satisfying, and she exercised until she went into a nursing home. Don't get me wrong, she wasn't perfect, but she taught me some valuable lessons about the agency we have, no matter what our age, to steer our own lives for the better. The more I thought about it, the more I found myself wanting to shift gears and do something new—although I am now in my 70s and certainly eligible for a conventional retirement. The result is this book.

I really want to help people over 50 see the value of their life and to make the most of it. While I still speak about and help people heal through the pathway of anger, this is my new "little corner of the world." You will find your own. And it doesn't have to be big to be significant. In fact, don't let the potential size of your audience deter you. It may be your family, your friends (or a particular friend), a museum or another organization that you serve as a volunteer, or a business that you grow. It can be anywhere that you can express an art, a talent, or wisdom that enhances others' lives. Improving even one other life on this planet is more than important. Besides, you never know the ripple effect down the line. Again, just be true to your heart about whom you are meant to serve.

Serve the Well-Being of Others

This simple goal can be your purpose wherever you go, no matter how old you are. If we see this as our overarching theme, purpose, or goal, we know it doesn't matter what our specific gifts are or how we're administering them to others—it only matters that we are doing what we can in each circumstance. Our conscious intent to love transforms whatever we do into a life-changing effort.

So, just ask yourself where love or help is needed. Wherever you invest or extend your love, you are letting your own light shine. You are giving a gift to the world. We all have the power to help others heal and to awaken their hearts. Our willingness and conviction are what put that power to use. This ensures much more than success; it gives us significance. In the widest sense, our life is a corner of the universe, and by improving that corner through everything we touch, we change everything. It's a place where your gift may find you.

Be a Mentor—Formally or Informally

There's one group I see as a particularly important target for your help as you grow older: anyone younger, but especially those who are in their teens or 20s, the years when so many youngsters struggle to find their way in a world where values they observe are often at cross-purposes. Researchers have documented the difference that a wise adult with loving intent can make in youngsters' lives.

Ann Masten and Norman Garmezy are among the scholars who have pioneered the study of resilience and how it can make all the difference between youngsters who thrive despite adverse childhoods and those who are unable to escape the difficult circumstances in which they were born. While early research focused on the personal qualities of the children, as time went on, the search turned to adults in the child's environment. Investigators concluded that the presence of a loving adult was critical; while parents or teachers often filled that role, the researchers found "in the end it does not matter so much who steps up, but that *someone* steps up and encourages the child to believe in herself." To say, "You can be somebody."[156]

Tony LoRe, founder of Youth Mentoring Connection, has seen this happen. By providing youth with mentors who can help them see their gifts while also acknowledging their wounds, he has helped thousands of at-risk youth believe in themselves and strive for a bright future. They are building a vibrant community. In 2016, 96 percent of mentored teens graduated from high school, with 90 percent going on to college. Compare that to the average graduation rate in the area— South Central Los Angeles—of only 56 percent.[157]

"Charismatic adult" is what the late Dr. Julius Segal, a distinguished clinical psychologist, called people like Tony and the mentors who help him.[158] You can be that supportive person, too. Perhaps there is already a youngster in your circle—a niece or nephew, a neighbor, or a friend's child—who could benefit from your companionship and support. The thing is, you don't have to write a textbook or set up classes. In fact, your example may be almost as important as your encouragement, and this can work two ways— both positively and negatively. Sandy grew up in a very traditional family where her mother stayed at home and mostly submitted to the decisions of Sandy's father. In her first job, Sandy saw a number of women who were living their lives in a different way—working while raising their families and fully participating in the decisions that the family faced. Some of them had chosen a life course that didn't include marriage and a family. It opened a door that Sandy had never peeked through—one she had never imagined existed. Sandy began to see that, contrary to how she had seen her mother behave, women could define their own roles in life.

"Mentoring isn't just something nice you do, or even necessarily a conscious choice," Marianne Williamson points out in *The Age of Miracles*. She remembers the essential contribution an adult made to the path she chose "just at the moment when I needed to see it." In turn, "a younger friend, who is like a little sister to me, has said to me more than once, 'You think I'm ignoring you, but I am listening to every word.'"[159]

This means reflecting on the message we are communicating to those who may be reading lessons from who we are and what we do, not just what we say. Certainly, none of us are perfect, but we need to have an intent, especially when we are around younger people, to model the values and traits we would like to see them adopt. We must make it our intention to be of valuable guidance to those younger than ourselves, to use our gifts with them and pass them on. The older we are, the more we bring depth, heart, knowledge, and wisdom. Just by being ourselves, we can change the lives of people around us.

And the converse is also true. True mentoring means that we allow others to be their true selves. It entails realistic positivity. While accepting them for who they are, we see their gifts and hold the space and expectation of their highest possibility. In this way, we bring out the best that is within them and give them the support to develop it. At every phase of life, we as humans benefit from the support and example of people who've gone before us, who value us, who listen to our thoughts and feelings, and who provide unconditional support. Who in your life could you be that person for?

Experiences like those mentioned above provide us with the clues to how we can use our own gift: serve wherever you are and where you have influence—it doesn't have to be in the United Nations. Remember Susie and David from earlier in this chapter? Although they moved across the country to be near Susie's grandchildren, they found other contributions they could make. Susie helped David to start a real estate business, and she joined and then served as president of a women's social club. Having retired from a career in healthcare management, she volunteered one day a week at a local hospital. She also regularly helped a friend in her 90s who needed some assistance opening and sorting her mail. In all of these endeavors, she never really considered herself "on a mission." When we look at the values and purposefulness behind her choices, however, we can see that her purpose in life is to love and support the people in her family and to be an active participant in her community in ways she both enjoys and sees as contributions to its welfare.

People appreciate her efforts. Ten years after this crucial turn in her life, her son-in-law makes a long-running joke as family and friends gather around the Thanksgiving dinner table at his house and share what they are most thankful for: "Have I thanked Susie and David lately for moving to California?" Their choices have made a hugely positive difference in other people's lives.

You can find the same satisfaction in your own way, creating a legacy that will live beyond your years.

exercises

Timeline Review: Service to Others

1. Divide your life into decades. In each decade, make a note of what you did that made a difference in the larger world around you. This might be in your career or volunteer work, but it could also include family and friends you helped or guided, possibly by example.

2. Now look over what you wrote. What rewards did you take away?

3. Finally, consider how you have been served by others throughout your life and what you have learned from them. This review may give you ideas about what service might be calling to you today.

Values Inventory

1. Take an inventory of the values you live by. I'm offering a list of suggestions here, but in truth, you may not find your values here—or they might need different words to become familiar to you. Try to come up with the top five on your own, then look at the list if you're feeling stumped.

The Values I Live By

My top five values (from list or others)	A recent instance where I saw it in my life—or saw that it was missing	On a scale from 1 to 10, how much of an influence is this value having in my life?
1.		
2.		
3.		
4.		
5.		

Examples

Acceptance by others	Fun	Privacy/solitude
Accomplishment/results	Honesty	Recognition
Achievement	Humor	Risk-taking
Adventure/excitement	Integrity	Romance/magic
Aesthetics/beauty	Intimacy	Safety/security

Altruism	Joy	Power
Autonomy	Kindness	Self-expression
Commitment	Leadership	Sensuality
Community	Love	Service/contribution
Compassion	Loyalty	Spirituality
Connecting/bonding	Openness	Trust
Control	Personal growth/	Vitality
Creativity	learning	
Discipline	Orderliness/accuracy	
Freedom	Passion	

2. Ask yourself:

- How and why did these values become important to me? Was I imitating someone else or thinking for myself?

- How do I display or incorporate these values in my everyday life?

- If others made a list for me, would it have the same values?

- How hard was it to think of an example where my value could be seen? Do I need to change my values or work harder to implement them?

Get Clear about Your Mission

1. What would you like to do? (Is this your natural gift or something you will need to learn?)

2. Who would you like to do it for? (Do you know these people now or have access to this circle? Is there a group you could join that shares your mission?)

3. What is the difference you hope to make? (What is the change you'd like to see happen in the people you touch? How will you know if it has happened?)

4. What inner shifts need to take place in you for that to occur?

5. What outer support will you need to ensure that you remain focused even when things get challenging? (Remember, resistance arises within us when we dare to go for our dreams, our goals; the mind quickly begins to throw at us all the reasons we can't or shouldn't go for what we want. And, as is the nature of life, obstacles will rise in the road to test our resolve. So, to be successful, we need to anticipate that. This is part of being realistically positive. And so is planning for the support we will need in overcoming challenges and staying the course.)

I'll use myself as an example here:

- *What would you like to do?*

   To inspire and teach others to embrace their potential and live their best life. To help them live as their true self.

- *Who would you like to do it for?*

   People aged 50 and older.

- *What is the difference you hope to make?*

   For them to get beyond their limiting beliefs and make choices for their life based not on fears and insecurities but rather on what they would love.

- *What inner shifts or support need to take place in you for that to occur?*

   So that I might not fear changing course at this point late in life, I need to make it okay to fail. I need to make "going for my dream" and living according to what's true for me today the reward in and of itself.

- *What outer support will you need to ensure that you remain focused even when things get challenging?*

   I'll need the support of my collaborator and the book's publisher to create the book. I'll need the support of my husband, my publisher, and my publicist for doing workshops and a speaking tour. I'll need the support of my personal assistant to help me manage the many day-to-day and ongoing tasks.

"I would like to be of use. Anyone who can't be of use is useless.
I'm not here for no reason. I am here for a purpose.
So, I am a member of different organizations, trying to make
a better world. I am of use, yes, people can count on me.
I will do the best I can."

—Maya Angelou

Much of this book has been about how to make ourselves the most emotionally well, healthy, and vibrant we can be. I think I've saved the best for last, the key component: a "why?" beyond this "project of the self," as I call it, that gives meaning and purpose to it all. That "why?" is others. To be of use, as the quote from Maya Angelou above says.[160] To do the best we can, to help others also have a wonderful life. Our greatest meaning, fulfillment, and happiness come when we live with others' well-being in our intentions, when we dedicate our energy and life to making their lives better as well. We do that by giving of ourselves in whatever ways we feel called to and by contributing the gifts that are uniquely ours to give. There is no higher calling, and I know you are up to the task!

That's where I'll leave you on this journey. Remember, the present is where we can make a difference, and the future is always filled with possibility. We create a tomorrow we love by what we intend, believe, and do today.

notes & credits

1. Carolyn Gregoire, "7 Cultures that Celebrate Aging and Respect Their Elders," *Huffington Post*, February 25, 2014 (accessed February 21, 2017, http://www.huffingtonpost. com/2014/02/25/what-other-cultures-can-teach_n_4834228.html).

2. Check your beliefs and self-image against this list: "Top 20 Stereotypes of Older People," *Senior Citizen Times*, November 22, 2011 (accessed February 21, 2017, https://the-senior-citizen-times.com/2011/11/23/top-20-stereotypes-of-older-people).

3. *The Economist* reports on the so-called U-bend phenomenon at "The U-Bend of Life," *The Economist*, December 18, 2010 (accessed February 21, 2017, http://www.economist. com/node/17722567). For more details, see Arthur A. Stone, Joseph E. Schwartz, Joan E. Broderick, and Angus Deaton, "A Snapshot of the Age Distribution of Psychological Well-Being in the United States," *PNAS*, June 1, 2010 (accessed February 20, 2017, http://www.pnas.org/content/107/22/9985.full.pdf).

4. Andrea Brandt, *8 Keys to Eliminating Passive-Aggressiveness* (New York: W. W. Norton & Company, 2013) and Andrea Brandt, *Mindful Anger: A Pathway to Emotional Freedom* (New York: W. W. Norton & Company, 2014).

5. Bill Crawford, "Realistic Optimism," *Crawford Performance Solutions*, no date (accessed February 23, 2017, http://www.billcphd.com/quotes.php?quote_id=148).

6. Sarah Griffiths, "The Glass Really IS Half Full: Realistic Optimists Are Happier and More Successful than Other Personality Types," *Daily Mail*, August 27, 2013 (accessed February 23, 2017, http://www.dailymail.co.uk/sciencetech/article-2402601/The-glass-really-IS-half-Realistic-optimists-happier-successful-personality-types.html).

7. Crawford, "Realistic Optimism."

8. See http://www.taoporchon-lynch.com

9. Throughout the book, I refer to the stories of a variety of people. Some of these are widely reported stories of public figures; others are more personal stories of my friends and clients. In the latter case, I have tended to only give people's forenames to protect their anonymity and some names have been changed.

10. John J. Ratey and Eric Hagerman, *Spark: The Revolutionary New Science of Exercise and the Brain* (New York: Little, Brown, 2013), p. 224.

11. "Neuroplasticity," *Hopes*, June 26, 2010 (accessed February 23, 2017, http://web. stanford.edu/group/hopes/cgi-bin/hopes_test/neuroplasticity).

12. Katrina Schwartz, "A Growth Mindset Could Buffer Kids from Negative Academic Effects of Poverty," *MindShift*, July 26, 2016 (accessed February 23, 2017, https://ww2. kqed.org/mindshift/2016/07/26/a-growth-mindset-could-buffer-kids-from-negative-academic-effects-of-poverty).

13. Lisa Feldman Barrett, "How to Become a 'Superager'," *New York Times*, December 31, 2016 (accessed February 23, 2017, http://www.nytimes.com/2016/12/31/opinion/sunday/how-to-become-a-superager.html?_r=0).

14. William Whitecloud, *The Magician's Way: What It Really Takes to Find Your Treasure* (Novato, CA: New World Library, 2009).

15. Marianne Williamson, *The Age of Miracles: Embracing the New Midlife* (Carlsbad, CA: Hay House, 2008), p. v.

16. Whitecloud, *The Magician's Way*.

17. Daniel J. Siegel, *The Mindful Brain: Reflection and Attunement in the Cultivation of Well-Being* (New York: W.W. Norton, 2007), p. 128.

18. Katty Kay and Claire Shipman, *The Confidence Code: The Science and Art of Self-Assurance—What Women Should Know* (New York: HarperCollins, 2014), p. 65.

19. Marci Shimoff and Carol Kline, *Happy for No Reason: 7 Steps to Being Happy from the Inside Out* (New York: Atria, 2008), p. 126.

20. Carl Jung, *Modern Man in Search of a Soul* (New York: Harcourt Harvest, 1955), p. 112.

21. "Stress Symptoms: Effects on Your Body and Behavior," *Mayo Clinic*, no date (accessed February 23, 2017, http://www.mayoclinic.org/healthy-lifestyle/stress-management/in-depth/stress-symptoms/art-20050987). The following article includes some advice on managing stress: "5 Things You Should Know About Stress," *National Institutes of Health*, no date (accessed February 23, 2017, https://www.nimh.nih.gov/health/publications/stress/index.shtml).

22. Deborah S. Hartz-Seeley, "Chronic Stress Is Linked to the Six Leading Causes of Death," *Miami Herald*, March 21, 2014 (accessed February 23, 2017, http://www.miamiherald.com/living/article1961770.html). This article also includes ways to address stress.

23. Roy Nichols and Jane Nichols, "Funerals: A Time for Grief and Growth," *Death: The Final Stage of Growth*, ed. Elizabeth Kubler-Ross (New York: Simon and Schuster, 2009), p. 96. © 1975 by Roy Vaughn Nichols and Jane A. Nichols. Used with permission of Roy Nichols.

24. Siegel, *The Mindful Brain*.

25. Susan David, *Emotional Agility: Get Unstuck, Embrace Change, and Thrive in Work and Life* (Avery, 2016).

26. Gay Hendricks, *Learning to Love Yourself: The Steps to Self-Acceptance, the Path to Creative Fulfillment* (Amare, 2014), p. 31.

27. Hendricks, *Learning to Love Yourself*, p. 39.

28. Bryan E. Robinson, excerpts from *Overdoing It: How to Slow Down and Take Care of Yourself* (Deerfield Beach, FL: Health Communications, 1992), pp. 30–31. Copyright © 1992 by Bryan E. Robinson. Reprinted with the permission of The Permissions Company, Inc., on behalf of Health Communications, Inc., www.hcibooks.com.

29. Haruki Murakami and Philip Gabriel, *Kafka on the Shore* (New York: Alfred A. Knopf, 2005), 6.

30.   "John Locke," *Wikipedia*, April 14, 2017 (accessed April 18, 2017, https://en.wikipedia. org/wiki/John_Locke).

31.   David Doughan, "J. R. R. Tolkien: A Biographical Sketch," *The Tolkien Society*, November 20, 2016 (accessed February 23, 2017, https://www.tolkiensociety.org/ author/biography).

32.   "Hillary, Barbara (1931–)," *Black Past: Remembered and Reclaimed*, no date (accessed February 23, 2017, http://www.blackpast.org/aah/hillary-barbara-1931).

33.   Sara Schilling, "Bill Painter, Giant of Tri-Cities Outdoor Community, Dies at 93," *Seattle Times*, June 23, 2016 (accessed April 10, 2017, http://www.seattletimes.com/ seattle-news/northwest/bill-painter-giant-of-tri-cities-outdoor-community-dies-at-93).

34.   Ann Brenoff, "This May Be the Single Biggest Retirement Mistake You Can Make," *Huffington Post*, January 17, 2017 (accessed February 23, 2017, http://www. huffingtonpost.com/entry/this-may-be-the-single-biggest-retirement-mistake-you-can-make_us_579f7870e4b0e2e15eb686a3). For more on the study, including a list of what survey respondents said, see Steve Doughty, "So Much for a New Lease of Life! Joy of Retirement Wears Off after Just TEN MONTHS as Bickering and Daytime TV Take Their Toll," *Daily Mail*, November 14, 2013 (accessed February 23, 2017, http://www. dailymail.co.uk/news/article-2507404/Joy-retirement-wears-just-TEN-MONTHS-bickering-daytime-TV-toll.html).

35.   "The Retirement Problem: What to Do With All That Time?" *Knowledge@Wharton*, January 14, 2016 (accessed February 23, 2017, http://knowledge.wharton.upenn.edu/ article/the-retirement-problem-what-will-you-do-with-all-that-time).

36.   Les Brown, *Live Your Dreams* (New York: William Morrow, 1994), p. 75.

37.   "Oldest Graduate: Dr. Allan Stewart Sets World Record," *World Record Academy*, May 4, 2012 (accessed February 23, 2017, http://www.worldrecordacademy.com/society/ oldest_graduate_Dr_Allan_Stewart_sets_world_record_112861.html).

38.   "Nola Ochs," *Wikipedia*, February 1, 2017 (accessed February 23, 2017, https:// en.wikipedia.org/wiki/Nola_Ochs).

39.   Ina Jaffe, "Dance Returns the 'Joy of Movement' to People with Parkinson's," *NPR*, January 23, 2016 (accessed February 23, 2017, http://www.npr.org/sections/health-shots/2016/01/23/463222589/dance-returns-the-joy-of-movement-to-people-with-parkinsons).

40.   Marie Kondo, *Spark Joy: An Illustrated Master Class on the Art of Organizing and Tidying Up* (New York: Ten Speed Press, 2016), p. 40.

41.   Definition of "joy," *Dictionary.com* (accessed February 23, 2017, http://www.dictionary. com/browse/joy?s=t). Used with permission of Dictionary.com.

42.   Iain S. Thomas, "The Grand Distraction," *I Wrote This For You and Only You* (Chicago: Central Avenue Publishing, 2015). Used with permission of Iain S. Thomas.

43. Wendy Koreyva, "Learn to Meditate in 6 Easy Steps," *The Chopra Center*, September 3, 2016 (accessed February 23, 2017, http://www.chopra.com/articles/learn-to-meditate-in-6-easy-steps).

44. Priscilla L. Moulton and Bethe Lee Moulton, *Molly Waldo! A Young Man's First Voyage to the Grand Banks of Newfoundland, Adapted from the Stories of Marblehead Fishermen of the 1800s* (Boca Raton, FL: Glide Press, 2013).

45. Joseph Campbell, Phil Cousineau, and Stuart L. Brown, *The Hero's Journey: Joseph Campbell on His Life and Work* (Novato, CA: New World Library, 2003), 217.

46. Lawrence Robinson, Melinda Smith, and Jeanne Segal, "Laughter Is the Best Medicine: The Health Benefits of Humor and Laughter," *HelpGuide*, January 2017 (accessed February 23, 2017, http://www.helpguide.org/articles/emotional-health/laughter-is-the-best-medicine.htm).

47. Stephen Cope, *The Great Work of Your Life: A Guide for the Journey to Your True Calling* (New York: Random House, 2012), 88.

48. Carina Storrs, "Stand Up, Sit Less, Experts Say; Here's How to Do It," *CNN*, August 7, 2015 (accessed February 23, 2017, http://www.cnn.com/2015/08/06/health/how-to-move-more).

49. "The Transformative Effect of Sleep," *Pearson Practice*, September 29, 2015 (accessed April 19, 2017, https://www.pearsonpractice.com/the-transformative-effect-of-sleep/).

50. Jo Ann Jenkins with Boe Workman, *Disrupt Aging: A Bold New Path to Living Your Best Life at Every Age* (Philadelphia, PA: Perseus Books, 2016).

51. Maia Szalavitz, "Touching Empathy: Lack of Physical Affection Can Actually Kill Babies," *Psychology Today*, March 1, 2010 (accessed February 23, 2017, https://www.psychologytoday.com/blog/born-love/201003/touching-empathy).

52. Definition of "emotional intelligence," OxfordDictionaries.com (accessed February 23, 2017 https://en.oxforddictionaries.com/definition/emotional_intelligence). Used by permission of Oxford University Press.

53. Daniel Goleman, *Emotional Intelligence: Why It Can Matter More Than IQ* (New York: Bantam Books, 1995).

54. Carl W. Buehner, in Richard L. Evans, *Richard Evans' Quote Book* (Salt Lake City: Publishers Press, 1971), p. 244.

55. Brené Brown, *Daring Greatly: How the Courage to Be Vulnerable Transforms the Way We Live, Love, Parent, and Lead* (London: Penguin, 2013).

56. This is summarized from an interview Dr. Brown did with *Forbes* magazine: Dan Schawbel, "Brené Brown: How Vulnerability Can Make Our Lives Better," *Forbes*, April 21, 2013 (accessed February 23, 2017, https://www.forbes.com/sites/danschawbel/2013/04/21/brene-brown-how-vulnerability-can-make-our-lives-better/#5bff9f7d36c7). Dr. Brown's work is highly regarded in the business world, and she has given a TED talk that is on the top 10 list. You can listen, too, at Brené Brown, "Brené Brown: The Power of Vulnerability TED Talk," *TED.com*. June 2010 (accessed February 23, 2017, https://www.ted.com/talks/brene_brown_on_vulnerability?language=en#t-116918).

57.   Maria Shriver, "It's Important to Be Vulnerable: Here's Why," *MariaShriver.com*, October 8, 2014 (accessed February 23, 2017, http://mariashriver.com/blog/2014/10/ why-its-important-to-be-vulnerable-in-life-work-sarah-vermunt).

58.   Martin E. P. Seligman, *Flourish: A Visionary New Understanding of Happiness and Well-Being* (New York: Atria, 2013), p. 20.

59.   James R. Doty, "Why Kindness Heals," *The Center for Compassion and Altruism Research and Education*, January 26, 2016 (accessed April 19, 2017, http://ccare.stanford.edu/ the-huffington-post/why-kindness-heals/).

60.   Kimberly Fulcher, *Remodel Your Reality: Seven Steps to Rebalance Your Life and Reclaim Your Passion* (San Jose, CA: River Rock Press, 2006), pp. 129–162.

61.   Elizabeth Fishel and Jeffrey Jensen Arnett, "Are You a Good Friend to Your Grown-Up Kid? 5 Tips for Relating to Your Now-Adult Child," *AARP*, April 3, 2013 (accessed March 1, 2017, http://www.aarp.org/home-family/friends-family/info-04-2013/ parenting-adult-children-family-relationships.html). Used with permission of AARP Magazine and the authors. See also Arnett and Fishel's book Getting To 30: *A Parent's Guide to the 20-Something Years* (New York: Workman Publishing, 2014).

62.   This and other research is discussed at "Research," *Pets for the Elderly*, no date (accessed March 1, 2017, http://petsfortheelderly.org/research.html).

63.   Dale Carnegie, *How to Win Friends and Influence People* (Magdalene Press, 2015).

64.   Kathy Davis, *The Love of My Life* greeting ecard, *Bluemountain.com* (accessed April 24, 2017, https://www.bluemountain.com/ecards/valentines-day/the-love-of-my-life-kathy-davis/card-3269510). Used with permission of Kathy Davis.

65.   Judith Claire and Frank Wiegers, *So THAT'S Why They Do That: Men, Women, and Their Hormones* (Santa Monica, CA: Top Gun Love, 2014).

66.   Story drawn from information and quotations in Sharath Ahuja, "Did You Know the World's Oldest Marathon Runner Is an Indian? Meet the Turbaned Tornado Fauja Singh!" *The Better India*, July 15, 2015 (accessed March 1, 2017, http://www. thebetterindia.com/23273/story-of-fauja-singh-worlds-oldest-marathon-runner).

67.   See http://www.elizabethlayton.com.

68.   Recommendations from the National Institute on Aging are available at "Healthy Eating after 50," *National Institutes of Health*, no date (accessed March 1, 2017, https:// www.nia.nih.gov/health/publication/healthy-eating-after-50).

69.   Eliza Barclay, "Eating to Break 100: Longevity Diet Tips from the Blue Zones," *NPR*, April 11, 2015 (accessed March 1, 2017, http://www.npr.org/sections/ thesalt/2015/04/11/398325030/eating-to-break-100-longevity-diet-tips-from-the-blue-zones).

70.   Dan Buettner, "10 Blue Zones[*] Food Guidelines," *Blue Zones Project by Healthways*, 2015 (accessed March 1, 2017, https://www.bluezones.com/wp-content/uploads/2015/06/ Blue-Zones-Food-Guidelines-2015.pdf).

71.   William J. Evans, "What is Sarcopenia?" *Journals of Gerontology, Series A: Biological Sciences and Medical Sciences* 50A (1995): 5–8.

72.   This section is adapted from "You're Never Too Old to Start Weight Training," *Mercola. com*, January 23, 2015 (accessed March 1, 2017, http://fitness.mercola.com/sites/fitness/archive/2015/01/23/weight-training-older-adults.aspx).

73.   Philip A. Ades, "Weight Training Improves Walking Endurance in Healthy Elderly Persons," *Annals of Internal Medicine* 124, no. 6 (1996): 568–572, doi:10.7326/0003-4819-124-6-199603150-00005.

74.   Gary R. Hunter, Margarita S. Treuth, Roland L. Weinsier, Tamas Kekes-Szabo, Sherron H. Kell, David L. Roth, and Christal Nicholson, "The Effects of Strength Conditioning on Older Women's Ability to Perform Daily Tasks," *Journal of the American Geriatrics Society* 43, no. 7 (1995): 756–760, doi:10.1111/j.1532-5415.1995.tb07045.x.

75.   Teresa Liu-Ambrose, Karim M. Khan, Janice J. Eng, Patti A. Janssen, Stephen R. Lord, and Heather A. Mckay, "Resistance and Agility Training Reduce Fall Risk in Women Aged 75 to 85 with Low Bone Mass: A 6-Month Randomized, Controlled Trial," *Journal of the American Geriatrics Society* 52, no. 5 (2004): 657–665, doi:10.1111/j.1532-5415.2004.52200.x.

76.   Chris Woolston, "Seniors and Weightlifting: Never Too Late," *HealthDay*, January 20, 2017 (accessed March 1, 2017, https://consumer.healthday.com/encyclopedia/aging-1/misc-aging-news-10/seniors-and-weightlifting-never-too-late-647213.html).

77.   The Active Times, "Sitting Is the New Smoking: Ways a Sedentary Lifestyle Is Killing You," *Huffington Post*, September 29, 2014 (accessed March 1, 2017, http://www.huffingtonpost.com/the-active-times/sitting-is-the-new-smokin_b_5890006.html).

78.   Mary MacVean, "'Get Up!' or Lose Hours of Your Life Every Day, Scientist Says," *Los Angeles Times*, July 31, 2014 (accessed March 1, 2017, http://www.latimes.com/science/sciencenow/la-sci-sn-get-up-20140731-story.html).

79.   Ratey and Hagerman, *Spark*, pp. 225–226.

80.   IOS Press, "Tai Chi Increases Brain Size, Benefits Cognition in Randomized Controlled Trial of Chinese Elderly," *EurekAlert!* June 19, 2012 (accessed March 1, 2017, http://www.eurekalert.org/pub_releases/2012-06/ip-tci061912.php).

81.   Studies as reported in Roger Jahnke, Linda Larkey, Carol Rogers, Jennifer Etnier, and Fang Lin, "A Comprehensive Review of Health Benefits of Qigong and Tai Chi," *American Journal of Health Promotion* 24, no. 6 (2010): e1–e25, doi:10.4278/ajhp.081013-lit-248.

82.   "Top 10 Health Benefits of Water Aerobics," *Health Fitness Revolution*, May 20, 2015 (accessed March 1, 2017, http://www.healthfitnessrevolution.com/top-10-health-benefits-water-aerobics).

83.   Molly Hurford, "8 Ways Cycling Will Make You Healthier," *Bicycling*, May 25, 2016 (accessed March 1, 2017, http://www.bicycling.com/training/motivation/8-ways-cycling-will-make-you-healthier).

84. "The Top Ten Health Benefits of Hiking," *GoodHiker.com*, May 25, 2011 (accessed March 1, 2017, http://www.goodhiker.com/2011/05/25/health-benefits-hiking).

85. Julie Rose, "Running for Seniors: Why You Should Try Jogging," *SilverSneakers*, December 2, 2016 (accessed March 2, 2017, https://www.silversneakers.com/blog/running-seniors-try-jogging-older-years).

86. K. Aleisha Fetters, "Benefits of Pilates: 8 Reasons Every Woman Should Try Pilates," *Fitness Magazine*, no date (accessed March 2, 2017, http://www.fitnessmagazine.com/workout/pilates/benefits-of-pilates).

87. Laura Johannes, "New Research Reveals the Intriguing Health Benefits of the Ancient Chinese Practice of Qigong," *Wall Street Journal*, September 30, 2013 (accessed March 2, 2017, https://www.wsj.com/articles/SB100014240527023043731045791071905269 46048).

88. Ryan Malone, "The 12 Benefits of Tai Chi for Seniors," *Inside Elder Care*, March 2, 2010 (accessed March 2, 2017, http://www.insideeldercare.com/health/the-12-benefits-of-tai-chi-for-seniors).

89. Michael Cramton, "5 Health Benefits of Playing Tennis," *ACTIVE.com*, no date (accessed March 2, 2017, http://www.active.com/tennis/articles/5-health-benefits-of-playing-tennis).

90. Bob Barnett, "6 Surprising Health Benefits of Walking," *Grandparents.com* (accessed April 20, 2017, http://www.grandparents.com/health-and-wellbeing/health/health-benefits-walking).

91. "10 Benefits of Strength Training for Seniors," *MyBodyZone*, February 22, 2016 (accessed March 2, 2017, http://www.mybodyzone.com/2008/12/11/10-benefits-of-strength-training-for-seniors).

92. Amy Paturel, "Yoga Health Benefits as You Age," *AARP: The Magazine*, November 2016 (accessed March 2, 2017, http://www.aarp.org/health/healthy-living/info-11-2013/health-benefits-of-yoga.html).

93. "Walking: Trim Your Waistline, Improve Your Health," *Mayo Clinic*, March 3, 2016 (accessed March 2, 2017, http://www.mayoclinic.org/healthy-lifestyle/fitness/in-depth/walking/art-20046261).

94. Patti Neighmond, "Walking 2 Minutes an Hour Boosts Health, but It's No Panacea," *NPR*, May 1, 2015 (accessed March 2, 2017, http://www.npr.org/sections/health-shots/2015/05/01/403523463/two-minutes-of-walking-an-hour-boosts-health-but-its-no-panacea).

95. Bob Dylan, lyrics from "It's Alright, Ma (I'm Only Bleeding)." Copyright © 1965, Warner Bros Inc., renewed 1993 by Special Rider Music.

96. Constance Gustke, "For Effective Brain Fitness, Do More than Play Simple Games," *New York Times*, July 8, 2016 (accessed March 2, 2017, http://www.nytimes.com/2016/07/09/your-money/for-effective-brain-fitness-do-more-than-play-simple-games.html).

97.   Pilar Escuder-Mollon, Roger Esteller-Curto, Luis Ochoa, and Massimo Bardus, "Impact on Senior Learners' Quality of Life through Lifelong Learning," *Procedia—Social and Behavioral Sciences* 131 (May 15, 2014): 510–516, doi:10.1016/j.sbspro.2014.04.157.

98.   Thomas M. Brod, "Neurofeedback Training Improves Cognition in the Elderly," *EEGYM*, July 14, 2014 (accessed March 2, 2017, http://eegym.com/neurofeedback-improves-cognition). This article summarizes the research and provides links to other sources.

99.   As told in Ratey and Hagerman, *Spark*, p. 243. See also David Snowdon, *Aging with Grace: What the Nun Study Teaches Us about Living Longer, Healthier, and More Meaningful Lives* (New York: Bantam Books, 2002). Snowdon has retired, but research on the nuns' community continues at the University of Minnesota.

100.   Daniel Tomasulo, "Proof Positive: Can Heaven Help Us? The Nun Study—Afterlife," *PsychCentral*, November 3, 2010 (accessed March 2, 2017 https://psychcentral.com/blog/archives/2010/10/27/proof-positive-can-heaven-help-us-the-nun-study-afterlife).

101.   Ratey and Hagerman, *Spark*, p. 242.

102.   Research in this area is summarized in Mo Costandi, "Am I Too Old to Learn a New Language?" *The Guardian*, September 13, 2014 (accessed March 2, 2017, https://www.theguardian.com/education/2014/sep/13/am-i-too-old-to-learn-a-language). The article also provides links to academic writing about the original research.

103.   Jennifer M. Ortman, Victoria A. Velkoff, and Howard Hogan, "An Aging Nation: The Older Population in the United States," *Current Population Reports*, May 2014 (accessed March 2, 2017, https://www.census.gov/prod/2014pubs/p25-1140.pdf).

104.   Data in this paragraph come from American Council on Education, *Framing New Terrain: Older Adults & Higher Education*, October 2007 (accessed March 2, 2017, http://plus50.aacc.nche.edu/documents/older_adults_and_higher_education.pdf).

105.   Here's one of many articles that explain how to get started as a blogger: Jessica Knapp, "How to Start a Blog: Beginner's Guide for 2017," *Blogging Basics 101: Social Media and Blogging Tips*, March 1, 2017 (accessed March 2, 2017, https://www.bloggingbasics101.com/how-do-i-start-a-blog).

106.   *Writer's Digest* is a longtime clearing house of information about writing and publishing. Here's what it has to say about self-publishing: "Directory of Self-Publishing Companies," *Writer's Digest*, January 17, 2013 (accessed March 2, 2017, http://www.writersdigest.com/writing-articles/by-writing-goal/get-published-sell-my-work/directory-of-self-publishing-companies).

107.   Lisa Fernandez, "More Retirees Are Self-Publishing Their Memoirs as a Family Legacy," *Mercury News*, August 13, 2016 (accessed March 2, 2017, http://www.mercurynews.com/2011/10/04/more-retirees-are-self-publishing-their-memoirs-as-a-family-legacy).

108.   Melissa Castoria-Binkley, Linda Noelker, Thomas Prohaska, and William Satariano, "Impact of Arts Participation on Health," *Journal of Aging, Humanities, and the Arts* 4 (2010): 352–367 (accessed March 2, 2017, http://www.neocca.org/presentations/2010-Impact_Arts_Participation.pdf).

109. Colin J. Greaves and Lou Farbus, "Effects of Creative and Social Activity on the Health and Well-Being of Socially Isolated Older People: Outcomes from a Multi-method Observational Study," *Journal of the Royal Society for the Promotion of Health* 126, no. 3 (2006): 134–142 (accessed March 2, 2017, http://journals.sagepub.com/doi/abs/10.11 77/1466424006064303?ssource=mfr&rss=1&).

110. *The Creativity and Aging Study: The Impact of Professionally Conducted Cultural Programs on Older Adults*, National Endowment for the Arts, April 30, 2006 (accessed March 2, 2017, https://www.arts.gov/sites/default/files/CnA-Rep4-30-06.pdf).

111. "Learn More about EngAGE," *EngAGE: The Art of Active Aging*, no date (accessed March 2, 2017, http://www.engagedaging.org/about-us).

112. "William Carlos Williams," *Wikipedia*, February 23, 2017 (accessed March 2, 2017, https://en.wikipedia.org/wiki/William_Carlos_Williams).

113. Jung, *Modern Man in Search of a Soul*, p. 112.

114. Martha R. Crowther, Michael W. Parker, W. A. Achenbaum, Walter R. Larimore, and Harold G. Koenig, "Rowe and Kahn's Model of Successful Aging Revisited: Positive Spirituality—The Forgotten Factor," *The Gerontologist* 42, no. 5 (2002): 613–620 (accessed March 2, 2017, http://gerontologist.oxfordjournals.org/content/42/5/613. full.pdf).

115. Helen Lavretsky, "Spirituality and Aging," *Aging Health* 6, no. 6 (2010): 749–769, doi:10.2217/ahe.10.70. Results of that research are included in the following paragraphs.

116. Lavretsky, "Spirituality and Aging."

117. These are just some possibilities. If you narrow your search by including your community—say, "Oakland spiritual group"—you will find options near you. See Jim Tolles, "Finding a Spiritual Community," *Spiritual Awakening Process*, October 5, 2010 (accessed March 2, 2017, http://www.spiritualawakeningprocess.com/2010/10/finding-spiritual-community.html) and Mackenzie Wright, "Finding Spiritual Community: Alternatives to Joining a Church," *Psychics Universe*, January 9, no year (accessed April 10, 2017, http://www.psychicsuniverse.com/articles/spirituality/living-spiritual-life/ spiritual-guidance/finding).

118. This article offers guidance for forming your own spiritual group: Alice Fryling, "What Happens in Group Spiritual Direction?" *Small Groups*, no date (accessed March 2, 2017, http://www.smallgroups.com/articles/2009/what-happens-in-group-spiritual-direction.html?paging=off).

119. Williamson, *The Age of Miracles*, p. 162.

120. The Dalai Lama, *Kindness, Clarity, and Insight: The Fourteenth Dalai Lama, His Holiness Tensin Gyatso*, trans. and ed. Jeffrey Hopkins, co-ed. Elizabeth Napper (Ithaca, NY: Snow Lion Publications, 1984; repr. Delhi: Motilal Banarsidass, 2006), 84.

121. "*Thinking, Fast and Slow*," *Wikipedia*, April 6, 2017 (accessed April 10, 2017, https:// en.wikipedia.org/wiki/Thinking,_Fast_and_Slow).

122. Walter Isaacson, "The Genius of Jobs," *New York Times*, October 29, 2011 (accessed March 2, 2017, http://www.nytimes.com/2011/10/30/opinion/sunday/steve-jobss-genius.html).

123. Doc Childre, Howard Martin, and Donna Beech. *The HeartMath Solution: The Institute of HeartMath's Revolutionary Program for Engaging the Power of the Heart's Intelligence* (San Francisco, CA: HarperSanFrancisco, 1999), p. 4.

124. Eli Goodstein, "Stanford University Study Says Spending Time in Nature Benefits Mental Health," *USA Today*, July 9, 2015 (accessed March 2, 2017, http://college. usatoday.com/2015/07/09/study-nature-good-for-mental-health).

125. U.S. Department of Agriculture Forest Service, Pacific Northwest Research Station, "Health and Wellness Benefits of Spending Time in Nature," no date (accessed March 2, 2017, https://www.fs.fed.us/pnw/about/programs/gsv/pdfs/health_and_wellness.pdf).

126. See Richard Louv, "Health Benefits of Being Outdoors," *Camptown*, July 23, 2012 (accessed April 10, 2017, http://camptown.net/2012/09/health-benefits-of-being-outdoors). This article also recounts the benefits of time spent outside.

127. Sarah Knapton, "First Hint of 'Life after Death' in Biggest Ever Scientific Study," *The Telegraph*, October 7, 2014 (accessed March 2, 2017, http://www.telegraph.co.uk/ science/2016/03/12/first-hint-of-life-after-death-in-biggest-ever-scientific-study

128. Sean Martin, "Life after Death: Scientists Reveal Shock Findings from Groundbreaking Study," *Express*, January 29, 2017 (accessed March 2, 2017, http://www.express.co.uk/ news/science/670781/There-IS-life-after-DEATH-Scientists-reveal-shock-findings-from-groundbreaking-study). Used with permission of Express Newspapers.

129. Judith Johnson, "Do You Have a Healthy Attitude about Death?" *Huffington Post*, January 8, 2013 (accessed March 2, 2017, http://www.huffingtonpost.com/judith-johnson/death-and-dying_b_2432780.html).

130. Mona Simpson, "A Sister's Eulogy for Steve Jobs," *New York Times*, October 30, 2011 (accessed April 25, 2017, http://www.nytimes.com/2011/10/30/opinion/mona-simpsons-eulogy-for-steve-jobs.html?pagewanted=all).

131. Marcia Carteret, "Cultural Aspects of Death and Dying," *Dimensions of Culture*, 2011 (accessed March 2, 2017, http://www.dimensionsofculture.com/2010/11/ cultural-aspects-of-death-and-dying).

132. http://www.nhpco.org is the national website.

133. Yasmine Hafiz, "American Attitudes towards Death: 12 Facts from New Pew Research Center Survey," *Huffington Post*, November 21, 2013 (accessed March 3, 2017, http:// www.huffingtonpost.com/2013/11/21/death-america-pew-research_n_4312321. html).

134. Lewis Richmond, *Aging as a Spiritual Practice: A Contemplative Guide to Growing Older and Wiser* (New York: Avery, 2010).

135. Richmond, *Aging as a Spiritual Practice*, p. 133.

136. Jaweed Kaleem, "Death over Dinner Convenes as Hundreds of Americans Coordinate End of Life Discussions across U.S.," *Huffington Post*, August 18, 2013 (accessed March 3, 2017, http://www.huffingtonpost.com/2013/08/18/death-over-dinner_n_3762653. html?utm_hp_ref=death%E2%80%94dying).

137. Kaleem, "Death over Dinner." You can find out about the continuing project at http://deathoverdinner.org.

138. Annie Robinson, "How Mindfulness Can Ease the Fear of Death and Dying," *Sonima*, August 30, 2016 (accessed March 3, 2017, http://www.sonima.com/meditation/fear-of-death).

139. Mark Vanhoenacker, "My Deathbed Playlist (and Yours)," *New York Times*, November 5, 2016 (accessed March 3, 2017, https://www.nytimes.com/2016/11/06/opinion/sunday/my-deathbed-playlist-and-yours.html?_r=2).

140. "Bio—Artistic Director Homer Bryant," *Chicago Multicultural Dance Center*, no date (accessed March 3, 2017, http://cmdcschool.weebly.com/homer-hans-bryant.html).

141. Arianna Huffington, *On Becoming Fearless . . . in Love, Work, and Life* (New York: Little, Brown, 2006), p. 221.

142. As summarized in Robert Grimm, Jr., Kimberly Spring, and Nathan Dietz, *The Heath Benefits of Volunteering: A Review of Recent Research*, Corporation for National & Community Service, 2007 (accessed March 2, 2017, https://www.nationalservice.gov/pdf/07_0506_hbr.pdf).

143. Quoted in Jim Schnabel, "Can a Purpose-Driven Life Help Protect the Aging Brain?" *Dana Foundation*, December 30, 2013 (accessed March 3, 2017, http://dana.org/News/Can_A_Purpose-Driven_Life_Help_Protect_the_Aging_Brain_).

144. Described in Melanie Haiken, "Aging and Purpose: The New Movement in Positive Aging," *Caring.com*, September 10, 2014 (accessed March 3, 2017, https://www.caring.com/articles/aging-purpose-positive-aging).

145. Rosemarie Kobau, Joseph Sniezek, Matthew M. Zack, Richard E. Lucas, and Adam Burns, "Well-Being Assessment: An Evaluation of Well-Being Scales for Public Health and Population Estimates of Well-Being among US Adults," *Applied Psychology: Health and Well-Being* 2, no. 3 (2010): 272–297, doi:10.1111/j.1758-0854.2010.01035.x.

146. http://cbreaux.blogspot.com.

147. Betty Reid Soskin, "Last Week's Post-concussion Interview for ParkLeaders Online Program," *CBreaux Speaks: Blog of Betty Reid Soskin*, May 26, 2015 (accessed March 3, 2017, http://cbreaux.blogspot.com/2015_05_24_archive.html). Used with permission of Betty Reid Soskin.

148. "At the State University of New York, Lynn Videka-Sherman studied nearly 200 patients after they had lost a child. Her results showed significantly less depression among parents who reinvested their energies in another person or activity": Julius Segal, *Winning Life's Toughest Battles: Roots of Human Resilience* (New York: Ivy Books, 1987), p. 115.

149. Gayle Sulik, "The Unbearable Weight of the Pink Ribbon," *Pink Ribbon Blues*, March 2, 2015 (accessed March 3, 2017, http://pinkribbonblues.org/2015/03/resisting-the-unbearable-weight-of-the-pink-ribbon).

150. Laurie Beckland, "Op-Ed: As I Lay Dying," *Los Angeles Times*, February 20, 2015 (accessed March 3, 2017, http://www.latimes.com/opinion/op-ed/la-oe-becklund-breast-cancer-komen-20150222-story.html).

151. Leo Rosten, "Words To Live By: The Real Reason For Being Alive," *The Sunday Star (Evening Star)*, January 20, 1963, p. 2.

152. Huffington, *On Becoming Fearless*, pp. 217–218.

153. Norman MacEwan, quoted in *The Forbes Scrapbook of Thoughts on the Business of Life* (New York: B.C. Forbes & Sons, 1950), p. 378.

154. "Bio—Artistic Director Homer Bryant."

155. "Homer's Philosophy," *Chicago Multi-Cultural Dance Center*, no date (accessed April 10, 2017, http://www.cmdcschool.org).

156. Research as summarized in Michaela Haas, *Bouncing Forward: Transforming Bad Breaks into Breakthroughs* (New York: Enliven, 2015), p. 288.

157. "Census Profile: Los Angeles County (South Central)—LA City (South Central/Watts) PUMA, CA," *Census Reporter*, no date (accessed March 3, 2017, https://censusreporter. org/profiles/79500US0603751-los-angeles-county-south-central-la-city-south-centralwatts-puma-ca).

158. Haas, *Bouncing Forward*, p. 288.

159. Williamson, *The Age of Miracles*, p. 82.

160. Haas, *Bouncing Forward*, p. 25.

bibliography

"5 Things You Should Know About Stress." *National Institutes of Health*. No date. Accessed February 23, 2017. https://www.nimh.nih.gov/health/publications/stress/index.shtml.

"10 Benefits of Strength Training for Seniors." *MyBodyZone*. February 22, 2016. Accessed March 2, 2017. http://www.mybodyzone.com/2008/12/11/10-benefits-of-strength-training-for-seniors.

Ades, Philip A. "Weight Training Improves Walking Endurance in Healthy Elderly Persons." *Annals of Internal Medicine* 124, no. 6 (1996): 568–572. doi:10.7326/0003-4819-124-6-199603150-00005.

Ahuja, Sharath. "Did You Know the World's Oldest Marathon Runner Is an Indian? Meet the Turbaned Tornado Fauja Singh!" *The Better India*. July 15, 2015. Accessed March 1, 2017. http://www.thebetterindia.com/23273/story-of-fauja-singh-worlds-oldest-marathon-runner.

American Council on Education. *Framing New Terrain: Older Adults & Higher Education*. October 2007. Accessed March 2, 2017. http://plus50.aacc.nche.edu/documents/older_adults_and_higher_education.pdf.

Arnett, Jeffrey Jensen, and Elizabeth Fishel, *When Will My Grown-Up Kid Grow Up?* New York: Workman Publishing, 2013.

Barclay, Eliza. "Eating to Break 100: Longevity Diet Tips from the Blue Zones." *NPR*. April 11, 2015. Accessed March 1, 2017. http://www.npr.org/sections/thesalt/2015/04/11/398325030/eating-to-break-100-longevity-diet-tips-from-the-blue-zones.

Barnett, Bob. "6 Surprising Health Benefits of Walking." *Grandparents.com*. Accessed April 20, 2017. http://www.grandparents.com/health-and-wellbeing/health/health-benefits-walking.

Barrett, Lisa Feldman. "How to Become a 'Superager.'" *New York Times*. December 31, 2016. Accessed February 23, 2017. http://www.nytimes.com/2016/12/31/opinion/sunday/how-to-become-a-superager.html?_r=0.

Beckland, Laurie. "Op-Ed: As I Lay Dying." *Los Angeles Times*. February 20, 2015. Accessed March 3, 2017. http://www.latimes.com/opinion/op-ed/la-oe-becklund-breast-cancer-komen-20150222-story.html.

"Bio—Artistic Director Homer Bryant." *Chicago Multicultural Dance Center*. No date. Accessed March 3, 2017. http://cmdcschool.weebly.com/homer-hans-bryant.html.

Brandt, Andrea. *8 Keys to Eliminating Passive-Aggressiveness*. New York: W. W. Norton & Company, 2013.

Brandt, Andrea. *Mindful Anger: A Pathway to Emotional Freedom*. New York: W. W. Norton & Company, 2014.

Brenoff, Ann. "This May Be the Single Biggest Retirement Mistake You Can Make." *Huffington Post*. January 17, 2017. Accessed February 23, 2017. http://www.huffingtonpost.com/entry/this-may-be-the-single-biggest-retirement-mistake-you-can-make_us_579f7870e4b0e2e15eb686a3.

Brod, Thomas M. "Neurofeedback Training Improves Cognition in the Elderly." *EEGYM*. July 14, 2014. Accessed March 2, 2017. http://eegym.com/neurofeedback-improves-cognition.

Brown, Brené. "Brené Brown: The Power of Vulnerability TED Talk." *TED.com*. June 2010. Accessed February 23, 2017. https://www.ted.com/talks/brene_brown_on_vulnerabili ty?language=en#t-116918.

Brown, Brené. *Daring Greatly: How the Courage to Be Vulnerable Transforms the Way We Live, Love, Parent, and Lead*. London: Penguin, 2013.

Brown, Les. *Live Your Dreams*. New York: William Morrow, 1994.

Buettner, Dan. "10 Blue Zones® Food Guidelines." *Blue Zones Project by Healthways*, 2015. Accessed March 1, 2017. https://www.bluezones.com/wp-content/uploads/2015/06/Blue-Zones-Food-Guidelines-2015.pdf.

Campbell, Joseph, Phil Cousineau, and Stuart L. Brown. *The Hero's Journey: Joseph Campbell on His Life and Work*. Novato, CA: New World Library, 2003.

Carnegie, Dale. *How to Win Friends and Influence People*. Magdalene Press, 2015.

Carteret, Marcia. "Cultural Aspects of Death and Dying." *Dimensions of Culture*. 2011. Accessed March 2, 2017. http://www.dimensionsofculture.com/2010/11/cultural-aspects-of-death-and-dying.

Castoria-Binkley, Melissa, Linda Noelker, Thomas Prohaska, and William Satariano. "Impact of Arts Participation on Health." *Journal of Aging, Humanities, and the Arts* 4 (2010): 352–367. Accessed March 2, 2017. http://www.neocca.org/presentations/2010-Impact_Arts_Participation.pdf.

"Census Profile: Los Angeles County (South Central)—LA City (South Central/Watts) PUMA, CA." *Census Reporter*. No date. Accessed March 3, 2017. https://censusreporter.org/profiles/79500US0603751-los-angeles-county-south-central-la-city-south-centralwatts-puma-ca.

Childre, Doc, Howard Martin, and Donna Beech. *The HeartMath Solution: The Institute of HeartMath's Revolutionary Program for Engaging the Power of the Heart's Intelligence*. San Francisco, CA: HarperSanFrancisco, 1999.

Claire, Judith, and Frank Wiegers. *So THAT'S Why They Do That!: Men, Women, and Their Hormones*. Santa Monica, CA: Top Gun Love, 2014.

Cope, Stephen. *The Great Work of Your Life: A Guide for the Journey to Your True Calling*. New York: Random House, 2012.

Costandi, Mo. "Am I Too Old to Learn a New Language?" *The Guardian*. September 13, 2014. Accessed March 2, 2017. https://www.theguardian.com/education/2014/sep/13/am-i-too-old-to-learn-a-language.

Cramton, Michael. "5 Health Benefits of Playing Tennis." *ACTIVE.com*. No date. Accessed March 2, 2017. http://www.active.com/tennis/articles/5-health-benefits-of-playing-tennis.

Crawford, Bill. "Realistic Optimism." *Crawford Performance Solutions*. No date. Accessed February 23, 2017. http://www.billcphd.com/quotes.php?quote_id=148.

Crowther, Martha R., Michael W. Parker, W. A. Achenbaum, Walter R. Larimore, and Harold G. Koenig. "Rowe and Kahn's Model of Successful Aging Revisited: Positive Spirituality—The Forgotten Factor." *The Gerontologist* 42, no. 5 (2002): 613–620. Accessed March 2, 2017. http://gerontologist.oxfordjournals.org/content/42/5/613.full.pdf.

The Dalai Lama, *Kindness, Clarity, and Insight: The Fourteenth Dalai Lama, His Holiness Tensin Gyatso*, trans. and ed. Jeffrey Hopkins, co-ed. Elizabeth Napper (Ithaca, NY: Snow Lion Publications, 1984; repr. Delhi: Motilal Banarsidass, 2006), 84.

David, Susan. *Emotional Agility: Get Unstuck, Embrace Change, and Thrive in Work and Life*. Avery, 2016.

Davis, Kathy. *The Love of My Life* greeting ecard. *Bluemountain.com*. No date. Accessed April 24, 2017. https://www.bluemountain.com/ecards/valentines-day/the-love-of-my-life-kathy-davis/card-3269510.

Definition of "emotional intelligence." *OxfordDictionaries.com*. No date. Accessed February 23, 2017. https://en.oxforddictionaries.com/definition/emotional_intelligence.

Definition of "joy." *Dictionary.com*. No date. Accessed February 23, 2017. http://www.dictionary.com/browse/joy?s=t.

"Directory of Self-Publishing Companies." *Writer's Digest*. January 17, 2013. Accessed March 2, 2017. http://www.writersdigest.com/writing-articles/by-writing-goal/get-published-sell-my-work/directory-of-self-publishing-companies.

Doty, James R. "Why Kindness Heals." *The Center for Compassion and Altruism Research and Education*. January 26, 2016. Accessed April 19, 2017. http://ccare.stanford.edu/the-huffington-post/why-kindness-heals.

Doughan, David. "J. R. R. Tolkien: A Biographical Sketch." *The Tolkien Society*. November 20, 2016. Accessed February 23, 2017. https://www.tolkiensociety.org/author/biography.

Doughty, Steve. "So Much for a New Lease of Life! Joy of Retirement Wears Off after Just TEN MONTHS as Bickering and Daytime TV Take Their Toll." *Daily Mail*. November 14, 2013. Accessed February 23, 2017. http://www.dailymail.co.uk/news/article-2507404/Joy-retirement-wears-just-TEN-MONTHS-bickering-daytime-TV-toll.html.

Escuder-Mollon, Pilar, Roger Esteller-Curto, Luis Ochoa, and Massimo Bardus. "Impact on Senior Learners' Quality of Life through Lifelong Learning." *Procedia—Social and Behavioral Sciences* 131 (May 15, 2014): 510–516. doi:10.1016/j.sbspro.2014.04.157.

Fernandez, Lisa. "More Retirees Are Self-Publishing Their Memoirs as a Family Legacy." *Mercury News*. August 13, 2016. Accessed March 2, 2017. http://www.mercurynews.com/2011/10/04/more-retirees-are-self-publishing-their-memoirs-as-a-family-legacy.

Fetters, K. Aleisha. "Benefits of Pilates: 8 Reasons Every Woman Should Try Pilates." *Fitness Magazine*. No date. Accessed March 2, 2017. http://www.fitnessmagazine.com/workout/pilates/benefits-of-pilates.

Fishel, Elizabeth, and Jeffrey Jensen Arnett. "Are You a Good Friend to Your Grown-Up Kid? 5 Tips for Relating to Your Now-Adult Child." *AARP*. April 3, 2013. Accessed March 1, 2017. http://www.aarp.org/home-family/friends-family/info-04-2013/parenting-adult-children-family-relationships.html.

Fryling, Alice. "What Happens in Group Spiritual Direction?" *Small Groups*. No date. Accessed March 2, 2017. http://www.smallgroups.com/articles/2009/what-happens-in-group-spiritual-direction.html?paging=off.

Fulcher, Kimberly. *Remodel Your Reality: Seven Steps to Rebalance Your Life and Reclaim Your Passion*. San Jose, CA: River Rock Press, 2006.

Goleman, Daniel. *Emotional Intelligence: Why It Can Matter More Than IQ*. New York: Bantam Books, 1995.

Goodstein, Eli. "Stanford University Study Says Spending Time in Nature Benefits Mental Health." *USA Today*. July 9, 2015. Accessed March 2, 2017. http://college.usatoday.com/2015/07/09/study-nature-good-for-mental-health.

Greaves, Colin J., and Lou Farbus. "Effects of Creative and Social Activity on the Health and Well-Being of Socially Isolated Older People: Outcomes from a Multi-method Observational Study." *Journal of the Royal Society for the Promotion of Health* 126, no. 3 (2006): 134–142. Accessed March 2, 2017. http://journals.sagepub.com/doi/abs/10.1177/1466424006064303?ssource=mfr&rss=1&.

Gregoire, Carolyn. "7 Cultures that Celebrate Aging and Respect Their Elders." *Huffington Post*. February 25, 2014. Accessed February 21, 2017. http://www.huffingtonpost.com/2014/02/25/what-other-cultures-can-teach_n_4834228.html.

Griffiths, Sarah. "The Glass Really IS Half Full: Realistic Optimists Are Happier and More Successful than Other Personality Types." *Daily Mail*. August 27, 2013. Accessed

February 23, 2017. http://www.dailymail.co.uk/sciencetech/article-2402601/The-glass-really-IS-half-Realistic-optimists-happier-successful-personality-types.html.

Grimm, Robert, Jr., Kimberly Spring, and Nathan Dietz. *The Heath Benefits of Volunteering: A Review of Recent Research.* Corporation for National & Community Service, 2007. Accessed March 2, 2017. https://www.nationalservice.gov/pdf/07_0506_hbr.pdf.

Gustke, Constance. "For Effective Brain Fitness, Do More than Play Simple Games." *New York Times.* July 8, 2016. Accessed March 2, 2017. https://www.nytimes.com/2016/07/09/your-money/for-effective-brain-fitness-do-more-than-play-simple-games.html?_r=0.

Haas, Michaela. *Bouncing Forward: Transforming Bad Breaks into Breakthroughs.* New York: Enliven, 2015.

Hafiz, Yasmine. "American Attitudes towards Death: 12 Facts from New Pew Research Center Survey." *Huffington Post.* November 21, 2013. Accessed March 3, 2017. http://www.huffingtonpost.com/2013/11/21/death-america-pew-research_n_4312321.html.

Haiken, Melanie. "Aging and Purpose: The New Movement in Positive Aging." *Caring.com.* September 10, 2014. Accessed March 3, 2017. https://www.caring.com/articles/aging-purpose-positive-aging.

Hartz-Seeley, Deborah S. "Chronic Stress Is Linked to the Six Leading Causes of Death." *Miami Herald.* March 21, 2014. Accessed February 23, 2017. http://www.miamiherald.com/living/article1961770.html.

"Healthy Eating after 50." *National Institutes of Health.* No date. Accessed March 1, 2017. https://www.nia.nih.gov/health/publication/healthy-eating-after-50.

Hendricks, Gay. *Learning to Love Yourself: The Steps to Self-Acceptance, the Path to Creative Fulfillment.* Amare, 2014.

"Hillary, Barbara (1931–)." *Black Past: Remembered and Reclaimed.* No date. Accessed February 23, 2017. http://www.blackpast.org/aah/hillary-barbara-1931.

"Homer's Philosophy." *Chicago Multi-Cultural Dance Center.* No date. Accessed April 10, 2017, http://www.cmdcschool.org.

Huffington, Arianna. *On Becoming Fearless . . . in Love, Work, and Life.* New York: Little, Brown, 2006.

Hunter, Gary R., Margarita S. Treuth, Roland L. Weinsier, Tamas Kekes-Szabo, Sherron H. Kell, David L. Roth, and Christal Nicholson. "The Effects of Strength Conditioning on Older Women's Ability to Perform Daily Tasks." *Journal of the American Geriatrics Society* 43, no. 7 (1995): 756–760. doi:10.1111/j.1532-5415.1995.tb07045.x.

Hurford, Molly. "8 Ways Cycling Will Make You Healthier." *Bicycling.* May 25, 2016. Accessed March 1, 2017. http://www.bicycling.com/training/motivation/8-ways-cycling-will-make-you-healthier.

IOS Press. "Tai Chi Increases Brain Size, Benefits Cognition in Randomized Controlled Trial of Chinese Elderly." *EurekAlert!* June 19, 2012. Accessed March 1, 2017. http://www.eurekalert.org/pub_releases/2012-06/ip-tci061912.php.

Isaacson, Walter. "The Genius of Jobs." *New York Times.* October 29, 2011. Accessed March 2, 2017. http://www.nytimes.com/2011/10/30/opinion/sunday/steve-jobss-genius.html.

Jaffe, Ina. "Dance Returns the 'Joy of Movement' to People with Parkinson's." *NPR.* January 23, 2016. Accessed February 23, 2017. http://www.npr.org/sections/health-shots/2016/01/23/463222589/dance-returns-the-joy-of-movement-to-people-with-parkinsons.

Jahnke, Roger, Linda Larkey, Carol Rogers, Jennifer Etnier, and Fang Lin. "A Comprehensive Review of Health Benefits of Qigong and Tai Chi." *American Journal of Health Promotion* 24, no. 6 (2010): e1–e25. doi:10.4278/ajhp.081013-lit-248.

Jenkins, Jo Ann, with Boe Workman. *Disrupt Aging: A Bold New Path to Living Your Best Life at Every Age.* Philadelphia, PA: Perseus Books, 2016.

Johannes, Laura. "New Research Reveals the Intriguing Health Benefits of the Ancient Chinese Practice of Qigong." *Wall Street Journal.* September 30, 2013. Accessed March 2, 2017. https://www.wsj.com/articles/SB10001424052702304373104579107190526946048.

Johnson, Judith. "Do You Have a Healthy Attitude about Death?" *Huffington Post.* January 8, 2013. Accessed March 2, 2017. http://www.huffingtonpost.com/judith-johnson/death-and-dying_b_2432780.html.

Jung, Carl. *Modern Man in Search of a Soul.* New York: Harcourt Harvest, 1955.

Kaleem, Jaweed. "Death over Dinner Convenes as Hundreds of Americans Coordinate End of Life Discussions across U.S." *Huffington Post.* August 18, 2013. Accessed March 3, 2017. http://www.huffingtonpost.com/2013/08/18/death-over-dinner_n_3762653.html?utm_hp_ref=death%E2%80%94dying.

Kay, Katty, and Claire Shipman. *The Confidence Code: The Science and Art of Self-Assurance—What Women Should Know.* New York: HarperCollins, 2014.

Knapp, Jessica. "How to Start a Blog: Beginner's Guide for 2017." *Blogging Basics 101: Social Media and Blogging Tips.* March 1, 2017. Accessed March 2, 2017. https://www.bloggingbasics101.com/how-do-i-start-a-blog.

Knapton, Sarah. "First Hint of 'Life after Death' in Biggest Ever Scientific Study." *The Telegraph.* October 7, 2014. Accessed March 2, 2017. http://www.telegraph.co.uk/science/2016/03/12/first-hint-of-life-after-death-in-biggest-ever-scientific-study.

Kobau, Rosemarie, Joseph Sniezek, Matthew M. Zack, Richard E. Lucas, and Adam Burns. "Well-Being Assessment: An Evaluation of Well-Being Scales for Public Health and Population Estimates of Well-Being among US Adults." *Applied Psychology: Health and Well-Being* 2, no. 3 (2010): 272–297. doi:10.1111/j.1758-0854.2010.01035.x.

Kondo, Marie. *Spark Joy: An Illustrated Master Class on the Art of Organizing and Tidying Up.* New York: Ten Speed Press, 2016.

Koreyva, Wendy. "Learn to Meditate in 6 Easy Steps." *The Chopra Center.* September 3, 2016. Accessed February 23, 2017. http://www.chopra.com/articles/learn-to-meditate-in-6-easy-steps.

Lavretsky, Helen. "Spirituality and Aging." *Aging Health* 6, no. 6 (2010): 749–769. doi:10.2217/ahe.10.70.

"Learn More about EngAGE." *EngAGE: The Art of Active Aging.* No date. Accessed March 2, 2017. http://www.engagedaging.org/about-us.

Liu-Ambrose, Teresa, Karim M. Khan, Janice J. Eng, Patti A. Janssen, Stephen R. Lord, and Heather A. Mckay. "Resistance and Agility Training Reduce Fall Risk in Women Aged 75 to 85 with Low Bone Mass: A 6-Month Randomized, Controlled Trial." *Journal of the American Geriatrics Society* 52, no. 5 (2004): 657–665. doi:10.1111/j.1532-5415.2004.52200.x.

Louv, Richard. "Health Benefits of Being Outdoors." *Camptown.* July 23, 2012. Accessed April 10, 2017. http://camptown.net/2012/09/health-benefits-of-being-outdoors.

MacEwan, Norman. Quoted in *The Forbes Scrapbook of Thoughts on the Business of Life.* New York: B.C. Forbes & Sons, 1950.

MacVean, Mary. "'Get Up!' or Lose Hours of Your Life Every Day, Scientist Says." *Los Angeles Times.* July 31, 2014. Accessed March 1, 2017. http://www.latimes.com/science/sciencenow/la-sci-sn-get-up-20140731-story.html.

Malone, Ryan. "The 12 Benefits of Tai Chi for Seniors." *Inside Elder Care.* March 2, 2010. Accessed March 2, 2017. http://www.insideeldercare.com/health/the-12-benefits-of-tai-chi-for-seniors.

Martin, Sean. "Life after Death: Scientists Reveal Shock Findings from Groundbreaking Study." *The Express*. January 29, 2017. Accessed March 2, 2017. http://www.express.co.uk/news/science/670781/There-IS-life-after-DEATH-Scientists-reveal-shock-findings-from-groundbreaking-study.

Moulton, Priscilla L., and Bethe Lee Moulton. *Molly Waldo! A Young Man's First Voyage to the Grand Banks of Newfoundland, Adapted from the Stories of Marblehead Fishermen of the 1800s*. Boca Raton, FL: Glide Press, 2013.

Murakami, Haruki, and Philip Gabriel. *Kafka on the Shore*. New York: Alfred A. Knopf, 2005.

Neighmond, Patti. "Walking 2 Minutes an Hour Boosts Health, but It's No Panacea." *NPR*. May 1, 2015. Accessed March 2, 2017. http://www.npr.org/sections/health-shots/2015/05/01/403523463/two-minutes-of-walking-an-hour-boosts-health-but-its-no-panacea.

"Neuroplasticity." *Hopes*. June 26, 2010. Accessed February 23, 2017. http://web.stanford.edu/group/hopes/cgi-bin/hopes_test/neuroplasticity.

"Nola Ochs." *Wikipedia*. February 1, 2017. Accessed February 23, 2017. https://en.wikipedia.org/wiki/Nola_Ochs.

"Oldest Graduate: Dr. Allan Stewart Sets World Record." *World Record Academy*. May 4, 2012. Accessed February 23, 2017. http://www.worldrecordacademy.com/society/oldest_graduate_Dr_Allan_Stewart_sets_world_record_112861.html.

Ortman, Jennifer M., Victoria A. Velkoff, and Howard Hogan. "An Aging Nation: The Older Population in the United States." *Current Population Reports*. May 2014. Accessed March 2, 2017. https://www.census.gov/prod/2014pubs/p25-1140.pdf.

Paturel, Amy. "Yoga Health Benefits as You Age." *AARP: The Magazine*. November 2016. Accessed March 2, 2017. http://www.aarp.org/health/healthy-living/info-11-2013/health-benefits-of-yoga.html.

Ratey, John J., and Eric Hagerman. *Spark: The Revolutionary New Science of Exercise and the Brain*. New York: Little, Brown, 2013.

"Research." *Pets for the Elderly*. No date. Accessed March 1, 2017. http://petsfortheelderly.org/research.html.

Richmond, Lewis. *Aging as a Spiritual Practice: A Contemplative Guide to Growing Older and Wiser*. New York: Avery, 2013.

Robinson, Annie. "How Mindfulness Can Ease the Fear of Death and Dying." *Sonima*. August 30, 2016. Accessed March 3, 2017. http://www.sonima.com/meditation/fear-of-death.

Robinson, Bryan E. *Overdoing It: How to Slow Down and Take Care of Yourself*. Deerfield Beach, FL: Health Communications, 1992.

Robinson, Lawrence, Melinda Smith, and Jeanne Segal. "Laughter Is the Best Medicine: The Health Benefits of Humor and Laughter." *HelpGuide*. January 2017. Accessed February 23, 2017. http://www.helpguide.org/articles/emotional-health/laughter-is-the-best-medicine.htm.

Rose, Julie. "Running for Seniors: Why You Should Try Jogging." *SilverSneakers*. December 2, 2016. Accessed March 2, 2017. https://www.silversneakers.com/blog/running-seniors-try-jogging-older-years.

Rosten, Leo. "Words To Live By: The Real Reason For Being Alive." *The Sunday Star (Evening Star)*. January 20, 1963.

Roy Nichols and Jane Nichols, "Funerals: A time for Grief and Growth," *Death: The Final Stage of Growth*, ed. Elizabeth Kubler-Ross (New York: Simon and Schuster, 2009), p. 96.

Schawbel, Dan. "Brené Brown: How Vulnerability Can Make Our Lives Better." *Forbes*. April 21, 2013. Accessed February 23, 2017. https://www.forbes.com/sites/danschawbel/2013/04/21/brene-brown-how-vulnerability-can-make-our-lives-better/#5bff9f7d36c7.

Schilling, Sara. "Bill Painter, Giant of Tri-Cities Outdoor Community, Dies at 93." *Seattle Times*. June 23, 2016. Accessed April 10, 2017. http://www.seattletimes.com/seattle-news/northwest/bill-painter-giant-of-tri-cities-outdoor-community-dies-at-93.

Schnabel, Jim. "Can a Purpose-Driven Life Help Protect the Aging Brain?" *Dana Foundation*. December 30, 2013. Accessed March 3, 2017. http://dana.org/News/Can_A_Purpose-Driven_Life_Help_Protect_the_Aging_Brain_.

Schwartz, Katrina. "A Growth Mindset Could Buffer Kids from Negative Academic Effects of Poverty." *MindShift*. July 26, 2016. Accessed February 23, 2017. https://ww2.kqed.org/mindshift/2016/07/26/a-growth-mindset-could-buffer-kids-from-negative-academic-effects-of-poverty.

Segal, Julius. *Winning Life's Toughest Battles: Roots of Human Resilience*. New York: Ivy Books, 1987.

Seligman, Martin E. P. *Flourish: A Visionary New Understanding of Happiness and Well-Being*. New York: Atria, 2013.

Shimoff, Marci, and Carol Kline. *Happy for No Reason: 7 Steps to Being Happy from the Inside Out*. New York: Atria, 2008.

Shriver, Maria. "It's Important to Be Vulnerable: Here's Why." *MariaShriver.com*. October 8, 2014. Accessed February 23, 2017. http://mariashriver.com/blog/2014/10/why-its-important-to-be-vulnerable-in-life-work-sarah-vermunt.

Siegel, Daniel J. *The Mindful Brain: Reflection and Attunement in the Cultivation of Well-Being*. New York: W.W. Norton, 2007.

Simpson, Mona. "A Sister's Eulogy for Steve Jobs." *New York Times*. October 30, 2011. Accessed April 25, 2017. http://www.nytimes.com/2011/10/30/opinion/mona-simpsons-eulogy-for-steve-jobs.html?pagewanted=all.

Snowdon, David. *Aging with Grace: What the Nun Study Teaches Us about Leading Longer, Healthier, and More Meaningful Lives*. New York: Bantam Books, 2002.

Soskin, Betty Reid. "Last Week's Post-concussion Interview for ParkLeaders Online Program." *CBreaux Speaks: Blog of Betty Reid Soskin*. May 26, 2015. Accessed March 3, 2017. http://cbreaux.blogspot.com/2015_05_24_archive.html.

Stone, Arthur A., Joseph E. Schwartz, Joan E. Broderick, and Angus Deaton. "A Snapshot of the Age Distribution of Psychological Well-Being in the United States." *PNAS*. June 1, 2010. Accessed February 20, 2017. http://www.pnas.org/content/107/22/9985.full.pdf.

Storrs, Carina. "Stand Up, Sit Less, Experts Say; Here's How to Do It." *CNN*. August 7, 2015. Accessed February 23, 2017. http://www.cnn.com/2015/08/06/health/how-to-move-more.

"Stress Symptoms: Effects on Your Body and Behavior." *Mayo Clinic*. No date. Accessed February 23, 2017. http://www.mayoclinic.org/healthy-lifestyle/stress-management/in-depth/stress-symptoms/art-20050987.

Sulik, Gayle. "The Unbearable Weight of the Pink Ribbon." *Pink Ribbon Blues*. March 2, 2015. Accessed March 3, 2017. http://pinkribbonblues.org/2015/03/resisting-the-unbearable-weight-of-the-pink-ribbon.

Szalavitz, Maia. "Touching Empathy: Lack of Physical Affection Can Actually Kill Babies." *Psychology Today*. March 1, 2010. Accessed February 23, 2017. https://www.psychologytoday.com/blog/born-love/201003/touching-empathy.

The Active Times. "Sitting Is the New Smoking: Ways a Sedentary Lifestyle Is Killing You." *Huffington Post*. September 29, 2014. Accessed March 1, 2017. http://www.huffingtonpost.com/the-active-times/sitting-is-the-new-smokin_b_5890006.html.

The Creativity and Aging Study: The Impact of Professionally Conducted Cultural Programs on Older Adults. National Endowment for the Arts, April 30, 2006. Accessed March 2, 2017. https://www.arts.gov/sites/default/files/CnA-Rep4-30-06.pdf.

"The Retirement Problem: What to Do With All That Time?" *Knowledge@Wharton*. January 14, 2016. Accessed February 23, 2017. http://knowledge.wharton.upenn.edu/article/the-retirement-problem-what-will-you-do-with-all-that-time.

"The Top Ten Health Benefits of Hiking." *GoodHiker.com*. May 25, 2011. Accessed March 1, 2017. http://www.goodhiker.com/2011/05/25/health-benefits-hiking.

"The Transformative Effect of Sleep." *Pearson Practice*. September 29, 2015. Accessed April 19, 2017. https://www.pearsonpractice.com/the-transformative-effect-of-sleep.

"The U-Bend of Life." *The Economist*. December 18, 2010. Accessed February 21, 2017. http://www.economist.com/node/17722567.

"*Thinking, Fast and Slow*." *Wikipedia*, April 6, 2017. Accessed April 10, 2017, https://en.wikipedia.org/wiki/Thinking,_Fast_and_Slow.

Thomas, Iain S. "The Grand Distraction." *I Wrote This For You and Only You*. Chicago: Central Avenue Publishing, 2015.

Tolles, Jim. "Finding a Spiritual Community." *Spiritual Awakening Process*. October 5, 2010. Accessed March 2, 2017. http://www.spiritualawakeningprocess.com/2010/10/finding-spiritual-community.html.

Tomasulo, Daniel. "Proof Positive: Can Heaven Help Us? The Nun Study—Afterlife." *PsychCentral*. November 3, 2010. Accessed March 2, 2017. https://psychcentral.com/blog/archives/2010/10/27/proof-positive-can-heaven-help-us-the-nun-study-afterlife.

"Top 10 Health Benefits of Water Aerobics." *Health Fitness Revolution*. May 20, 2015. Accessed March 1, 2017. http://www.healthfitnessrevolution.com/top-10-health-benefits-water-aerobics.

"Top 20 Stereotypes of Older People." *Senior Citizen Times*. November 22, 2011. Accessed February 21, 2017. https://the-senior-citizen-times.com/2011/11/23/top-20-stereotypes-of-older-people.

U.S. Department of Agriculture Forest Service, Pacific Northwest Research Station. "Health and Wellness Benefits of Spending Time in Nature." No date. Accessed March 2, 2017. https://www.fs.fed.us/pnw/about/programs/gsv/pdfs/health_and_wellness.pdf.

Vanhoenacker, Mark. "My Deathbed Playlist (and Yours)." *New York Times*. November 5, 2016. Accessed March 3, 2017. https://www.nytimes.com/2016/11/06/opinion/sunday/my-deathbed-playlist-and-yours.html?_r=2.

"Walking: Trim Your Waistline, Improve Your Health." *Mayo Clinic*. March 3, 2016. Accessed March 2, 2017. http://www.mayoclinic.org/healthy-lifestyle/fitness/in-depth/walking/art-20046261.

Whitecloud, William. *The Magician's Way: What It Really Takes to Find Your Treasure*. Novato, CA: New World Library, 2009.

"William Carlos Williams." *Wikipedia*. February 23, 2017. Accessed March 2, 2017. https://en.wikipedia.org/wiki/William_Carlos_Williams.

Williamson, Marianne. *The Age of Miracles: Embracing the New Midlife*. Carlsbad, CA: Hay House, 2008.

Woolston, Chris. "Seniors and Weightlifting: Never Too Late." *HealthDay*. January 20, 2017. Accessed March 1, 2017. https://consumer.healthday.com/encyclopedia/aging-1/misc-aging-news-10/seniors-and-weightlifting-never-too-late-647213.html.

Wright, Mackenzie. "Finding Spiritual Community: Alternatives to Joining a Church." *Psychics Universe*, January 9, no year. Accessed April 10, 2017, http://www.psychicsuniverse. com/articles/spirituality/living-spiritual-life/spiritual-guidance/finding.

"You're Never Too Old to Start Weight Training." *Mercola.com*. January 23, 2015. Accessed March 1, 2017. http://fitness.mercola.com/sites/fitness/archive/2015/01/23/weight-training-older-adults.aspx.

index

A

AARP 90, 156
accept death mindfully 167
accepting your mortality 166
action steps 92, 114, 141
address conflict in a spirit of love 109
allow others to help you 113
All Souls Day 165
apprecionado 20
aqua aerobics 126, 131
Arianna Huffington 172, 177
art as therapy 144
atonement 57
attachments 48
authentic relationships 111
authentic self 39, 68, 125
authority figure 105
avoid criticism 110
avoid negative language 110

B

Barbara Hillary 65
basic mindfulness 28
Battle of Evermore 85
be a mentor 183
beauty aficionado 20
becoming the kind of friend you'd like
    to have 98
be flexible 88
beginner's mind 70, 144, 155
being more creative 143
be proactive and resourceful 89
be true to your heart 182
Betty Reid Soskin 174
be useful and relevant 176
Bill Painter 65
Blue Zone Diet 125
bone density 129
brain plasticity 136
brain training 138
Brené Brown 99
Buddhism 157, 165, 167

C

cardiovascular health 129
Carl W. Buehner 99
chair yoga 130
challenge to possibility: part 1 30
challenge to possibility: part 2 30
charismatic adult 184
Chicago Multi-Cultural Dance Center 179
choral singing 143
Christian belief 157
chronic pain 129
circle of support 91
Cirque du Soleil 179
COAL (curiosity, openness, acceptance,
    love) 14, 40, 81, 169
cognitive skills 128
coloring books for grown-ups 145
color outside the lines 145
community service 172
compassion 26, 101, 109, 116, 153
compensating tendencies 11
connect through touch 108
cooking 143
core beliefs 10
core values 179
Cornelius Vanderbilt 65
counterwill 85, 89, 110
courage 153
create a workable plan 86
create, definition 143
create emotional safety 108
creating a legacy 185
creating a vision 66
creativity 149
crossword puzzles 138
cycling 131

D

Dalai Lama 154
Dale Carnegie 113
Dance Theatre of Harlem 179
dancing 131

Daniel Goleman 99
dark night of the soul 179
Day of the Dead 165
Death over Dinner 167
death playlist 168
developing your spiritual side 147
diet recommendations 125
different views of death 165
discover and name your
   "Gift to Others" 181
disempowering your fears 21
don't multitask during communication 111
do what you love together 106
drama 143

E

eating mindfully 14, 71
Elizabeth Layton 123
embrace differences as opportunities
   to grow 112
embracing your mortality 160
emotional intelligence 98
emotional mindfulness 40
emotional safety 43
empathy 99, 109, 153
empowering self-talk 18
endorphins 75
energy in motion 11, 22
energy of emotions 36
EngAGE 143
engaging your mind 123, 135, 137
enhancing your body 123, 125
enjoy special time together 117
essential connections, forging 104
establish a blog 139
evaluating your joy 77
exercise as a social event 132
exercise doesn't have to be formal 133
exercise options chart 131
exercises, Chapter 1 28
exercises, Chapter 2 59
exercises, Chapter 3 (finding your joy) 76
exercises, Chapter 3 (living your dream) 91
exercises, Chapter 4
   (existiing relationships) 113
exercises, Chapter 4
   (friendship qualities) 101
exercises, Chapter 4
   (intimate partnerships) 119

exercises, Chapter 5
   (engaging your mind) 140
exercises, Chapter 5
   (enhancing your body) 134
exercises, Chapter 5
   (expressing your creativity) 145
exercises, Chapter 6 (mortality) 169
exercises, Chapter 6 (spirituality) 158
exercises, Chapter 7 186
exercising for fun 130
explore something new 135
expressing your creativity 123, 141
extend appreciation often 110
extend your love unconditionally 116

F

false self 38, 59, 79
Fauja Singh 5, 123
faulty thinking 46, 60
faulty thinking, types of 47
fear and resistance, dealing with 85
fear into love 29
fear of death 150
feeling our feelings 37
feeling our feelings, step by step 41
finding and giving your gifts to
   the world 181
finding the life we love 69
finding your joy 65, 68, 76, 124
find the people you want to serve 182
fitness trackers 134
flexibility 88
flourishing in every decade xiv
forging healthy connections 108
forgiveness 57, 153
Four Noble Truths 157
Frank Lloyd Wright xvi
friendly universe 150
friendship IQ 101

G

gardening 143
general fitness 131
generosity 153
gentle yoga 130
gift of change 23
gift of death 27
gift of forgiveness 52
gift of loss 24

gifts of pain 25
go back to school 137
golf 131
gratitude 20, 72, 77, 153
gratitude-appreciation one-two punch 30
grieve the loss 118
Grim Reaper 165
growth mindset 8
gym workouts 131

H

habits 83
healing power of mindfulness 40
heart has its own intelligence 155
heart's desire 13
Higher-Self quality 153, 160
hiking 131
Homer Bryant 171, 180
hospice 166
humor 75

I

immune health 129
improved endurance 127
improved leg strength 127
innovation 149
insight 149
instrumental music 143
integrity 153
intent to love 100
internal motivation 99
intimate partners 114
intimate relationships 116
intuition 154

J

jazz dance 143
Jesus 157
jigsaw puzzles 138
Jill Lesly Jones 178
jogging/running 131
John Locke 65
John Orne Johnson ("JOJ") Frost 73
joint pain, less 128
JOJ Frost 86
joy 153
joy, definition of 69
joyful experience 71
joy, opening ourselves to 70

joy rating 78, 80
joy, strategies for finding 71
J. R. R. Tolkien 65

K

kindness 100, 153

L

laughter 75
Laurie Becklund 175
learn a foreign language 136, 137
learn how to play a musical instrument 136
learning bucket list 141
leave a legacy 177
Leo Rosten 176
let go 58
letting go of regrets and resentments 58
letting go of what is no longer serving you 55
life's structure 82
limiting beliefs 46
limiting beliefs, setting aside 67
listen more than you talk 106, 109
listen to your body 132
living your dream 65, 81
longevity bonus xiii
love 153

M

make room for significant others in adult
    children's lives 106
mantra 81
mapmakers 10
Marbleheaders 73
Marie Kondo 68, 69
Maya Angelou 189
meditation 72, 148, 151, 152, 153, 155
memories 48
mental acuity 128
mindful breathing 77
mindfulness 14, 40, 71, 100, 103, 109, 121,
    148, 153, 155, 157, 162, 167
mindfulness in creating positive change 14
mindfulness meditation 151
mindset of innocence 155
My true religion is kindness 154

N

namaste 150
near-death experiences 163

need for connection 97
neurofeedback 136
neuroplasticity 8
Norman MacEwan 178

O

observe respectful boundaries 105
online search for love/friendship 120
opening ourselves to joy 70
open your heart fearlessly 116
opportunity of a lifetime xi
osteoporosis 128
our perceptions 9
oxytocin 19

P

Pablo Picasso 65
paint positive pictures 110
passive-aggression 55
pattern interrupts 83
pedometers 134
perceptions 9
percolating with a feeling 42
perfectionism 47
pets are good for your heart 106
physical dexterity 129
physical exercise 126
Pilates 129, 131
play more, using your brain 138
pole dancing 130
positive communication 110
positive spirituality 151
positivity 13
practice positive communication 113
prayer 151, 155
preparing for the adventure 1
provide honest feedback 111
psychological safety 40
publish your own book 139

Q

qigong 128, 131, 152
quality of life 136

R

range of motion 128
realistic optimism 4
realistic positivity 4, 15, 31, 33, 68, 79, 85, 97, 124, 185

recognizing our value xii
regrets 53
relationship categories 104
relationships with children/dependents 105
relationships with friends 107
relationships with parents/authority figures 104
religious rituals 151
replacing losses 118
research a topic 138
resentments 51
resilience 149
risk of falls, reduced 128
rituals 58
road cycling 132
role models 21
Rosie the Riveter National Historical Park 174
rowing 132

S

safe 10
sarcopenia 127
seek out new friends 113
self-actualize 177
self-awareness 99, 119
self-compassion 119
self-doubt into confidence 29
self-exploration 55, 181
self-fulfilling prophecy 9
self-regulation 99
sense of purpose 173
serendipity 71
serenity 153
service, benefits of 174
set ground rules for how to disagree 106
setting aside limiting beliefs 67
sex 117
sex, benefits of 118
show appreciation to your partner 116
Sister Bernadette 136
sitting is the new smoking 128
sitting/standing ratio 84
skills 178
sleep, benefits of 84
sleep patterns, tracking 134
social connections 121
social network 95, 143
social skills 99
solution specialist 17

spend time in nature 156
spiritual destiny 125
spiritual dimension 152
spirituality 147
spirituality, developing your 149
spirituality, physical advantages of 151
start right now 86
step counters 134
Stephen Cope 82
step into the unknown 144
stepping into wonder 76
strategies for finding your joy 71
strategy games 138
strength training 127, 132
superagers 8
support your partner's independence 116
swimming 131
synchronicity 71

T

tai chi 128, 131, 152
talents 178
Taoism 157
Tao Porchon-Lynch 5
tennis 132
tether points 33, 35
the benefits of exercise 127
The Chopra Center 72
the purpose of life 176
things I like about me 101
THINK before you speak 112
Timeline Review: Aging 28
Timeline Review: Creative Activities 145
Timeline Review: Educational Activities 140
Timeline Review: Joy 76
Timeline Review: Physical Activity/
    Exercise 134
Timeline Review: Relationships 103
Timeline Review: Resentments and
    Regrets 60
Timeline Review: Service to Others 186
Timeline Review: Spirituality 158
Timeline Review: The False Self 59
Tony LoRe 183
transcendent sex 117
transform your community 171
trauma 35, 175
treadmill desk 128
true self 39

U

unconditional self-worth 153
unconditional support 185
undivided attention, give 111
untrue agreements 45
use empowering feedback 110
using rituals to let go 58

V

values inventory 186
voices of your fear and your love 91
volunteering 172

W

walking 132
walking health benefits 133
weekly arts programs, benefits of 143
weight training 127, 132
what happens after death? 163
what kind of friend are you? 102
whole picture 12
wisdom 149
write about your life 146
write a memoir 139
writing 138

Y

yoga 132, 151, 152
your best years 3
your healing 179
your insight 179
your joy 180
your loves 180
your mission 187
your passions 180
your transformation 179
your values 178
Youth Mentoring Connection 183

Z

Zumba Gold 131